The Gun Book for Girls

Silvio Calabi, Steve Helsley & Roger Sanger

SHOOTING
SPORTSMAN
BOOKS

ISBN 978-1-60893-203-0

Library of Congress Cataloging-in-Publication Data available upon request

Printed in the USA

 Books

Distributed to the trade by National Book Network

Designed by Rich Eastman

This book is for all the girls (of every age) who have contributed so much to the shooting sports. We admire and appreciate your accomplishments.

One of these "girls"—Nancy Tompkins, whose husband and daughters are also shooting champions—wrote something memorable in the introduction to her own book *Prone and Long Range Rifle Shooting*. We'd like to repeat it here:

Of all the reasons that I shoot, the most precious to me is not the medals, the records, national championships or even world championships; it is the incredible, wonderful friends I have made from all over the world. Shooters are some of the most caring, sharing, wonderful people I have ever met.

Contents

Lock & Load!

How This Book Happened & What It's About

Maybe you've seen the first volume in this series, called *The Gun Book for Boys*. People's reactions to it are always the same: "Hey, this is cool!" And then, "What do you mean 'boys'? Aren't you forgetting something—or someone?"

No, we didn't forget. We know many women of all ages who are target shooters or hunters or who own guns for self-defense or work in some part of the shooting business. So at first we wanted to call it *The Gun Book for Kids*. Then we found some new information that opened our eyes wide: In the US, female participation in target shooting grew by 51.5 percent between 2001 and 2011, to a total of more than 5 million girls and women.

Internationally, the number of women shooting for medals at the Olympic Games increased from 77 in 1984 (in Los Angeles) to 145 in 2008 (in Beijing) to 159 in 2012 (in London). In total, 390 shooters from 108 countries competed at the London Games—and a woman shooter named Kim Rhode became the first American in any sport to win a medal in five consecutive summer Olympics.

Female participation in hunting in America grew by almost 42 percent from 2001 to 2011, to more than 2½ million. (That's out of a total of 15 million hunters.)

Overall, 23 percent of women in the US now own a gun, and that number is growing quickly.*

In 2012, June 9 was officially declared National Take Your Daughter to the Range Day, which should encourage even more girls to take up the sport.

In the face of a trend this strong, we decided it would be much better to write a separate book, one that focuses specifically on things that matter to female shooters, especially those who are just starting out.

Welcome to *The Gun Book for Girls*.

* These statistics were gathered by the National Sporting Goods Association, the National Shooting Sports Foundation, the Gallup Poll and the International Shooting Sports Federation.

Girls & Shooting

Writing the boys' book wasn't that difficult. It's been a long time since we were 14, but we remember what we went through when we were learning about guns and shooting. And we're males, which helped with the boys' book but puts us at a disadvantage here. However, we know what we don't know, and we have many female shooters to turn to for help and advice. (You'll see some of them in the photos; others are listed in the Acknowledgements at the back of the book.)

Even without their input, we know that there's much more to building guns for girls than just slapping on a pink stock. We also know from experience that girls learn skills such as shooting in ways that are somewhat different from the way boys learn. (We have daughters and even granddaughters. Wives too.) Shooting coaches always prefer female students because they tend to listen and to do as they're taught. Girls often have no shooting experience at all and so haven't developed any bad habits. They aren't shy about ad-

In July 2012 Nur Suryani Mohamed Taibi became the first woman ever to represent Malaysia as a shooter in the Olympic Games. Not only that, but when she competed in the 10-meter air rifle qualification event, she was eight months pregnant.

mitting ignorance of guns or fear of recoil either, which is not only honest but also useful for an instructor to know.

Women—adults, that is, not girls—are often interested in guns, especially handguns, as a way to protect themselves. This takes guns out of the area of "fun" and makes shooting not a hobby but a necessity. We will go over these issues in this book, but we're not going to recommend that you train and then apply for a permit to carry a concealed weapon. You might, however, decide to do so when you're older, and this book can help prepare you for this serious step. Using or carrying a gun for self-defense comes with huge responsibilities.

Generally, women are less interested in hunting than men are. Hunting comes with responsibilities too, which we'll describe for you. You may think that killing wild animals for meat is needless (yes, we have supermarkets) and for trophies is cruel, but the whole story will surprise you. The chapter called "Game: Animals & Birds" will give you a better understanding of hunting as well as wilderness and conservation. This is important even if you never go hunting.

Target shooting, on the other hand, seems to appeal to boys and girls about equally, just as school sports do. Unlike soccer or basketball, target shooting is an individual skill, like tennis or skiing, but all of these activities make us focus on technique and physical and mental conditioning. Placing a bullet precisely into the X-ring of a distant target or smashing a speeding clay pigeon can be every bit as satisfying as booting a ball into the other team's goal or swimming the 200-yard freestyle in less than two minutes.

Plinking—shooting at improvised targets like Necco wafers, tin cans or milk jugs full of water—can be even more fun.

Knowledge is power, so much of this book is about the technical aspects of guns and shooting and especially the safety rules and considerations. These are the same whether you're male or female, so parts of this book are very similar to what's in the boys' book.

Beyond that, however, this book contains more information than the boys' version. The girls and women who helped us were especially interested in things like recoil (does it hurt?) and modern guns designed for them, with smaller grips or stocks that are easier to hold. Other questions often were about shooting clothing that fits them, not males. The idea of careers that are related to guns or shooting sparked considerable interest too.

Being male, when we were kids we wanted to know about guns and shooting, snipers and rogue elephants, and man-eating tigers and blowing up stuff. How far will a bullet go, anyway? Were those $15 war-surplus guns in the magazine ads any good? Is my .22 enough for hunting deer? How about an old army rifle? Can I get ammo for that relic pistol Granddad gave me? Isn't shooting birds with clusters of pellets cheating? Does a bulletproof vest stop all types of bullets? Why is it dangerous to shoot at the water? Will firing a machine gun for a long time melt the barrel? Why is my mother so freaked out about BB guns?

In order, the answers are: It depends. Some of them. It can be. Sure. Probably not. No way. No way. Because it's like skipping a stone. Yes, sort of. Because she's your mother (and loves you).

We've been working on the answers to these questions—and a whole lot more—ever since we were kids ourselves. Then finally it seemed like a good idea to share them with you. No shooter knows everything, and all shooters have questions. Thanks to the Internet, answers are easy to find, but they aren't always complete answers or even the right answers. We're here to help sort out the right answers from the junk.

You don't have to read this book from the beginning. It's set up like a box of chocolates: You can dip into it anywhere and find something interesting. However, you probably should read (or at least look at) the chapter titled "Talking the Talk" next. It explains a lot of the language of guns and shooting. You may think you know this stuff already, but even a lot of adults who've owned guns for years get some of the lingo wrong. Then later on, if you find a word you don't know while you're reading, flip back to that chapter and look for it. If the word isn't there, it's probably explained somewhere else. For example, if you don't know what a percussion cap is, it's not in the alphabetic listing; it's in the chapter "Making It Go *BOOM!*"

Guns Are Tools

Some adults won't like this book. As you probably already know, to some people guns have become symbols of crime and violence, and a few people believe no one should own guns any more.

However, from the days of the Pilgrims up until about when your parents were born, most of us regarded guns as everyday items. We began to get a lot more uptight about them after the Vietnam War, which ended in 1975. Also, at the same time, the population of our country was growing quickly, and more and more people were living in cities, where they learned nothing about hunting and not much about self-reliance, which is what guns were for during most of America's history.

(History is everything. In Japan there are almost no shootings. Japan has a culture of blade-making, though, that goes back more than a thousand years. When criminal violence occurs in Japan, it's often with knives or swords.)

Too many people now are freaked out about guns. But guns are just tools, and every tool has a purpose. Use any tool, from a hammer to a lawn mower, the wrong way and it can become dangerous. No one has a problem with chain saws, but no one would use a chain saw to carve the Thanksgiving turkey, either. The same thing is true for guns. They don't belong in school. They're not toys. You don't use them to settle arguments.

A Russian SVD, the *Snayperskaya Vintovka Dragunova*, or Dragunov sniper rifle. Some people would call this a scary gun. Guns aren't scary, but what *is* scary are some people with guns. This book can make you a safe shooter who really knows her way around firearms.

Guns aren't scary, but what *is* scary are some people with guns—people who have bad intentions or who are just ignorant or careless. This book may or may not affect your intentions, but it can make you a safe shooter who really knows her way around firearms.

How times have changed: an advertisement said to be from *Harper's Weekly* Magazine in 1904. Today no one would dream of allowing a child to play with a gun, "absolutely safe" or not, in bed or otherwise, but this indicates how commonplace guns were at that time. Along with attitudes about guns, safety habits have changed tremendously too.

You Can't Argue with History

Quick: What's the single most important manmade item in history?

You probably thought, *Oh, easy: the automobile.* Or maybe the computer.

We think the most important manmade item in history, so far anyway, is the gun. Some of the biggest breakthroughs in technology came about because someone wanted a better gun or ammunition, and then these breakthroughs were applied to making other things. You may have learned in history class that Henry Ford invented the assembly line, where

mass-produced parts were put together in a standardized way to produce the Model T car quickly and inexpensively. Ford may have been the first to build automobiles this way, but gunmakers like Eli Whitney and John Hall beat him to the basic idea a century earlier.

(In fact, an 1882 report to the US Census Bureau on *The Manufacture of Firearms and Ammunition* declared that this "interchangeable system" of manufacturing "has been one of the chief influences in the rapid increase in the national wealth" in the previous 50 years.)

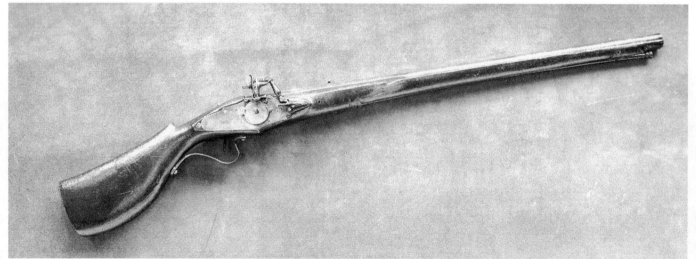

Pilgrim John Alden's wheellock rifle. Alden sailed to America on the *Mayflower* in 1620, when he was 20 years old, and became a member of Capt. Miles Standish's Plymouth Colony militia. Without their guns, the colonists might have been forced to return to England. The rifle was found hidden in the walls of the Alden family home in 1924.

National Firearms Museum

Here's another absolutely key advancement that came courtesy of the gun business: The most basic concept in precision manufacturing is the ability to shape things consistently to within a few thousandths of an inch. (A motor, for example, won't run if its parts don't fit together this closely.) The first person to work to such tight dimensions—he "invented" the thousandth of an inch—was Joseph Whitworth, an English engineer who designed a more accurate rifle for the British Army in the 1850s. Queen Victoria knighted him for his work.

The Bessemer process of smelting iron ore efficiently came about in part because the gun industry needed better steel. And so on and so forth. Today the huge and growing demand for guns of all kinds (military and police as well as civilian) is driving advances in engineering, metallurgy, plastics and manufacturing around the world.

Now look beyond manufacturing and you'll see that the importance of guns in all of history is impossible to ignore.

The first Europeans known to have reached North America were Vikings who arrived in Newfoundland a thousand years ago. Their settlement failed. Some historians think it's possible the Norsemen were driven away because their swords, axes and bows were no better than the native Indians' weapons. Six hundred years later English settlers established Jamestown in what became Virginia, and the Pilgrims landed on what is now Cape Cod. They had guns, though. They were able to hold off the Indians, and they stayed and prospered. The rest, as they say, is history—America's history.

In the chapter titled "You'll Put Your Eye Out!" you'll read about what might have been the single most important gun in American history: the air rifle that in 1804 was the Lewis & Clark Expedition's "secret weapon."

Going much farther back in time, the most important weapon in England's history (which, thanks to those colonists and their guns, is where modern American history began) was the longbow, a fearsome and far-reaching killing device that was the forerunner of the rifle. It was the first weapon that allowed a peasant on foot to topple an armored nobleman from his horse—to stand up for himself, in other words, and refuse to be treated like a slave. This was the beginning of the end of

Guns in America

y 1630 the Massachusetts Bay Colony required that all men, including servants, be "furnished with good & sufficient arms" and provided guns to those who couldn't afford them.

One hundred and sixty years later, the first official census found that 3,929,214 "free white persons and slaves" (Indians weren't counted) lived in America. This probably meant upward of 650,000 families, most of which were involved in farming. It's likely that each of these households had at least one gun. Much of the rest of America's population probably also had guns, even if only a pocket pistol kept in a nightstand in a house in Boston, New York or Philadelphia.

Then, just 70 years after that, the enormous armies of the Civil War—about 3¼ million soldiers in a country of just 31½ million people—needed so many guns that when the war ended there was a huge surplus of them.

If anyone you know is worried about an oversupply of guns in our country today, tell them it's too late: Guns proliferated here centuries ago.

the feudal system of kings, vassals and serfs. It took centuries—and proclamations like Magna Carta, the Constitution and the Bill of Rights—for the rights of the common person to be fully nailed down, but standing behind these rights was always the threat of armed resistance to the abuse of authority.

The first shots of the American Revolution were fired on April 19, 1775, when British troops marched out of Boston to seize colonists' guns and ammunition. Americans have been a bit touchy about this subject ever since.

It's Not Dangerous If You Know What You're Doing

The National Rifle Association, the National Shooting Sports Foundation, 4-H clubs and many other organizations across America have helped teach good gun handling to millions of people, young and not so young. As a result, shooting has become one of the safest of all sports. There are many, many fewer accidents in shooting than in volleyball or bowling, for example, or tennis or even swimming.

Read this book. Pay attention. Become a skilled, smart, safe shooter, and represent our sport well. Hey, we're all in this together.

The National Rifle Association of America, the NRA, was created in 1871 to teach firearms skills. It's still doing this today. Thanks to the NRA and other groups, including Scouting and the National Shooting Sports Foundation, shooting has become one of the safest of all sports. There are many, many fewer accidents in shooting than in, for example, volleyball or skateboarding.

More Books on Guns

If you really get interested in shooting, you're eventually going to own a library of books on the subject. If this copy of The Gun Book for Girls belongs to you, your library is already off to a good start. On the subject of guns and cartridges, we recommend the following three reference books. You don't have to read them from start to finish; just use them as sources when you want to look up something specific.

Small Arms of the World, by Edward Clinton Ezell. This is one of the bibles of the shooting sports, with hundreds of pages of text and pictures. It's been around forever and is now in its 12th edition, but the older versions are just as interesting as the newer ones. You can get used paperback copies very inexpensively.

Frank Barnes's *Cartridges of the World* is another must-have-yet-low-priced shooting book. The current edition is the 10th, revised and expanded to include descriptions of more than 1,500 cartridges—American, British, European, new, old, military, wildcats (see "Talking the Talk"), obsolete, for rifle, pistol and shotgun. All the editions are useful, but the newer ones have more information.

The Gun and Its Development, by W.W. Greener. The author was one of England's best-known and most successful gunmakers. His book has been through at least nine editions since it was first published, back in 1881, and has been reprinted time and again. It's long and sometimes difficult to follow, but no shooting library is complete without it. New or secondhand copies are available for just a few bucks.

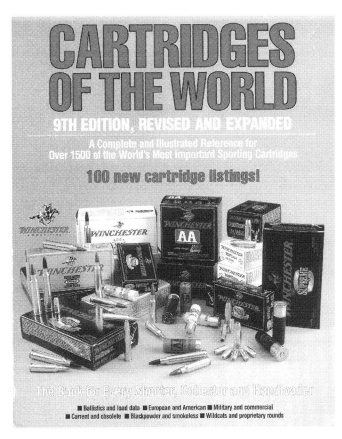

There are hundreds if not thousands more books on guns, gunmakers, ammunition and shooting (competition, military and hunting), and we've recommended a few more throughout these pages. Plus there are magazines, Websites and blogs that cover every one of the shooting sports, from collecting old guns to self-defense and from target shooting to hunting big game and everything in between. More and more of this content is being written by and for women shooters.

By the way, on the subject of books: Don't leave this one where your mom or dad can find it. They might get so wrapped up in it that you won't get it back for a while.

And here's another thought: "Books are weapons in the war of ideas." This saying was used on an anti-Nazi poster during World War II, when the Germans publicly burned books written by people they didn't like. It is still true today in the Internet Age, when anyone can post anything online at any time without having to prove themselves first.

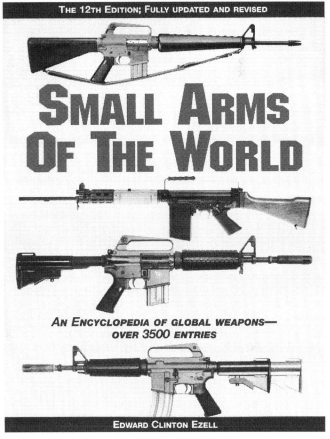

'You've Come a Long Way, Baby'

That Was Then; This Is Now

"You've come a long way, baby" was an advertising slogan for cigarettes in the 1960s, when the Women's Liberation movement was gaining momentum in America. It was meant to encourage women to smoke as a way of declaring their independence. (It seems amazing now, but that ad campaign also included photos of women hanging laundry outside, captioned "Back then, every man gave his wife at least one day a week out of the house.") Smoking aside, it was a catchy phrase and wound up being applied to all sorts of other things that girls and women began to do more openly. One of those things was shooting. Women always have had guns for self-defense, and there always have been women target shooters and hunters, but now any limits (real or imagined) have been blown away.

More and more women are embracing hunting as a soul-restoring, natural pastime and a source of healthful meat. The only American to win medals in five consecutive Olympic Games is a woman shooter named Kim Rhode. The top long-range match shooters in America are Sherri Jo Gallagher, Michelle Gallagher and Nancy Tompkins, mother and daughters who take turns winning long-range rifle championships.

More women and more opportunities for women appear in the "Professions with Passion" chapter. The chapter you're reading right now focuses on what might be called the non-recreational aspects of shooting for women: self-defense, politics and military service. Most of this book is devoted to enjoying shooting as a hobby, but let's never forget that even air guns aren't toys; they can be used as deadly weapons.

When she was 17, in 1996, American Kim Rhode became the youngest female gold medalist in Olympic shooting history. At the 2012 London games she became the first American to win a medal in five consecutive Olympics.

Self-Defense & 'Concealed Carry'

In the 1850s, if you lived on a ranch in the Nebraska Territory, you probably kept a rifle close at hand to deal with marauders, both four- and two-legged; women in wild-and-wooly San Francisco might have tucked a small handgun into their clothing somewhere. There were no 9-1-1 calls (or telephones) and no fast-response law enforcement as we know it today. To a great degree, self-defense was one's own responsibility.

Much has changed since then, but at least one thing has not: Today, even with virtually instant communication and professional police departments, each of us is still the "first responder" for our own personal defense. This can be an especially critical issue for women, who may be victimized more often than men and who are often smaller and weaker than a male attacker. A gun is a great "equalizer." More than half of American women who own guns bought them for protection.

Any gun, whether it's for self-defense or target shooting or hunting, has to be stored safely and legally. (There's a lot of information on this later in the book.) At the same time, a gun that's meant to be used in case someone breaks into your home should be fairly easy to get to. Until you are an adult, these matters are the responsibility of your parents or guardians. However, anyone who can reach that gun in an emergency should fully understand the consequences of using it. Shooting someone or even just threatening someone with a gun is a serious matter that requires study, family discussions and clear thinking.

OK, that's when you're at home. Carrying a gun for self-defense in public is even more serious. Most states and some cities have laws about carrying a gun, whether openly or hidden in your car or on your person. Carrying a concealed gun legally usually requires a special permit, and to qualify for the permit you may have to be specially trained. You also have to be an adult.

More and more women are learning to shoot and are buying guns to protect themselves.

Then: This Savage Arms Co. ad, probably from the 1920s, advises, "Fathers, it is your serious duty in these times to arm your home."

Now: The modern approach to self-defense for women is total self-reliance. This poster is from the National Association for Gun Rights.

Many of them also are getting concealed-carry permits so they can keep a handgun with them. Gun companies, in turn, are making lighter, more compact revolvers and pistols for people with smaller hands. At the same time, clothing, purse and holster manufacturers are coming up with new ways to carry these guns.

Anyone who carries a gun for self-defense should practice frequently with it—drawing it, shooting it, loading it and unloading it—and must be mentally prepared: *Do I use it now?*

If you think you'll want to apply for a concealed-carry permit when you're old enough, reading this book will go a long way toward preparing you. It's not about gun fighting, but it has everything you need to know to become a safe, responsible and skilled shooter.

Don't Mess with These Women

In the 1950s law enforcement was male only. Not only were there no female cops, but some police departments wouldn't even accept men who weren't at least 5 feet 8 inches tall. The few women in law-enforcement agencies were secretaries or they worked with children or searched female prisoners; the real cop duties went to men. There weren't many police academies, and "professional education" was mostly OJT (on-the-job training). Formal firearms instruction was even harder to find. At the time, most cops were veterans of World War II or the Korean War and knew one end of a gun from the other. Besides, Americans are all descendants of Daniel Boone—we were born knowing how to shoot! (Wrong, wrong, wrong.)

Into this environment came Lucy—Lucille—Chambliss, who started shooting at the age of 10, in 1941, at her father's Winter Haven Rifle Club, in Florida. After high school she went to college to study commercial art, but a career in art wasn't for her. Instead, with strong mentors from the club, Lucy turned to competitive pistol shooting. Soon she was winning matches. The Winter Haven Police Department noticed. The chief hired Lucy as a secretary—and firearms instructor. She never worked as a street cop, but because she had sworn peace-officer status, she could represent her department in shooting matches. She was Winter Haven's "ringer."

In 1958 Lucy also began to train police recruits at the Polk County academy. She kept competing too. Lucy won the Florida Women's Pistol Championship 11 times, the US National Women's Pistol Championship four times (and was runner-up four times), the National Women's Combat Pistol Championship twice and the Florida Open Pistol Championship once. She also won medals in the 1970 World Shooting Championships. In 1978 she was elected to the board of directors of the National Rifle Association. The US Government awarded her the 139th Distinguished Shooters Badge and, in 1983,

Then: Lucy Chambliss demonstrating what was considered good revolver shooting form in the late 1950s—the same formal stance that a duelist used a century earlier. She wears no hearing or eye protection.

Florida Governor Bob Graham nominated her for the state's hall of fame.

What a difference a generation can make. In the 1970s police agencies began accepting women in significant numbers. Now women are police chiefs, sheriffs and heads of state and federal law-enforcement agencies. Shooting techniques and competitions have changed too. So has firearms training. Today one of the best of the new wave of shooting instructors is a woman named Il Ling New.

Like Lucy Chambliss, Il Ling New was introduced to shooting by her father. She was 6 when she fired a pellet gun for the first time. At 10 she was duck hunting with her dad in the flooded ricefields of the Sacramento Valley, in California, and at 17 she became a licensed hunting guide. After high school she went to Yale, where she earned degrees in business. Il Ling also became captain of the Yale shooting team and won a Silver medal in American skeet and a Bronze in International Skeet in NCAA (National Collegiate Athletic Association) competition.

While walking to her apartment one beautiful morning during her student days in Connecticut, she suddenly found herself grabbed, with

Now: Il Ling New in a stable crouch and ready to fire her scoped Ruger Super Redhawk revolver, which is braced on shooting sticks. She wears full protection and specialized gloves.

a hand over her mouth and a gun in her back. Luckily, she lost only her purse and a bracelet to the mugger. She gained something possibly more valuable: The realization that she couldn't defend herself. After graduation her dad paid for Il Ling to take a handgun course at Gunsite Academy, in the Arizona desert.

Gunsite is one of the best places in the US to learn modern pistol shooting. Back in Lucy Chambliss's day, handgun fire was slow and deliberate, from one position and holding the gun with just one hand. Il Ling learned to shoot and reload quickly and fluidly, on the move, and using both hands.

After school Il Ling joined an advertising agency that sent her to its office in Korea and then to San Francisco. But after years as a workaholic executive, Il Ling decided it was time for something altogether different: She returned to Gunsite, where the determination that had served her so well in a global ad agency also made her stand out as a shooter. Il Ling became Gunsite's first female instructor and an expert with handguns, rifles and shotguns.

Then, to polish her craft as a guide, Il Ling hunted for more than a decade with some of the top professionals in Africa, Asia, Australia and Britain as well as the US. Today her hunting clients and shooting students include soldiers and cops, as well as moms, dads and kids.

In 2005 Il Ling said of her earlier years, "I was walking through life, not paying enough attention to what was around me." She gave an example of how that changed: While hunting in northern California, her Jack Russell terrier suddenly came tearing back to her.

"A mountain lion was right behind my dog in a full-on chase," she said, and the dog was leading the lion straight to her.

"I reacted on instinct." Il Ling's training kicked in, and she went straight to muscle memory: *eyes, muzzle, target*. The rifle came up and fired, the cougar went down, and the dog wasn't hurt. Neither was she.

In 2012 Il Ling New was inducted into the California Outdoors Hall of Fame. The official citation called her "America's No. 1 female firearms instructor and hunting guide." If Lucy Chambliss had been there, she'd probably have said, "You go, girl!"

Women, Guns & Politics

In this series of books we focus on facts, people and history and leave politics to others. However, as you get into shooting, you'll hear more about the controversies over gun ownership. And so, since this is *The Gun Book for Girls*, it seems appropriate to talk about the significant roles that women have played in gun politics in the US.

The NRA (National Rifle Association), founded in 1871, is the oldest gun-owners' group in America. For most of its history the NRA was almost exclusively male. Usually the president was a former military officer such as Gen. Ulysses S. Grant, who also became President of the United States. This too began to change in the 1970s as women joined the NRA's new political division, the Institute for Legislative Action. (The NRA had always been involved in legislative lobbying, but the issue of legal gun control really started to heat up in the late 1960s.)

In 1994 a woman named Tanya Metaksa was appointed NRA's chief lobbyist. (See "Professions with Passion.") Metaksa had gotten involved in gun-rights issues in Connecticut in the late 1960s and later became the chief legislative aide for New York Senator Alphonse D'Amato. The president of the NRA then was also a woman, Marion Hammer, and she teamed up with Metaksa in the political arena.

Hammer had gained a lot of lobbying experience in Florida. She was a pioneer in child and family firearms safety and was largely responsible for the NRA's Eddie Eagle GunSafe Program for kids.

It was also during the 1990s that a woman emerged as a leader of the gun-control movement: Sara Brady, whose husband, Jim, had been seriously injured in 1981 during an assassination attempt on

Then: After Ulysses S. Grant was the 18th President of the United States, he became the 8th president of the National Rifle Association, in 1883–84.

President Ronald Reagan. The lobbying organization she founded was called Handgun Control, Inc., and later it was renamed the Brady Campaign to Prevent Gun Violence.

At the NRA, as Marion Hammer was completing her term as president, Sandy Froman was elected one of the association's vice presidents.

Froman, a Harvard-educated lawyer, had never touched a gun until she was 32 years old. That was when, while living alone in Los Angeles, she was awakened one night by a racket at her door. Someone was trying to break in. She called the

Now: Sandy Froman, a lawyer, was president of the NRA in 2005–2007. She bought her first gun after someone tried to break into her house one night.

police. Then she called her neighbors, turned on the lights and her stereo, and began beating on her side of the door to try to drive the intruder away. It worked; the attacker slipped away into the darkness before the police arrived.

During those terrifying minutes, Froman realized she had no real way to protect herself. She decided never to be defenseless again. She took a shooting course, bought a handgun and started practicing. Much to her surprise, she loved shooting and turned into a good shot. Through this new interest she met a man named Bruce Nelson, a special agent with the California Department of Justice who also happened to be a top competitive shooter and a founding member of the International Practical Shooting Confederation.

Nelson and Froman married and moved to Arizona, where they both got involved in the politics of gun ownership. Like Lucy Chambliss almost 15 years earlier, Froman was elected to the NRA board of directors. In 2005 she became president of the association. She is now a veteran shooting competitor, a big-game hunter, a collector of military arms and a top-flight legislative advocate—all because of a thug who tried to break into her house.

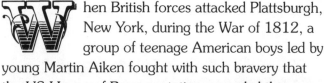

The Silver Star

When British forces attacked Plattsburgh, New York, during the War of 1812, a group of teenage American boys led by young Martin Aiken fought with such bravery that the US House of Representatives awarded them rifles for their "gallant and meritorious conduct."

In those days outstanding military acts by Americans were acknowledged, if at all, with an engraved sword or some sort of paper citation. In this case the rifles—Model 1819 Hall breechloading flintlocks, the most advanced military arm of the day—weren't delivered until 1826. The process of officially thanking the nation's heroes was a bit slapdash, at least until the Congressional Medal of Honor was created. (Read "Killer Apps.")

But that was just one award, and there are different levels of heroism. In 1918 Congress authorized more decorations that together make up the Pyramid of Honor: At the top is the Medal of Honor; next come the Distinguished Service Cross (Army), the Navy Cross (Navy, Marine Corps, Coast Guard) and the Air Force Cross. The third level of the pyramid is the Silver Star; like the Medal of Honor, it is given to all branches of America's armed services.

The first woman to earn a Silver Star was Mary Louise Roberts, a nurse and operating-room supervisor for the US Army's 56th Evacuation Unit. In January 1944, during WWII, the 56th landed at Anzio as part of the Allied invasion of Italy. Lt. Wilson was honored with the Silver Star for her actions while shrapnel from German artillery tore through the tent where she and her staff were working. Two of her nurses, Elaine Roe and Virginia Rourke, also earned Silver Stars that day, but because of her rank, Wilson, "the Angel of Anzio," was the first. Six nurses were killed at Anzio.

The first woman to receive the Silver Star since World War II was Sgt. Leigh Ann Hester of the 617th Military Police Company of the Kentucky Army National Guard. The Armed Forces Press Service wrote:

> Hester's squad was shadowing a supply convoy March 20 [2005] when anti-Iraq fighters ambushed the convoy. The squad moved to the side of the road, flanking the insurgents and cutting off their escape route. Hester led her team through the "kill zone" and into a flanking position, where she assaulted a trench line with grenades and M203 grenade launcher rounds. She and Nein, her squad leader, then cleared two trenches, at which time she killed three insurgents with her rifle.

Sgt. Hester's Silver Star was presented by Lt. Gen. John Vines, who declared, "My heroes don't play in the National Basketball Association and don't play in the US Open at Pinehurst. They're standing in front of me today. These are American heroes."

Women have won far fewer military medals than men, but for more than 200 years women in America's armed forces were officially barred from positions that directly involved fighting. This is changing fast, however, as the wars in Iraq and Afghanistan put everyone in harm's way. Now women fly combat missions in helicopter gunships and fighter planes, command armed patrol boats, serve as military police, escort convoys through combat zones and patrol with infantry squads as "support teams." These women are fighting and being wounded and sometimes dying right alongside men.

In December 2012 Secretary of Defense Leon Panetta announced that the last barriers would be removed. Soon women in the US Army will be able to join ground combat units as full-fledged soldiers, provided they meet the same physical-fitness and skill standards as the men.

Mary Louise Roberts Wilson, the US Army lieutenant and nurse who became the first woman to win the Silver Star, passed away in Dallas, Texas, in November 2001 at the age of 87.

Sgt. Leigh Ann Hester, 617th Military Police Co. of the Kentucky Army National Guard. In talking about the day her convoy was ambushed in Iraq, she said, "Your training kicks in . . . You've got a job to do—protecting yourself and your comrades."

Talking the Talk

Learn the Language of Guns & Shooting

Shooting has its own vocabulary, and non-shooters often mix up words or use them incorrectly. A magazine, for example, is not the same thing as a clip, and a revolver isn't a pistol. Even shooters sometimes get confused about what is or isn't an assault rifle. If you run into a word in this book that you're not sure of, flip back to this section and look it up. If it's not here, go to the dictionary. Or to the Internet.

The word "gun" itself can be confusing. It actually means a shotgun, not a rifle or a pistol, but everyone uses it more loosely. In this book you'll be able to tell whether we're using "gun" to mean a shotgun or a rifle, some type of handgun, or something else (such as a ship's cannon, called a naval gun), or whether it doesn't matter.

We use **firearm** to mean a shotgun, rifle or handgun that launches a projectile through the ignition of an explosive (gunpowder), so a BB gun or a pellet gun is not a firearm because it uses compressed air or some other gas.

Federal law and most state laws also treat firearms and air guns as two different things for the

Is this a real gun? An orange plastic tip on the muzzle tells us it's an Airsoft replica, in this case of a US Army M4 carbine. In some places the law calls this a firearm; in others it's an air gun. You should know the difference, and which definition applies where you live.

same reason. But some towns and cities define "firearm" as something like "any instrument used in the propulsion of pellets, shot, shells or bullets by action of gunpowder, compressed air or gas exploded or released within it." This is important because (depending on where you live) it means you could get into legal trouble even with a BB gun. This is covered in the chapter called "Shooting at Stuff," so don't worry about it just yet.

Rifles

Rifles are designed to fire a single projectile: a bullet. "Rifle" comes from rifling, the half-dozen or so grooves cut along the bore (the inside of the barrel) in long spirals. The bullet is a tight fit in the bore; the rifling grips the bullet and makes it spin in the air to make it fly accurately. (The feathers on an arrow do the same thing. So does a spiral pass with a football.)

Ideally, a hunting rifle is accurate enough to put its bullets into a one-inch circle at 100 yards. This is known as minute-of-angle accuracy, or MOA. In geometry a circle is divided into 360 degrees, and each degree is divided into 60 minutes. At a distance of 100 yards, one minute—equal to $\frac{1}{60}$ of $\frac{1}{360}$ of a circle—is exactly 1.047 inches. Or, for practical purposes, one inch.

Dozens of terms describe this bolt-action hunting rifle. You can learn them and also something about the hundreds of years of history and technology that went into developing it and its ammunition.

Target rifles, however, and certain tactical rifles for police and military sharpshooters should put their bullets more or less into the same hole at 100 yards. Why? At 1,000 yards, a one-minute-of-angle rifle could be off target by 10½ inches, and wind could make this deviation much greater. That's the difference between a bull's-eye and a complete miss. A long-range target or sniper rifle might be built to shoot to 0.25 MOA, a quarter of a minute of angle. It gets harder and harder to achieve less deviation than that.

There are four basic types of repeating rifles: bolt-action, lever-action, pump-action and autoloading. There are also single-shot rifles and double-barreled rifles. Turn to the chapter "Guns, Guns, Guns" for explanations.

The power of rifles—the energy of their cartridges or, really, their projectiles—varies tremendously. At one end of the range we have "plinking" rifles like .22 rimfires, for shooting at tin cans or small game like squirrels. (As you'll see, though, .22s can be deadly.) At the other end are so-called stopping rifles, such as the .577 Nitro Express, which fire bullets the size of your thumb that can penetrate many inches of thick skin and heavy bone. In general, the more powerful a rifle, the heavier it is and the harder it recoils, or kicks.

On the military side there are rifles that fire the large .50-caliber Browning Machine Gun (BMG)

Steve Helsley

Cartridges (from left): A .22 Long Rifle generates about 125 foot-pounds of energy; a .308 Winchester creates 20 times that much; and the .700 Nitro Express makes 71 times more than the .22, or 8,900 foot-pounds.

cartridge and even 20-millimeter (.790-caliber) anti-tank rounds, which makes them far more powerful than any hunting or target rifle. But .50 BMG rifles weigh more than 20 pounds and a 20mm Anzio rifle weighs 60 to 130 pounds, so these things are fired from bipods or other supports.

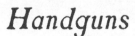

Handguns

Handguns fire bullets too and also have rifled barrels. There are three types of handguns: revolvers, pistols and single-shots. "Pistol" is like the word "gun"—it's used for all sorts of handguns, but it now means an autoloader or a single-shot.

Being usually less powerful than rifles, handguns are mostly for target shooting or for self-defense at close range. A few, mostly revolvers, are specially set up for hunting, with longer barrels and more powerful ammunition. Single-shot handguns often have longer barrels too, for better accuracy. Most cops and soldiers carry semi-automatic pistols.

The smallest common handgun is the .22; the largest is the .500 Smith & Wesson Magnum. Some single-shot hunting handguns take rifle ammunition,

which is even more powerful. Shooting these well takes practice. At least one self-defense revolver can fire .410 shotgun shells loaded with buckshot, which are large pellets that spread out in flight.

Steve Helsley

A Colt Model 1917 .45 revolver that was modified for fast-draw combat: The hammer spur and trigger guard were cut away and a carbine front sight added. The owner carried it in the jungles of Malaya in WWII. If only it could talk!

Handguns come in a huge variety of calibers and styles. This is a super-precise Anschutz air pistol for 10-meter international-match competition like in the Olympic Games. The shooter can adjust the grip to fit her hand like a glove. The tube under the barrel is the compressed-air reservoir.

Cartridges

Cartridges are single units of ammunition, sometimes called rounds. A rifle or handgun cartridge has a bullet wedged into the mouth of a metal case, or shell, which holds the gunpowder. A shotgun cartridge contains either shot pellets or a single large projectile called a slug. (Sometimes the word shell refers to a loaded cartridge.)

A cartridge's case contains a **primer**—a tiny explosive that is struck by the gun's firing pin, to light the gunpowder that drives the bullet or shot down the barrel. If the primer compound is contained inside the rim of the case (like most .22 ammunition), it's called a rimfire cartridge. More powerful ammunition has a separate primer set into the center of the base of the shell. This is called centerfire ammunition, and these cases often can be reloaded and reused.

A cartridge should fit precisely into the **chamber**, which is the first section of the gun barrel. After firing, the empty cartridge case (or shell) has to come out before the chamber can be reloaded for the next shot. Each type of firearm performs this process differently.

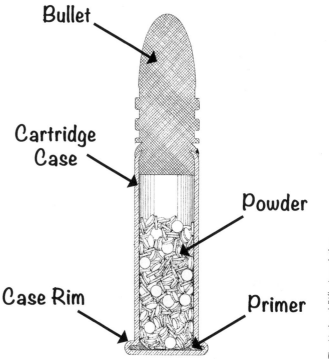

The National Rifle Association

The different parts of a .22 rimfire round. The primer may be in a different place and the projectile may be one bullet or many shot pellets, but basically all cartridges work the same way.

As guns progressed from smoothbore, single-shot muskets to modern repeating rifles, their projectiles evolved right along with them, from hand-cast lead balls to super-accurate bullets factory-made for dozens of specific purposes.

Caliber

The caliber of a rifle or handgun is the diameter of its bullet, which is also the diameter of its bore (the inside of the barrel, to the bottom of the rifling grooves). This is written in millimeters for European rifles and handguns and modern military weapons (9mm, for example, or 5.56mm or 7.62mm) and in decimal fractions of an inch (.308, for example, or .45 or .303) for American and British guns.

Just to be confusing, however, a cartridge's official name and the diameter of its bullet aren't always the same. For example, the British .450 Nitro Express and the American .458 Winchester Magnum use the same diameter bullet, which is in fact 0.458 inch across. This is because the Brits measure bore diameter between the tops of the rifling ridges (or "lands"), while Americans measure it between the bottoms of the rifling grooves. The difference is usually about .008", which just happens to be the difference between .450 and .458.

Sometimes, though, gun companies pick numbers just because they sound good or they're bigger than their competitors'. A .340 Weatherby Magnum bullet, for example, actually measures .338 inch in diameter—just like the .338 Winchester Magnum bullet.

Important: *Caliber* is also often used to mean *cartridge.* So we say, "Hey, what caliber is that rifle?"

If the reply is, "Three hundred," we have to ask again: "Which .300?"

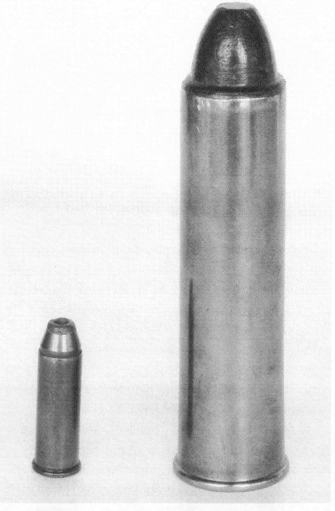

The word "Magnum" generally means a more powerful version of a certain cartridge. But power is relative. The .44 Magnum round (left) is puny compared to the massive 4-bore big-game cartridge from the 1880s.

Caliber Confusion

The self-contained cartridge was perfected 150 years ago and since then a lot of different ones have appeared. To be clear about which one we mean, we usually have to provide more than just the bore diameter. For example, 7.62mm is a very common bore size, so we can tell cartridges apart by the lengths of their cases, also in millimeters. There's a 7.62x22mm, a 7.62x38mm, a 7.62x39mm, a 7.62x51mm and a 7.62x54mm. (There may be more.) The shorter ones are for handguns and submachine guns; the others are for rifles. A couple of them have cases with rims that stick out at the base, so they have the letter R attached. There's also a 7.63x25mm pistol round and two 7.65mm pistol rounds: the German 7.65x22mm and the 7.65x17mm Browning.

And then, just to make things more confusing, some of the European metric cartridges have different names in English. The 7.65x17mm Browning is the same as the .32 ACP (Automatic Colt Pistol).

Seven-six-two em-em (as it's pronounced) is the metric equivalent of .30 inch, and there are even more .30-caliber cartridges, from the old .30-30 Winchester and .30-40 Krag to the .30 US M1 Carbine, the .30-06 Springfield, the .308 Winchester and on and on. These terms all mean something: The 30 and 40 refer to grains of gunpowder. (A grain is a unit of weight. There are 7,000 grains in a pound.) The .30-06 round was adopted by the American military in 1906; the .30 US Carbine was developed for the short, light, semi-auto M1 rifle of World War II.

Then, still in .30-caliber, there's a .300 Weatherby Magnum a .300 Winchester Magnum and a .300 Winchester Short Magnum, a .300 Holland & Holland (H&H) Magnum, a .300 Dakota Magnum, and more. The shapes and weights of the bullets vary and their cases have different dimensions and hold different amounts of powder, so they aren't interchangeable. A .300 Weatherby round won't chamber (fit) in a .300 H&H rifle.

"Magnum," by the way, just means "more powerful." An animal that is shot in the right place with a plain old .30-06 winds up just as dead as if it had been hit with a .300 Remington UltraMag, so the difference between a lot of these calibers amounts to one company trying to outsell another.

"Factory" loads are standard cartridges manufactured to precise dimensions that we can buy over the counter. One brand of factory-made ammunition will fit any gun chambered for that particular cartridge. Some people like to create their own cartridges by modifying a standard case (and chambering a gun barrel to fit). This is called a "wildcat" cartridge, and its name may be something like the .20 Practical. Sometimes a wildcat performs so well that it becomes a standard factory round.

There's one more type of cartridge designation that you should know about. Most of these are British and date from the late 1800s, but some of them are still used. A .500/.450 x 3¼, for example, has a case that's 3¼ inches long and originally was meant for a .510 bullet (what the British call .500-caliber), but its mouth has been reduced ("necked down") to take a smaller .450 bullet (that is, .458 in Brit-speak). Other common examples include the .577/.450 and the .500/.416. The case length is needed only where there's a choice.

If you've followed us this far, you already know more than many experienced shooters do. Don't let this confuse you. Just be aware that you need more than one number to identify most cartridges. Over time you'll get comfortable with the lingo. In the meantime, just flip back to these pages if you have questions.

Bullets

Bullets usually but not always contain lead (because lead has a very high specific gravity, meaning that it's heavy for its volume) and have some sort of jacket, or outer layer, of a metal such as copper or nickel.

The Hague Convention on land warfare of 1899 prohibited "the use of bullets which expand or flatten easily in the human body." Ever since then military bullets have had full metal jackets, which are supposed to drill right through and leave behind fairly clean, small holes. This may reduce the slaughter on a battlefield, but in hunting the goal is to kill the game as quickly and humanely as possible. Most hunting bullets have only partial jackets and soft (or hollow) points, so they "mushroom," or expand, when they hit in order to cut as many blood vessels and organs as possible.

Big animals with thick skins and heavy bones usually require heavier, stronger bullets. The lead may be mixed with other materials to make it harder or be replaced entirely by copper, bronze, brass or something else. Bullets that don't expand at all—for punching through heavy bone—are called "solids." Over about two centuries of development ammunition makers have learned to make bullets for different needs that perform very differently.

Bullet weights are given in grains. A 450-grain bullet weighs almost exactly one ounce. (Dig out five quarters; that's about one ounce.) A hollowpoint rimfire .22 bullet may weigh only 37 grains. The US Army's standard 5.56mm rifle bullet weighs 62 grains. Most .30-caliber hunting bullets weigh 150 to 180 grains. The largest .500 Smith & Wesson Magnum revolver bullet is 500 grains. Most cartridges are available with several sizes and types of bullets for different kinds of shooting or targets.

A round musket **ball** isn't the same thing as a streamlined, cone-shaped rifle **bullet**. Bullets have two great advantages over balls: First, they are more aerodynamically stable in flight and so more accurate. And second, a bullet can be made heavier just by making it longer, while a lead ball of a certain diameter (or gauge—see below) comes in just one weight.

Ballistics

The science of projectiles in flight is called ballistics. Shooters generally use two ballistic measurements to describe the performance of bullets: their speed (in feet per second) and the energy that they create (in foot-pounds). This is important, and there's more about it in "How Far & How Hard," but for now just know that a bullet of a certain weight, say 165 grains, might be traveling at 2,800 fps and generating 3,200 foot-pounds of energy. These numbers usually are measured at the gun's muzzle and sometimes 100 yards away in order to indicate how much the bullet has slowed down at that distance and how much power it has lost.

A bullet immediately starts to slow down (because of air resistance) and drop (because of gravity) when it leaves the muzzle, so it travels along a curve called the arc of **trajectory**. The bullet's velocity—the speed at which it flies—and shape determine how long it takes to get to the target, and this sets the trajectory.

A bullet that travels 2,000 feet in two seconds will drop 64 feet in that distance (if it doesn't hit the ground first). But if its speed can be doubled, to cover 2,000 feet in just one second, the bullet drops only 16 feet because gravity and air resistance have less time to affect it. The sights on a gun barrel are adjusted to tilt the barrel upward to compensate for the drop in trajectory.

Modern bullets achieve muzzle velocities of anywhere from about 1,000 to 4,000 fps. Their speed is measured using an instrument called a chronograph. The bullet's energy can then be calculated with a mathematical formula.

Shotguns

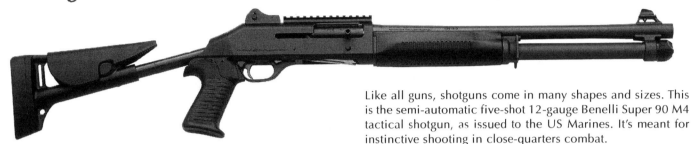

Like all guns, shotguns come in many shapes and sizes. This is the semi-automatic five-shot 12-gauge Benelli Super 90 M4 tactical shotgun, as issued to the US Marines. It's meant for instinctive shooting in close-quarters combat.

Shotguns are "smoothbores"; they have no rifling in their barrels. Shotguns are meant to shoot clusters of pellets, which spread out to make it easier to hit fast-moving targets such as birds in flight. Shotguns are short-range firearms.

The ounce or so of pellets in a normal shotgun cartridge needs a little distance to spread out, so inside of 20 feet a shotgun blast is highly lethal and destructive, no matter whether the gun is loaded with fine birdshot or large buckshot. Beyond that distance the spread of the pellets can be controlled somewhat by "choking" the barrel—shrinking its bore diameter slightly at the muzzle. A full-choke barrel delivers a tighter cloud of pellets downrange than an open-choke barrel; it should put nearly all of the shot inside a 30-inch circle at 40 yards.

Shotguns also can fire single projectiles called slugs loaded in special cartridges. Slugs are sort of halfway between a ball and a bullet in shape and will kill deer-size game out to about 125 yards. Some slugs are grooved to spin in flight, and it is possible to buy replacement rifled barrels for shotguns. Still, slugs don't have the range and accuracy of bullets.

Shotguns are measured in **gauge**. Gauge is the number of equal-size balls that could be made from one pound of pure lead that each just fits that-diameter barrel. A 12-gauge gun barrel would fit a ball that weighs one-twelfth of a pound. A 20-gauge gun barrel is smaller in diameter, to fit a ball that weighs one-twentieth of a pound.

This comes from old cannon designations: A 12-pounder cannon from the days of the American Revolution fired a 12-pound ball; a 12-gauge gun is a $1/12$-pounder. (By the way, those cannons were guns—no rifling—and their balls were iron, not lead. A 12-pound ball is about 4½ inches in diameter.) The designation was by weight instead of bore diameter, or caliber, because a ball that weighs X always has a certain diameter, while the weight of a bullet can be made more or less by changing its length, even though its diameter (caliber) stays the same.

A lead ball that weighs $1/12$ of a pound is 0.729 inch in diameter, so 12 gauge is .729 caliber. That's almost three-quarters of an inch, much bigger than any rifle or handgun caliber because of space needed for the hundreds of pellets in a shotgun cartridge. Twelve has been the most

A completely different sort of 12-gauge—a made-to-measure, double-barreled Rigby shotgun for hunting gamebirds. But it too is designed for fast, instinctive shooting without aiming.

popular shotgun gauge for hundreds of years. The most common other shotgun gauges today are 20 and 28. There are also 10- and 16-gauge guns. The smallest shotgun is the .410 bore, which is a true caliber, not a gauge size. (See "Shotguns for Birds" in the chapter "Game: Animals & Birds.")

There are different kinds of shotguns for target shooting, hunting and tactical use (military, police and self-defense).

The parts of a modern shotgun cartridge: The primer, gunpowder and (in a plastic shot-cup wad) shot pellets are packed into the plastic-and-brass case, which is then crimped shut.

Magazines

A magazine is a container built into a gun that holds the ammunition. A magazine has a spring in it that pushes the cartridges along so the "action" of the gun can grab each fresh one and feed it into the chamber for firing. A magazine is often called a clip, but this is wrong. A clip is a strip of metal that holds a row of cartridges so that they can be slid into the magazine or the cylinder of a revolver. (Filling a magazine by pushing each round in against spring pressure can be a pain.) Some clips go right into the magazine with the cartridges; a charger or stripper clip does not.

Rifle or shotgun magazines can be tubes under the barrel or in the buttstock that you fill from one end. Or they may be rectangular boxes that lock into the action just ahead of the trigger. Box magazines may fit within the stock or they may stick out, and they're either detachable or fixed in place.

A detachable magazine can be removed when it's empty and a fresh one snapped into place for quick reloading. The first detachable magazines appeared more than a century ago. Fixed box maga-

Box magazines and their clips. These are for the .30-caliber M1 carbine. A clip is a strip of metal that holds a row of cartridges to be slid into a magazine or into the cylinder of a revolver.

zines may have a floorplate that can be opened to dump out unused cartridges when it's time to unload the gun (instead of working the action to cycle the cartridges through the gun, which might result in an accidental discharge). Box magazines on hunting rifles usually hold two to four rounds. Assault rifles (and many of their look-alikes) usually have long magazines that hold 15 to 30 cartridges.

The Thompson submachine gun was sold with 50- and 100-round drum magazines in the 1920s, but high-capacity magazines go back at least to the late 1700s. The Girandoni air rifle that Lewis and Clark brought on their 1804–06 expedition across North America (see the chapter "You'll Put Your Eye Out!") held 20 to 30 lead balls that could be fired as fast as the shooter could flick the loading lever, cock the hammer and pull the trigger.

A pistol magazine generally holds from six to a dozen or more cartridges. It usually fits into the butt, or handle, of the gun. If it sticks out farther than the end of the grip, it's an extended magazine for more ammunition. However, high-capacity magazines of any kind, for rifles or pistols, are slow to load and have a tendency to misfeed, or jam.

Revolver magazines are called cylinders, which turn (revolve) to bring each cartridge in line with

A revolver's magazine is its cylinder; it swings out to the side for reloading. Revolver clips are half-moon shapes that fit the curve of the cylinder. On some old revolvers, the barrel and cylinder are hinged to tip down, so you reload from above.

the barrel for firing. Modern revolvers typically hold anywhere from five to 10 rounds.

Machine Guns

Dept. of Defense

A heavy machine gun lights up the night with a stream of .50-caliber tracer fire from the roof of a Humvee. The automatic gun changed warfare when it arrived on the battlefields of WWI.

By law and by sporting tradition and ethics, a rifle, shotgun or handgun meant for hunting fires one round at a time; the trigger has to be pulled once per shot. A firearm that shoots as long as its trigger is held back is a fully automatic weapon— also known as a machine gun.

Before the National Firearms Act of 1934, Americans could own machine guns with no re-

striction. Civilians can still own and shoot machine guns if the guns are properly registered.

Full-auto weapons, including a few combat shotguns, come in all shapes and sizes. A machine pistol is a handgun that can empty its magazine with just one squeeze of the trigger. A submachine gun is a compact, short-range, two-handed machine gun chambered for a pistol cartridge. An assault rifle is a full-size shoulder weapon for military use that fires a more powerful round. Many assault rifles can be switched from full- to semi-automatic fire, and some fire in three-shot bursts.

Non-military versions of these rifles fire only semi-automatically, meaning that the trigger has to be pulled separately for each shot.

And then there are light, medium and heavy machine guns, which are increasingly more powerful and are operated by a crew of two or more soldiers. Medium and heavy machine guns are usually mounted in aircraft or boats or on trucks or armored vehicles.

Antique Guns

Federal gun laws and regulations that apply across the whole country, not just in one state or another, are enforced by the Bureau of Alcohol, Tobacco, Firearms and Explosives. You should know that many of these laws do not apply to antique guns; and the BATFE (or ATF, as it's usually called) defines an "antique" gun two ways:

First, it is any firearm that was made in or before 1898. This means that a lever-action Winchester Model 1895 rifle, a bolt-action Mauser Model 1898, a Colt Single Action Army .45 revolver and a double-barreled Westley Richards shotgun, to name just four examples, qualify as "antiques" —provided they were made before 1899—even though many are still in use.

Any versions of such guns made after 1898 are not legally antiques—even if they are exactly the same model, made by the same company and fire the same ammunition. Go figure. The date a gun was manufactured can nearly always be determined by the gun's serial number (if you can locate the maker's records, that is).

And second, federal law says that an antique firearm is one that loads from the muzzle, uses black powder or its equivalent, and can't fire "fixed ammunition"—that is, modern-style, one-piece cartridges. In this definition, date of manufacture makes no difference; the gun could have been made last week.

There are a couple of other qualifications that have to do with using ammunition that "is not readily available in the ordinary channels of commercial trade," but they are minor. All this is important because such "antique firearms" can be sold, shipped around the country, and imported into the US without any legal restrictions.

The AR-15, the 'Modern Sporting Rifle'

Sooner or later you'll probably want a rifle that looks like an AR-15. To some people, even these lookalikes are "assault weapons" that don't belong in civilian hands. The shooting industry, however, calls them MSRs, Modern Sporting Rifles, and says they're the victims of misinformation. AR-type rifles have become very popular in America, and for good reason. Here's the background.

Whether they served in the Civil War, the Indian Wars, the Spanish-American War, World War I or II, Korea, Vietnam, Iraq or Afghanistan, generations of Americans learned to shoot with military rifles. When servicemen and women returned home, if they went hunting or target shooting, they often used what they were most comfortable with—the rifle they had been taught to shoot and that they had come to depend on.

From about 1860 to 1900, Americans' favorite rifles tended to be single-shots or lever-actions. These gave way to the bolt-action rifle, which dominated both world wars and, no surprise, became the standard for civilians too. Then, beginning in the 1950s and based on the US Army's M1 and M14 rifles, semi-automatics began to get more popular at home.

In the 1960s this led to the M16, the rifle that is still issued to US forces today. So far about 8 million of these have been produced, and it's a rare TV newscast that doesn't show M16s in the hands of American or other troops.

The M16 is the military designation for the AR-15, a rifle created by a man named Eugene Stoner in the 1950s and produced by the ArmaLite Corporation. "AR" stands for ArmaLite rifle, not assault rifle or automatic rifle.

However, the M16 and the original AR-15 are true assault rifles: fully automatic, shoulder-fired military weapons that take a medium-power cartridge. As you now know, any firearm capable of full-auto fire is a machine gun—it runs as long as the trigger is held back and there's ammo in the magazine—and machine guns have been closely restricted (not banned!) for civilians in the US since 1934. Civilian versions of such rifles fire only semi-automatically, meaning that the trigger has to be pulled separately for each shot.

OK, back to the story. By now millions of American servicemen and women have been trained to shoot the M16 and a shorter version of it called the M4. In this sense these guns are no different from the single-shot, bolt-action and semi-auto military rifles of earlier generations, so it's no surprise that civilian (semi-automatic) models of the M16/M4 have become very popular among hunters and target shooters. They are fairly light and easy to carry, rugged, dependable, accurate and, above all, familiar.

This is why the AR-type has been dubbed the "modern sporting rifle." However, it's impossible to tell at a glance whether a particular AR lookalike is capable of full-auto fire (and therefore a military

assault rifle) or if it's a civilian-legal semi-auto rifle. People who aren't aware—or don't care—that there's a difference just lump the two together. This led to the political and legal term "assault *weapon*," which is different from assault *rifle*.

Like other semi-autos, AR-type rifles (or Modern Sporting Rifles, or whatever you want to call them) are legal to own in all 50 states, provided the buyer meets federal, state and local requirements. (At least when this was written.) They're just ordinary semi-autos that happen to look like something else. You can say the same thing about some squirt guns.

But until you become an experienced shooter, it's easy to forget to "safe" a semi-auto gun (de-cock it, or at least flip on the safety catch) in between shots. And if you also forget about muzzle control—that is, where the gun is pointed—it's too easy to put a bullet somewhere it wasn't meant to go. An AR-type rifle is not the ideal beginner's gun.

Parts of a Modern Sporting Rifle

A "Modern Sporting Rifle"—a Patriot Ordnance Factory, Inc., Model P-415. This is a modular rifle; virtually every part can be changed, and a variety of accessories, from lasers to night sights, can be attached to the rails along the barrel.

Parts of a Bolt-Action Rifle

Rifles, shotguns and handguns have many similar parts. Shown here are the parts of a commonly used rifle—the bolt-action.

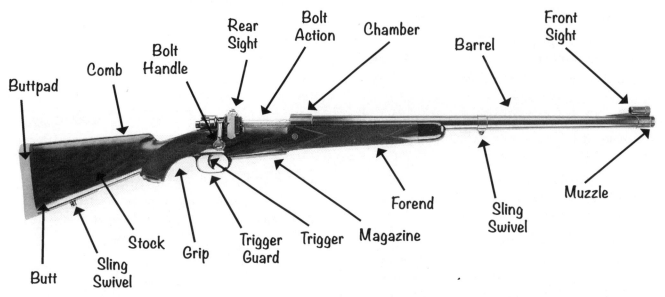

Parts of a Semi-Auto Pistol

A Ruger 22/45 Lite semi-automatic pistol. The knurled ring at the muzzle can be unscrewed and replaced by a suppressor (silencer).

Glossary

Action—the machinery of a gun that loads and fires the ammunition and then ejects the empty case.

Action body—the housing for the action, also called the receiver.

Assault rifle—a medium-weight military rifle that can be fired continuously as a machine gun, as well as semi-automatically, one round at a time.

Assault weapon—a political term: An "assault weapon" may look like an assault rifle, but it does not function like one; as defined by law in some states, most assault weapons are semi-automatics.

Barrel—the long tube through which a bullet or shot charge is fired.

Blunderbuss—a short-barreled muzzleloading smoothbore gun with a flared muzzle that is loaded with heavy balls and meant for close combat; fore-runner of the riot gun.

Bolt—the part of a gun's action that locks the cartridge into the chamber for firing.

Bore—the inside of the barrel.

Breech—the end of the barrel attached to the receiver, or action body, where the chamber is.

Breechloader—a firearm that is loaded from the breech, or the end of the barrel near the shooter. Successful breechloaders had to wait until one-piece metallic cartridges were perfected, around 1860. Breechloaders can be loaded and fired much faster than muzzleloaders.

Butt or **buttstock**—the part of a long gun (a shotgun or rifle) that fits against the shooter's shoulder.

Carbine—a compact, short-barreled rifle.

Centerfire—a cartridge with a separate primer in the center of the base of the case. These cases can be reloaded and reused.

Chamber—the first part of the barrel, where the cartridge fits.

Chamber pressure—a measure of the explosive energy of a cartridge. It's the pressure in pounds per square inch that the barrel, chamber and bolt have to withstand when the cartridge is fired.

Choke—in shotgun barrels, the constriction of the bore near the muzzle that helps control the spread of the shot pellets in flight.

Clip—a strip of metal that holds several cartridges so that they can be loaded into a magazine or, in a revolver, the cylinder.

Cylinder—see "revolver."

Damascus steel—strips of iron and steel heated and hammered together in a forge and then wound in a spiral around a long rod, or mandrel, to make a gun barrel. Damascus barrels faded away around 1910.

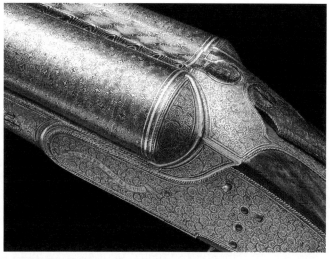

Steve Helsley

The many alternating spiral layers of forged metal give Damascus steel its unusual look. When steel-making and machining became cheaper, Damascus faded away. Today high-quality Damascus barrels are prized. The action of this Sauer shotgun was engraved to complement the pattern on the barrels.

Double action—a revolver with a hammer that can be cocked and fired with one (long) pull of the trigger. See "single action" too.

Double rifle—a rifle with two barrels, either side by side or one atop the other.

Drilling—a gun with three barrels, usually two shotgun barrels side by side on top and one rifle barrel underneath.

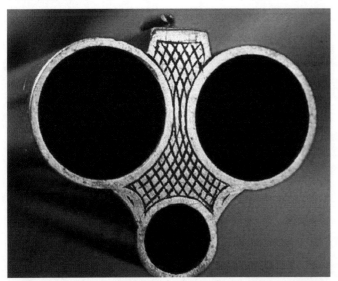

Three-barreled break-action guns called Drillings are popular in Germany. With shotgun and rifle barrels, the hunter is prepared for everything from birds to big game. *Dreiling* means triplet in German.

Dry-firing—working the action and pulling the trigger with no ammunition in the gun or with snap caps (dummy cartridges) in place of live ammunition.

Factory load—ammunition that can be bought over the counter in a store.

Flash hider—a cone-shaped device on a military rifle meant to cover up the muzzle flash of firing in the dark in order to keep the shooter from being blinded.

Flintlock—a muzzleloading gun whose powder charge is fired by sparks created by a piece of flint dragged across a steel "frizzen."

Full-automatic—a machine gun.

Hair trigger—a trigger that fires the gun with very little finger pressure. Dueling pistols often had hair triggers; now they're used on target rifles and

handguns. A hair trigger is sometimes confused with a set trigger.

Iron sights—also called open sights; that is, not telescopic, optical or electronic. (They haven't actually been made of iron for more than a century.)

Kentucky rifle—a light, long-barreled, full-stocked smallbore (.32 to .50 caliber) flintlock from the 1700s when Kentucky was the frontier, where civilization ended and the wilderness began. Kentucky rifles were actually made by German gunsmiths who settled in Pennsylvania. They were beautifully built and highly accurate. America's reputation as a "land of riflemen" began with the Kentucky/Pennsylvania rifle.

National Firearms Museum

A flintlock "Kentucky" rifle made by Mathias Miller of Pennsylvania around 1780. America's reputation as a "land of riflemen" began with these rifles, which helped win the American Revolution.

Lockwork—the part of the action that fires the cartridge; includes the hammer, spring and firing pin.

Machine gun—a gun that keeps firing as long as its trigger is held back (and ammunition is available).

Magazine—a container that holds the ammunition in a repeating gun. It can be a tube under the barrel or a rectangular box that fits into the action.

Magnum—a more powerful version of a cartridge; usually not interchangeable in the same gun.

Metallic cartridge—a one-piece round with its bullet and powder contained in a metal (usually brass or steel) case, or shell.

Musket—a long-barreled military shoulder gun. At first, a musket was a smoothbore muzzleloader. The word "musket" was still used in the early 1900s, even after the military switched to breechloading rifles, but then it became obsolete.

Muzzle—the end of the barrel from which the bullet or shot exits.

Muzzle brake—holes or slots at the muzzle of a gun barrel that bleed off or redirect some of the powder gas to reduce recoil. Some muzzle brakes are machined right into the barrel; others are attached to it.

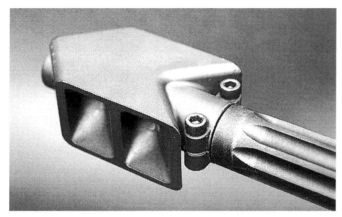

These backswept channels in the Barrett rifle's muzzle brake help tame the recoil of the .50 BMG cartridge by bleeding off and redirecting some of the combustion gas.

Muzzleloader—a firearm that's not a breechloader; its powder and ball or shot have to be rammed down the barrel from the muzzle with wads to hold them in place. Before about 1850 nearly all firearms—handguns, rifles, shotguns, cannons—were muzzleloaders.

Pennsylvania rifle—see "Kentucky rifle."

Percussion lock—a type of ignition system for muzzleloading guns that uses a metallic or paper primer held where the hammer can hit it.

Pistol—a semi-automatic or single-shot handgun.

Plinking—shooting for fun at improvised targets, almost always with a .22.

Point-blank range—a distance at which the bullet has not yet dropped significantly.

Primer—the part of a cartridge that is struck by the firing pin to ignite the gunpowder.

Receiver—the housing for the action, also called the action body.

Recoil pad—a section of soft material at the end of a gun's buttstock that absorbs some of the recoil.

Revolver—a handgun with a cylinder-shaped magazine that turns (revolves) to bring each cartridge in line with the barrel for firing.

Rifling—the spiral grooves cut into the bore that grip the bullet and make it spin in flight for stability and accuracy.

Rimfire—a cartridge with its primer powder inside the rim of the case.

Riot gun—a short-barreled pump-action or semi-auto shotgun issued to police. The term isn't used any longer.

A 12-gauge Winchester Model 1897 riot gun. The US Army added bayonets and called them trench guns. This was the tactical shotgun of its day, meant to deliver a lot of firepower at close range.

National Firearms Museum

Safety or **safety catch**—a mechanism that locks the trigger or action of a gun so that it can't be fired accidentally.

Self-loader—a full- or semi-automatic gun.

Semi-automatic—a firearm that reloads and cocks itself automatically and can be fired just by pressing the trigger. A machine gun is a fully automatic firearm that fires as long as the trigger is held back.

Serial number—today, by law, every gun has to be numbered by its maker to record its caliber and when and to whom it was sold. (Most makers record much more information than that.) Better-quality guns have had serial numbers for 200 years or more.

Set trigger—a trigger that can be "set" to fire at two different pull weights, for example four pounds and four ounces. The heavy setting is for normal hunting use. The light one is for extra-precise shooting from a rest at a faraway target. European hunting rifles often have set triggers.

Sights—the optical or mechanical fittings on a gun barrel that let the shooter aim precisely.

Single action—a handgun with a hammer that has to be cocked with the thumb before it can be fired with the trigger. See also "Double action."

Six-gun—a revolver with chambers for six cartridges; also known as a six-shooter.

Small arms—rifles, shotguns and handguns that are carried and used by one person.

Smoothbore—a firearm with no rifling in its barrel: a shotgun or cannon.

Snap cap—a dummy cartridge made for dry-firing.

Spitzer bullet—a modern-style bullet that comes to a point. The word comes from *Spitzgeschoss*, which is German for "pointy bullet."

Stock—the part of a long gun that holds the action and barrel and that the shooter holds. It can be wood, fiberglass, plastic or some other material. Stocks have been made of everything from rhino horn to mastodon ivory.

Submachine gun—a full-automatic weapon (machine gun) that fires a pistol cartridge.

Subsonic round—a cartridge with a reduced powder charge to drop the velocity of the bullet below the speed of sound (about 1,125 fps at sea level) to make it quieter.

Takedown—a rifle or shotgun that can be taken apart into two sections for easier transport or storage.

Tracer round—a bullet with a tiny powder charge in its base that burns in flight so the shooter can see where it goes.

A takedown rifle or shotgun is one that can be taken apart for easier transport or storage. This is a Krieghoff Semprio.

Wheelgun—another name for a revolver. (The cylinder turns like a wheel as the gun is fired.)

Wildcat—a custom-made cartridge, one that's not commercially available.

Everyday Shooting Expressions

uns and shooting have played enormous roles in American history. They also have left their footprints all over our language. Here's a list of firearms-related words and phrases that almost everyone uses, even people who don't know where they came from.

All up in arms—outraged, excited; from a police, militia or other first-response unit grabbing its guns to answer an alarm.

Big gun—an important person.

Big shot—another important person.

Bite the bullet—go ahead, do it, even if it hurts. Old-time medics supposedly gave injured soldiers a bullet (more likely a piece of leather or wood) to bite down on while they were removing a bullet or hacking off an arm.

Bull's-eye!—you're right on target with what you were saying (or doing).

Bullet—used to describe anything really fast, like Japan's bullet train.

Butt (of a joke)—the butt end of a gun is where it hurts (recoil).

Caliber—meaning quality, as in "he's of the right caliber."

Cannon fodder—something or someone that's expendable or of so little value that they could be marched into the enemy cannons or could be fired out of a cannon.

Cocked and locked—all set, good to go, ready to rock and roll.

Dodge a bullet—escape the consequences.

Drop the hammer—go ahead, do it; fire!

Firing a broadside—giving it all you've got. Battleships that shot every gun on one side of the ship at an enemy fired a broadside.

Firing a shot across the bow—traditionally, a military vessel fires a round from a deck gun into the water by the bow of a ship they're trying to stop; this indicates that the next one won't miss. Used generally to mean any threatening or confrontational warning.

Flash in the pan—a minor event that comes and goes quickly, like the flash of priming powder in a flintlock pan.

Full bore—using all the power available, like a cartridge loaded full of gunpowder.

Give 'em both barrels—let 'em have it!

Going great guns—furious activity, like a warship firing all of its great guns in broadsides.

Going off half-cocked—doing something before you're completely ready, as in dropping the hammer on a gun before it's fully cocked.

Gun-shy—afraid of the recoil or noise of a shot; used to describe anyone who's nervous about repeating something that caused a problem before. ("He broke his leg, so he's gun-shy about skiing again.")

Hang fire—a shot that hasn't gone off even though the trigger was pulled is "hanging fire"; so it means an unexpected delay.

He can't hit the broad side of a barn—he's incompetent.

He has a hair trigger—he's short-tempered; could go off half-cocked.

He has you in his sights—he's coming after you; look out!

He's gunning for you—look out, someone's after you.

Hired gun—an assassin or a mercenary soldier; generally anyone brought in to do an unpleasant or difficult job.

Hit or miss—maybe it'll work and maybe it won't; erratic.

Hoist with his own petard—he's the victim of his own attempt to harm somebody else. "Petard" is a French word for a type of explosive.

Hotter than a $2 pistol—even a long time ago, $2 was very little for a pistol, but sometimes a pistol had to be gotten rid of quickly and was sold cheap. Used to describe something dodgy or of questionable background.

In the crosshairs—under close scrutiny, as though being watched through a riflescope.

Jump the gun—start too early; like going off half-cocked.

Just a wild shot—a poor attempt; a shot in the dark.

Keep your powder dry—stay alert, be prepared; from the muzzleloading days when wet powder or primer meant a misfire.

Kentucky windage—adjusting to an unfamiliar situation; a guesstimate. Windage is how far a bullet is blown off course by the wind, and Kentucky windage was an unscientific guess about where to aim to compensate. Probably linked to the frontiersmen who used Kentucky rifles.

Loaded for bear—prepared for the worst; or really angry and looking for revenge.

Lock and load—get ready! Once you've done this, you're "cocked and locked."

Lock, stock and barrel—everything; the whole shootin' match.

Long shot—a difficult, possibly risky attempt that's unlikely to succeed.

Machine-gun speech—talkingwaytoofast.

On the right trajectory—heading in the correct direction, like a well-aimed bullet.

On target—absolutely right; bull's-eye!

Parting shot—the last word. Retreating troops fired a parting shot and left the scene.

Point-blank—at short range, used to mean blunt, or in your face. "I asked her point-blank why . . . ."

Potshot—an easy score or an unfair comment. From "shooting for the pot"—hunting up any animal for food as opposed to a challenging trophy.

A powder-keg situation—something that could blow up or go wrong any minute. When cannons were muzzleloaders, gunpowder was kept in kegs that could be blown up accidentally by sparks or even static electricity.

Quick on the draw—fast-reacting; almost the same as going off half-cocked. It comes from Western-style fast-draw handgun shooting.

Quick on the trigger—same as above.

Ramrod straight—usually used to describe a soldier's position at attention. A ramrod is used to push a bullet down a muzzleloader's barrel. Sometimes "ramrod stiff."

Riding shotgun—stagecoach guards in the old West were armed with double-barreled shotguns and sat next to the driver, so this means either sitting in the front passenger seat in a car or riding along as protection.

Right on target—absolutely correct; bull's-eye!

Shoot from the hip—instead of aiming with the sights, so it means to act quickly without preparing.

Shoot first, ask questions later—act too quickly.

Shoot off your mouth—talk foolishly or carelessly.

Shoot your wad—give it all you've got.

Shooting blanks—used to describe a male that's sterile.

Shot in the dark—a good-faith attempt that might or might not work.

Shotgun approach—trying everything possible; like spraying shot pellets all over a target.

Shotgun wedding—a forced or hurried wedding where the bride is pregnant and her father is supposedly holding a shotgun on the groom to make him marry her.

Smoking gun—evidence; a strong clue or hint, like a gun that's still smoking left at the scene of a crime.

Stick to your guns!—don't give up.

Straight shooter—a trustworthy, honest, reliable person.

Take a shot!—give it a try!

The whole shootin' match—everything; the whole banana, enchilada, etc.

Trigger-happy—inclined to act too quickly, to shoot first and ask questions later.

Under the gun—under a lot of pressure to act, as though someone's forcing you to do something at the point of a gun.

Zero in—take careful aim, or close in on something. Zeroing-in your sights means adjusting them for zero error so the gun shoots accurately.

Zombie gun—Mossberg's lever-action .30-30 "black rifle" that mixes new and old with pure fantasy.

Making It Go *BOOM!*

A Short History of Firearms & Ammunition

For more than 500 years, black powder and lead balls were the standard diet of firearms. Through all of those centuries the quality of gunpowder improved and the round balls eventually became conical bullets, but the biggest changes were in how the powder was ignited and the shot was fired. The earliest "hand gonnes" (portable firearms) had no moving parts, sights or shoulder stocks. They were basically small cannons: crude gun barrels loaded from the muzzle and mounted on a pole or rested on a support. The gunner held a burning stick or something similar to a small hole in the barrel to light the powder charge.

Early in the 15th Century (1400s) came the first advancement in ignition. For the next 400 years, until the percussion cap was invented, every gun barrel had a "pan," a small cup attached alongside the barrel at the breech to hold a bit of priming powder. A tiny hole in the barrel wall led from the pan to the chamber inside. Every gun also had some sort of mechanism called a "lock" that set off the priming charge. The flame traveled through the hole

A "hand gonne" was a smaller version of this—and this was a portable version of a cannon. The painting is from 1405; the downsizing continued until we had muskets and handguns.

and lit the main charge in the chamber. The pan stayed pretty much the same for four centuries, but the lock slowly evolved.

Early Guns: The Matchlock

A English royal .60-caliber matchlock. A clamp on the end of the curved arm (the serpentine) held the "match," a length of smoldering rope. Pulling the trigger (that bent piece of wire underneath) released the serpentine to snap down into the pan, where the match lit the priming powder—most of the time. (Here the match cord is missing and the serpentine is resting in the pan.) The matchlock was the first portable gun with a trigger and a stock, which helped aim and control the recoil.

he first gun with a priming pan and an action was the matchlock. It had a length of thick cord, the "match," clamped in a pivoting S-shaped arm called a serpentine. Before the battle, the gunner lit the end of the match—a fuse, really—that then smoldered. To fire the gun, he pulled on the lower end of the serpentine, which pivoted the burning cord into the priming powder in the pan. This was the first trigger, and it allowed aiming and a steadier, two-handed grip on the gun. Match cord was first soaked in saltpeter, a chemical that is a component of gunpowder; when it dried, the cord would burn evenly and slowly.

Some units of the Chinese army were still using matchlocks (as well as bows and arrows and spears) in the early 1900s, but the next step ahead in firearms technology came around 1500 in Italy.

Early Guns: The Wheellock

he wheellock's inventor was none other than the brilliant artist, engineer and scientist Leonardo da Vinci. Since it generated friction to create heat, the wheellock was the first true mechanical gun lock. It had a small steel wheel powered by a hairspring; next to it was a pivoting arm (the "dog") that held a piece of iron pyrite, for sparking. The shooter had to wind the spring with a special key before he put priming powder in the pan. Pulling the trigger released the wheel to spin and pressed the pyrite against it. Like a cigarette lighter, this made a shower of sparks that dropped into the pan to set off the charge—most of the time, anyway. It took the skills of both a watchmaker and a gunmaker to build a wheellock, so it was too expensive to be mass-produced for armies. Kings, princes, dukes and that sort ordered them. Since they could be fired with just one hand, the first pistols were wheellocks.

A highly decorated wheellock with two locks on the same barrel. The shooter loaded two charges, one behind the other, and then fired the front one first (or tried to, hoping that both didn't go off together). Under each round cover is a steel wheel; the two curved arms, the "dogs," held chunks of a mineral called iron pyrite. After loading the gun, the shooter used a key to wind a spring behind each wheel. Pulling the trigger released the wheel, so it could spin, and let the dog snap down onto it. The friction of the pyrite against the edge of the spinning wheel created sparks, which fell into the pan, inside, and lit the powder.

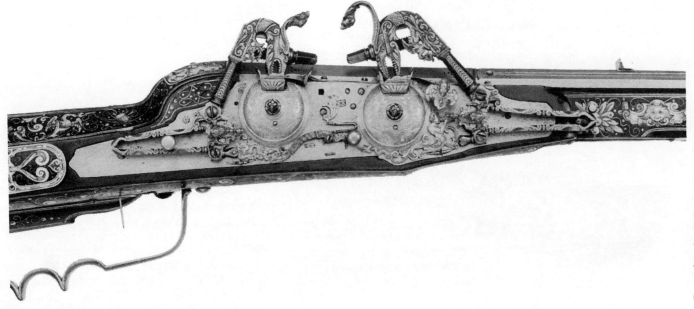

Tower of London Collection; George Swenson

Early Guns: The Flintlock

ast-forward another hundred years to the end of the 16th Century: Gunmakers in Holland invented the snaphance *(snap-hantz)*, a simpler and more reliable lock that didn't need a wheel. It had a hammer, called the cock, that held a piece of flint. The gunner thumbed back the hammer against a spring to "cock" it. When he released the hammer, by squeezing the trigger, the spring snapped it down onto a steel plate called the frizzen. Once again sparks were created that set off the priming charge.

Meanwhile, in Spain, gunmakers came up with a slightly different form of snaplock called a miquelet *(mick-elet)*. Like the snaphance, it was much cheaper to make than a wheellock, but it was still too expensive to supply to ordinary soldiers. So the matchlock stayed in service for a few more years. (As did the longbow, which was a lot faster and more accurate.)

The snaphance and the miquelet both had mechanical weaknesses, but these were soon fixed—this time by French gunmakers, who began to perfect the next evolution of the gun, the flintlock, early in the 17th Century.

As you might guess, the flintlock also struck flint against steel to produce sparks. A well-made flintlock proved to be very reliable and fairly inexpensive to make. The first troops to be armed with true flintlocks were five regiments of King Louis XIV's army of France in the middle 1600s.

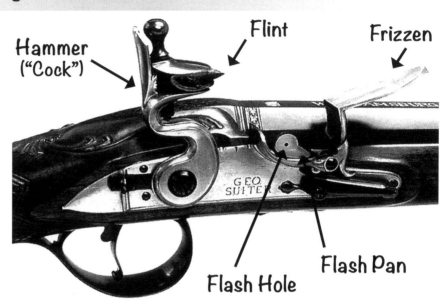

A flintlock. The hammer, or cock, has a piece of carefully shaped flint clamped into it. The curved piece on the right is the frizzen, or steel. When powder, wad and ball have been rammed down the barrel, the shooter pushes the frizzen forward (as shown) and pours priming powder into the flash pan below it. Then she pulls the frizzen back, to bring it into striking range of the flint. (This also covers the pan, to shield the priming powder from wind and rain.) Thumbing the hammer all the way back against its internal spring "cocks" the lock. Pulling the trigger lets the hammer snap forward, which drags the flint down along the face of the frizzen—and shoves it ahead, to uncover the pan—and the resulting shower of sparks falls into the flash pan, igniting the priming powder. The flame travels through the flash hole in the barrel and lights the main charge in the chamber. During two centuries of fine-tuning, the flintlock has become very reliable and effective. This new .62-caliber rifle was built by George Suiter, the gunmaker at Colonial Williamsburg.

The US Army used flintlocks into the 1840s.

But no matter how the priming charge in the pan was lit or how well protected it was against the elements, dampness was always a problem. Soggy powder won't ignite. And just keeping the rain off the gun wasn't enough; gunpowder attracts moisture from the air. (Soaking-wet bowstrings wouldn't pull well, either. Swords, spears and axes, however, worked fine in the rain. So did bayonets, which arrived on the battlefield around 1640.) A better ignition method was needed, and it was a scientifically minded Scottish clergyman named Alexander Forsyth who came up with it around 1805.

Early Guns: Percussion Fire

Reverend Forsyth was looking for practical uses of explosives such as fulminate of mercury (fulminate comes from the Latin word for lightning, *fulmen*). This was sometimes risky; according to family legend, one of Forsyth's experiments blew him out of his workshop. He discovered a "fulminating powder" that could be set off by whacking it with a hammer. Since he was a shooter and a hunter, Forsyth realized that this might be a better ignition method for firearms, so he designed and patented new gun locks for it that didn't required flint and steel

Other inventors went to work with Forsyth's fulminating powder too, looking for the most convenient and reliable way to use it in a gun. The big breakthrough was the percussion cap, which appeared early in the 1800s. (Several gunmakers claimed the credit, but it showed up in America and Britain at about the same time.) A percussion cap is a tiny copper cup with fulminate in its base. The shooter presses it onto a nipple, where the hammer strikes it. A hole through the nipple conducts the flash down to the gunpowder in the chamber.

The percussion cap proved safe, reliable, easy to use and reasonably weatherproof. It worked equally well on rifles, shotguns and handguns, and percussion locks were robust and easy to produce. It really was a breakthrough, and percussion guns and caps are still made today.

A percussion cap on the nipple of a double-barreled shotgun made in 1848 by William Powell. This was the first more-or-less weatherproof way to fire a gun; the next step was to put the cap directly into the cartridge.

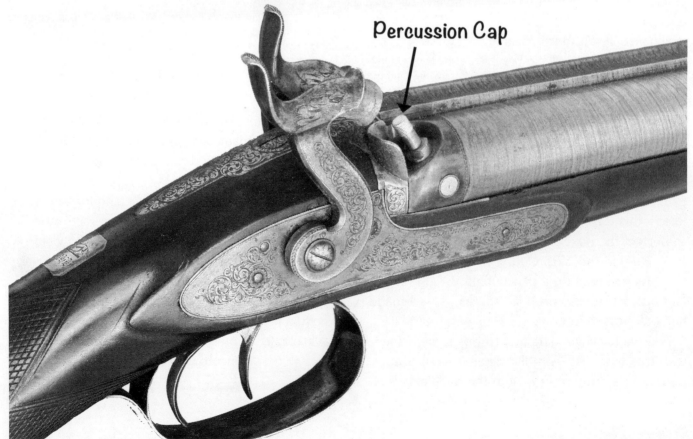

Percussion Cap

Steve Helsley

Early Guns: Needlefire & Pinfire

Now advancements in guns and ammunition started coming fast. Before long, guns were being loaded from the breech end of the barrels instead of the muzzle, with cartridges that had powder and ball and percussion caps contained in them.

The next step was pinfire cartridges. The pins stick up through notches in the ends of the barrels. The hammers drive the pins onto percussion caps, or primers, inside the cartridges. You didn't want to fall down with a dozen of these in your pocket.

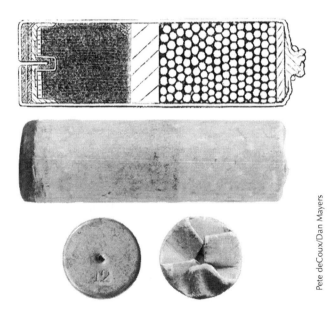

A 12-gauge needlefire shot cartridge with a metal base and a thick paper case. The "needle" was a long firing pin that punctured the bottom of the case and set off a percussion cap buried in the gunpowder. The white strip is the wad that separates the powder and shot.

The most successful of these were the needlefire and pinfire cartridges. Needlefire ammunition came in paper cases and turned out to be a technological dead-end. Pinfire cartridges

had metal cases, or just metal bases, and these evolved into modern-style shell cases with priming compound in their rims.

Then, in the 1850s and '60s, gunmakers in America, Britain and France introduced cartridges in metal cases with percussion caps set into their bases. Now it was all coming together, and finally two army officers, one British and the other American, brought the primer to its modern centerfire forms. (Centerfire, as opposed to rimfire, because the primers are set into the centers of the shell bases.)

Modern Guns: Primers & Metallic Cartridges

In the 1860s Col. Edward Boxer was the superintendent of the military arsenal at Woolwich, in London. The primer that bears his name is a little disk that contains an anvil

and explosive compound. This is pressed into a pocket in the bottom of the shell case. The gun's firing pin detonates the primer by hammering the compound against the anvil, and the flame reaches the powder charge through a hole in the bottom-center of the case.

On the other side of the Atlantic, Gen. Hiram Berdan had set up the famous Union Army sharpshooter regiments in the American Civil War. Along with being a marksman, he was also a gun and ammunition designer. His primer (Patent No. 53,388 of 1866) was a little different from Boxer's: The anvil is part of the shell case, not the primer, and there are two small flash holes leading to the gunpowder, not one.

Left: A Berdan primer sitting (upside-down) on its cartridge case, which has two flash holes, one on each side of the anvil pin. Right: a Boxer primer, which has its anvil built in and is pressed into a cartridge case that has just one hole. Both kinds are still used, but the Boxer is much easier to remove and replace.

Ironically, since the English Boxer primer is easier to remove and replace, it's most used in the United States, where many shooters reload their own ammo. And the American Berdan primer is the standard in European and other countries, where shooters usually don't reload their cases.

Just so you know, there are several primer sizes: large and small rifle, and large and small pistol. Also, modern priming compound is more "gun-friendly" than what Boxer and Berdan had to work with. The mercury fulminate and potassium chlorate (a form of salt) in their primers weakens shell cases and rusts gun barrels. These chemicals were replaced in commercial American ammunition by 1930, but some military primers were made with potassium chlorate until the late 1950s. A lot of foreign ammunition, especially military surplus, still has "salted" primers too. This type of ammunition generally shoots fine, but the gun barrel must be cleaned afterward.

What you've just read is hardly the whole story of how gunpowder was exploded over the centuries; we've only covered the methods that were successful enough to become popular. Here are a couple of other ways you might not have thought of: Around 1810 a Swiss gunmaker named Johannes Samuel Pauly, working in Paris, detonated cartridges with compressed air. (Compressed air gets very hot.) One hundred and fifty years later the Daisy VL round was fired by compressed air as well. And in the 1870s and '80s the British government issued patents to at least seven different gun locks that used electricity to fire cartridges. Electric ignition gets reinvented every few decades, but it has yet to catch on.

Rifling & the Devil

ith the wheellock came rifling. Gunmakers knew it made guns more accurate, but they didn't know why. From *The Age of Firearms*: "The Bavarian necromancer Moretius (Herman Moritz) found the explanation in 1522. A bullet fired from a rifled barrel flew true because no devil could remain astride a spinning object, as witness the rotating heavenly spheres (devil-free) and the stationary earth (devil-infested)."

Modern Guns: The Cartridge Case

oday top-quality rifle and pistol cartridge cases are made of brass, while shotgun shells are plastic or coated-cardboard tubes tucked into brass bases. It seems simple, but the cartridge took as long to improve as the gun. The two had to develop more or less together over hundreds of years. A better cartridge led to a better gun, and a better case meant a better cartridge.

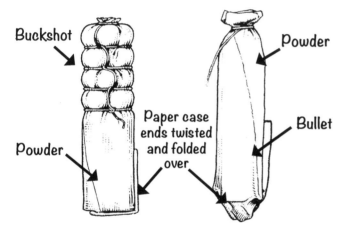

Buckshot

Powder

Powder

Paper case ends twisted and folded over

Bullet

Then: Paper cartridges with their ends tied off. One has buckshot over the gunpowder, the other has a Minié ball; both are for muzzleloading guns and could only be loaded by hand. The shooter tore the paper with his teeth, dumped the powder down the barrel, and then pushed the bullet or shot cluster after it with the ramrod. The paper became the wad.

By the end of the 16th Century one-piece cartridges had been invented for muzzleloaders: paper tubes filled with powder and ball with the ends tied off. The shooter tore open the tube with his teeth, poured the powder down the barrel and shoved the ball down after it with his ramrod; the paper served as the wad. The cartridge stayed in this basic form until the 1860s, when breechloading guns finally became practical. This happened partly because metallic cartridges had been invented; paper tubes don't work well in a breechloader and not at all in a repeater with a mechanical action.

However, primitive breechloaders had been around for a long time already too. England's King

Henry VIII (1491–1547) had a collection of guns that included early breechloaders. One, a wheellock, used *Eisenpatronen*, or iron cartridges, invented in Germany. The cartridge case was a small iron tube, loaded with powder and ball or shot, with a pan attached to the side that held the priming charge.

Later a breechloading flintlock's *Eisenpatrone* came with a complete pan and frizzen assembly.

Now: Flimsy paper cartridges won't work in mechanical repeating-rifle or machine-gun actions. These are military .338 Lapua Magnum rounds (about twice actual size) with brass cases and full-metal-jacketed bullets that won't mushroom.

As you can imagine, these guns and their ammo were clumsy, complicated and very expensive. And, like all muzzleloaders, they suffered from leaking combustion gas.

Muzzleloading gun barrels need a vent hole so the flash of the priming powder or percussion cap can get to the main charge. Holes go both ways, though, so some of the main explosion comes out this hole too, at least with a flintlock. This robs the gun of a bit of its power, and it leaves ash and other junk in the vent and all over the lock. A pressed-on percussion cap should seal the vent hole, but too heavy a main charge can blow back hard enough to break the hammer. And even with percussion caps, vent-hole ignition doesn't work well in rainy or even just damp weather.

For centuries gunmakers worked to improve locks, barrels, stocks, rifling, triggers, sights, powder and bullets, but the number-one challenge was to come up with a barrel-and-cartridge arrangement that completely sealed the breech when the gun fired.

Hand-in-hand with this, however, was the other number-one problem: priming powder and ignition. We've described how the metallic primer evolved, but without a practical case to put it in, it would have been worthless.

In addition to iron and paper, over the centuries people tried cartridge cases made of cardboard, varnished fabric, collodion (something like cellophane), pig gut, silk, metal foil, linen, rubber, copper and steel. The first breechloaders were generally single-shots, revolvers and break-action double-barreled guns. Shooters loaded them by hand, one cartridge at a time, so the cases could be fairly flimsy. But repeat-ers—guns with mechanical actions to load and eject cartridges—needed ammunition with stronger cases that could be yanked around without coming apart.

By the 1860s and '70s engineers had settled on brass as the ideal material for cartridge cases. Brass can be drawn (formed) into the right shapes, and it's both strong and slightly elastic. The case expands slightly when the cartridge fires, so it fills and seals the chamber snugly, and then it shrinks again, which makes it easier to pull out the empty. Brass is even somewhat self-lubricating, so the gun's action can handle it easily. Brass cases may also be reloaded and reused.

Then Col. Boxer's and Gen. Berdan's metallic primers were added to the new brass cases, and the modern cartridge with all its advantages was born. Since then ammo companies have used aluminum and plastic too, but nothing works as well as good old brass. However, to keep prices down a bit, many cartridges now come in less-expensive steel or aluminum cases, lacquered or brass-plated, for shooters who don't want to reload their ammunition.

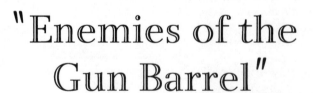

"Enemies of the Gun Barrel"

"A trigger is squeezed, primer struck. Gunpowder ignites and a projectile is launched. In that brief instant one of the most hostile places on earth is also created. Inside the gun barrel is a place that at the same time has the highest pressure, and highest temperature, and the strongest winds of anywhere on the planet. Accompanying these conditions is an atmosphere of poisonous and corrosive gasses . . . . The burning powder creates a mixture of toxic waste that includes: ammonia, water, carbon monoxide, carbon dioxide, methane, and hydrogen sulfide." —*George E. Kontis,* 2011 Small Arms Review

Evolution of the Bullet

Lead is heavy and fairly soft and melts at relatively low temperatures. In many ways it's the perfect metal for bullets. Until about 1900, with a few exceptions, it was the only metal used in bullets. And for centuries most bullets were just round lead balls that were loaded into the gun barrel from the muzzle.

The streamlined, pointed shape of the modern bullet seems obvious now, yet it was anything but. The first elongated bullets in wide use, around 1840, were shaped like eggs. Others had projections on their bases to tie a paper cartridge onto. The modern cone shape didn't become standard until the Minié bullet came along in the 1850s. (See "Gunsights: Then & Now.") This, especially in a rifled barrel, made it possible to shoot accurately at much longer ranges. It also allowed the weight of the bullet to vary without changing the caliber (just make it longer or shorter).

However, lead bullets have limits, even if they're hardened. They can't be fired at really high speeds without being damaged, and they tend to leave residue in the barrel, which destroys accuracy. Smokeless powder, which arrived in the 1880s, could drive bullets much faster than black powder.

Swiss gunmakers began to experiment with bullets that were jacketed, or coated, with harder metals. But then, instead of lead in the barrel, deposits from the jacket metal became the problem.

People tried different types of jacketing—wrapping bullets in paper, even greasing them with tallow or beeswax. Nothing completely eliminated this fouling, but it has been much reduced.

In 1898 the French designed a revolutionary bullet called the Balle D. Instead of a flat nose it had a sharp point, which made it much more aerodynamic, and two other revolutionary features: It was solid brass, and it had a tapered "boattail" base, which reduces aerodynamic drag and therefore increases how far the bullet can fly. This turned out to be especially valuable for machine guns, which could then be used for very-long-range area fire. Area fire means they were used like artillery, dropping rounds into a general area instead of sighting on specific targets. This is what makes the boattail bullet so useful for crew-served machine guns, as opposed to infantry rifles.

Just a very few of the many different kinds of bullets. Left to right: A 115-grain softnose bullet from an old Winchester .32-20 cartridge; a 500-grain .458-caliber bullet with grooves for lubrication; the 123-grain steel core from an AK-47 round—caliber 7.62x39mm—next to its jacketed lead cap (the core elongates the bullet for better aerodynamics; the cap was cut off for demonstration purposes); a massive .840-caliber 1,610-grain bullet from an 8-bore blackpowder big-game rifle; a modern 37-grain .17-caliber boattail hollowpoint; a 240-grain partly jacketed .44 Magnum bullet; a 493-grain lead slug for a 16-gauge shotgun; a 750-grain softnose .577 Nitro Express bullet; and an unusual 29-grain caseless VL .22 round made by Daisy in the 1960s.

Steve Helsley

The world's major armies redesigned their ammunition. Germany adopted a spitzer (pointed) bullet in 1905, the United States in 1906, Russia in 1909 and England in 1910. For more about the differences between military and hunting ammunition, read the section about bullets in "Talking the Talk."

Warfare calls for a lot of special ammunition, such as incendiary, tracer, door-breaching or armor-piercing rounds, and bullets with steel, tungsten or even (in 20mm—.790 caliber—and larger sizes) depleted-uranium cores. Depleted uranium is waste fuel from nuclear reactors and is extremely dense and heavy; not only can it punch through thick steel plate, but it also will explode when it does. Yes, it's radioactive too. Very nasty stuff.

Still, the shape of bullets and how they are constructed hasn't changed all that much in the past century. Most bullets are still mostly lead, hardened somewhat by adding tin, zinc or a metal called antimony, and have copper or nickel jackets that vary in thickness depending on the speed at which they are to be fired and the toughness of the target. For greatest "mushrooming" (expansion), a bullet will have a hollow nose, which might be filled with a little plastic tip to get the aerodynamic benefits of a point.

In recent years, however, concern about the effects of lead (which is toxic) on wildlife and the environment has forced ammo companies to come up with new materials. For hunting waterfowl, in many places traditional lead shot has been replaced by pellets made of steel, bismuth or tungsten.

Some rifle and pistol bullets are now solid copper, brass (like the Balle D) or bronze, and others are made from sintered metals, which are certain metallic powders fused together under pressure and heat. These were invented not because of concerns over lead as a poison but because they perform better on particularly big-boned or thick-skinned large animals.

Perhaps the most "striking" new trend in bullets is the popularity of .17- and .20-caliber cartridges. These tiny bullets can be driven at very high velocities, because they're mostly jacket and very little lead, and are very accurate. Since they're so small, they have the added benefit of producing almost no recoil.

Guns, Guns, Guns

Basic Types of Guns & How They Work

A picture, they say, is worth a thousand words. So on the next few pages we show you a common example of each of the basic types of long guns and handguns, with their actions open and closed. Study the photos and captions, and flip back to the general explanations on this page as needed. Don't forget that you can also find various definitions in the chapter "Talking the Talk."

• Most firearms have hammers, which either hit the primer directly or drive the firing pin into it, to detonate the cartridge. Some guns have external, or outside, hammers that can be cocked manually by pulling them back with your thumb. Hammerguns, particularly old ones, often don't have safety catches; you "safe" them just by de-cocking them (lowering the hammers, carefully) with your thumb. Lever-action rifles, which don't necessarily have outside hammers, generally do have safety catches.

• Guns with internal hammers cock themselves mechanically when the shooter opens or closes the action. You can't see or touch these hammers, so safety catches are needed to keep the gun from going off accidentally. Different guns have their safety catches in different places, but they should be easy to reach with a finger or thumb. Most are for right-handed shooters.

• Except for revolvers, every repeating gun has a bolt (or breechblock) that the action moves forward—to push the cartridge into the chamber and lock (bolt) it in place for firing—and then pulls backward, to extract the empty case. The bolt also contains the firing pin. Bolts are moved by different sorts of levers or handles, and this is what gives each type of gun action its name.

• It's easy to see when bolt-actions or lever-actions are open and the guns are safe. It's harder to tell with semi-automatics and pump-action guns. You can spot an open (safe) break-action gun from a long way off, which is one reason some shooters like them.

• Break-action guns usually have two barrels, but some have three or even four—or just one. The lever or other device that unlocks these guns and lets them "break" open may be on top of the action body, under it or alongside it.

So many different guns have been made by so many clever people over so many centuries that just about every idea has been tried at least once. What you'll see here are the basic types of firearms actions—the most successful and popular ones.

Somewhere in this collection is every imaginable type of gun—and plenty of other weapons.

Single-Shot vs. Lever-Action

These actions may look similar, but they're not. Lever-actions are repeaters and can shoot faster; single-shots are considered to be more accurate.

Single-Shot

A single-shot gun has to be reloaded every time it's fired; there's no magazine for extra ammunition. There are many different single-shot actions. This Ruger No. 1 rifle is a "falling-block" type: Pushing the lever forward lets the breechblock—as this kind of bolt is called—drop down; it also extracts the empty shell and recocks the hammer. The shooter pushes a fresh cartridge into the chamber with her fingers and closes the lever, which raises the breechblock and locks it into place. Good to go!

Lever-Action

This Marlin Model 336 has a tubular magazine inside the wooden forend, which is loaded through the little door in the side. Pushing the lever forward after firing drives the bolt backward, which pulls the empty shell from the chamber and kicks it out through the slot on the side; it also re-cocks the hammer. A spring in the magazine tube pushes each round backward into the action; closing the lever runs the bolt forward again, which shoves the new cartridge into the chamber and locks up everything for firing. (In the photo above, the hammer is cocked.)

Bolt-Action vs. Double Rifle

These are shown together because rifles for big game are usually one or the other. A big-bore bolt-action holds three or four cartridges; the double rifle holds only two, but it can fire them faster.

Bolt-Action

Turning the knobbed handle of this Winchester Model 70 upward unlocks the bolt so the shooter can pull it back, extracting the empty case and throwing it aside. A spring in the box magazine (inside the stock in front of the trigger) raises a fresh cartridge so it lines up with the barrel. The shooter then pushes the bolt forward, shoving the cartridge into the chamber, and then turns the bolt downward to lock the action so the rifle can be fired.

Double Rifle

This old Holland & Holland rifle has two single-shot barrels side-by-side and a locking lever under the trigger guard. Pushing the lever to the side unlocks a hinge, which lets the barrels drop open. The shooter pulls out the empties, slides in two fresh cartridges, then closes the barrels and swings the lever back to the trigger guard, to lock everything up. This rifle's hammers have to be cocked by hand (pulled back with your thumb) and it has two triggers, one for each barrel.

Semi-Auto vs. Pumpgun

These actions look somewhat alike and operate basically the same way, but a pumpgun has to be worked ("pumped") by hand.

Semi-Automatic

The box magazine is in front of the trigger guard of this Browning semi-auto rifle. The shooter pulls back the small cocking lever to open the bolt and let a cartridge rise up from the magazine; a spring then snaps the bolt forward, to load the round into the chamber and lock the action. When the rifle fires, the force of the explosion shoves the bolt backward and ejects the empty. Then the return spring takes over and the process repeats itself until the magazine is empty. A semi-auto requires one trigger pull per shot; a full-automatic (machine gun) fires as long as the trigger is held back.

Pumpgun

A pump- or slide-action gun works the same way as a semi-automatic, except that the shooter has to operate the action by hand, by pulling the forend backward and then pushing it ahead again. The tube under the barrel of this Remington Model 760 rifle is not the magazine but rather the rail that the pump handle slides along. (This rifle has a box magazine.) The slot in the action body is the port through which empty shells are ejected.

Side-by-Side vs. Over/Under

Mechanically, these actions are the same. However, there are some subtle differences in how these two types of guns feel, so some shooters prefer one or the other for different kinds of shooting.

Side-by-Side

Like the double rifle and the over/under, this shotgun (a Boswell) has two single-shot barrels joined together and is a break-action gun. Pushing the lever (this one is on the top of the gun) to the side unlocks the hinge so the action can "break" open for reloading. Like the double rifle, it has a trigger for each barrel. The front trigger usually fires the right, more-open-choked barrel first.

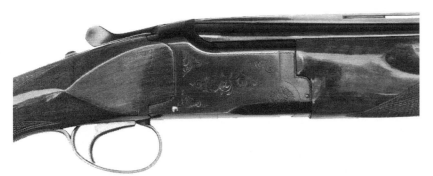

Over/Under

Double guns and rifles may have their barrels arranged horizontally or one above the other, like this, but the basic operating principle is the same. This Browning Citori shotgun has a single trigger, which fires first one barrel and then the other. (A selector switch lets you choose which barrel fires first.) Like the double rifle and the side-by-side shotgun, above, its hammers are inside the body of the gun; opening the action cocks them mechanically for firing.

Revolver vs. Semi-Automatic

These are the two most common types of handguns. Revolvers are more popular for hunting, while semi-autos are generally for police, military or self-defense use.

Revolver

The cylinder in this Smith & Wesson Model 19 swings out to the side for loading. Most revolvers hold six rounds, so they're also called six-guns or six-shooters—or even, because the cylinders turn to line up each round with the barrel, wheelguns. If the hammer has to be cocked with the thumb, it's a single-action revolver; if pulling the trigger can both cock and release the hammer, it's a double-action. The M19 is a double-action revolver.

Semi-Automatic

This Glock 17 pistol works the same way as the Browning semi-auto rifle, but instead of a cocking lever it has a slide, which the shooter pulls back. This lets a cartridge rise out of the magazine, inside the grip, and on most pistols this also cocks the action. Releasing the slide lets it slam forward, loading the chamber and making the pistol ready to fire. The little "finger" on the trigger is Glock's safety catch, which the shooter has to press to release the main trigger.

All photos by Steve Helsley

Gunsights: Then & Now

Taking Aim & Hitting Your Target

The Whites of Their Eyes

Two hundred and seventy years ago, Lt. Col. Sir Andrew Agnew's advice was right on target, so to speak. He actually said (or, more likely, roared at the top of his lungs, as one did on a battlefield), *"Dinna fire till ye see the whites of their e'en!"*

That is, "Don't shoot until you see the whites of their eyes!"

Sir Andrew led the 21st Foot of the Scots Fusiliers Regiment of the British Army, and he probably gave his famous order in their own Scottish accent. Fusiliers were infantry armed with *fusils,* French for muskets, muzzleloading smoothbore guns.

After the first volley, a battlefield was blanketed with a dirty white fog of smoke that smelled like rotten eggs. Unless the wind blew it away, troops couldn't see to aim, and they had to breathe the nasty stuff too.

The occasion was the Battle of Dettingen, in Germany in 1743, during the War of the Austrian Succession. The 21st Foot was being charged by French "heavy horse"—armored cavalry. Sir Andrew

had devised the unusual tactic of splitting his soldiers into two columns with an open lane in between. The French galloped right into this trap, and the Fusiliers turned and caught them in a dreadful crossfire. (Cavalry of all armies were famous for their dash and bravery, not their brains.) Sir Andrew had to keep his troops from giving away the surprise by opening fire too soon, and thus his famous order about holding fire till the very last second.

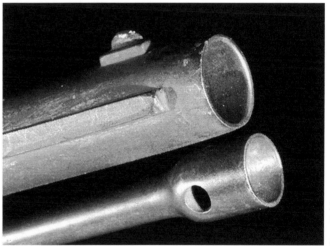

The crude front sight of a big-bore French *fusil.* (The end of the ramrod, underneath, is shaped to fit over a Minié bullet without flattening its point.) Many military muskets had no rear sights at all, but they were so inaccurate that it hardly mattered.

(Supposedly, at the end of the day, when the victorious British were mopping up, King George II came by and remarked, "Sir Andrew, I hear the French rode through your regiment today." Agnew is said to have replied, "Aye, yer Majesty, but they dinna git oot again.")

Sir Andrew knew that his men had to make their first volley count, and that meant letting the enemy get close. Soldiers then were not trained in marksmanship as we know it, but just to stand in rows and load, aim and fire, over and over again, in the direction of the enemy. The enemy, if they were infantry also, would do the same thing. The loser was the army that broke and ran first.

At a hundred yards military muskets were likely to miss a target the size of a man's head and probably the man himself. Not only that, but after the first volley a battlefield was blanketed with a foul-smelling, whitish fog of blackpowder smoke. Accuracy was impossible.

Everyone knew muskets were far less accurate than muzzleloading rifles but they cost much less and, because the balls were a sloppy fit in the barrels, they could be reloaded and fired much more quickly. Most muskets had only a front sight that was little more than a bump near the muzzle and no rear sight at all.

Just point, grit your teeth and yank the trigger. Reload and do it again. And again and again and again.

I n 1814 Gen. George Hanger wrote in his book, *To All Sportsmen, Farmers, and Gamekeepers*: "A soldier's musket, if not exceedingly ill-bored and very crooked, as many are, will strike the figure of a man at 80 yards; it may even at a hundred; but a soldier *must be very fortunate indeed* who shall be wounded by a *common musket* at 150 yards, PROVIDED HIS ANTAGONIST AIMS AT HIM; and, as to firing at him at 200 yards with a common musket, you may just as well fire at the moon and have the same hopes of hitting your object. I do maintain, and I will prove, whenever called on, that NO MAN WAS EVER KILLED, AT TWO HUNDRED YARDS, by a common soldier's musket, BY THE PERSON WHO AIMED AT HIM."

Cutting spiral grooves, rifling, into a gun barrel to spin the ball or bullet in flight greatly improves accuracy. The notion of rifling was understood, although the technology was still crude, by the end of the 16th Century. From then on, both front and rear sights were installed on rifles. Two sights let the shooter line up his barrel just so, for aiming. But, with a few exceptions, it wasn't until the mid-1800s that regular American soldiers had rifles instead of muskets.

Around 1856 a Frenchman named Claude Étienne Minié got his name on a projectile that changed the way wars would be fought. It was a true bullet, conical in shape, but its base was hollowed out. It could be rammed down a gun barrel easily because it didn't fit too tightly in the bore, yet the hollow base made the soft lead expand when the bullet was fired, to grip the rifling. (At first it had a wooden wedge in

Steve Helsley

A highly accurate single-shot 1863 Sharps buffalo rifle (converted from percussion fire) with an aperture sight that could be adjusted precisely up and down for distance and also moved sideways to make up for crosswinds that might blow the bullet off-target. Pushing the trigger guard down opens the action for loading.

its base; then someone discovered the bullet would expand all by itself.) The Minié bullet proved accurate out to 500 yards. To take advantage of this, more sophisticated sights were installed on infantry rifles.

(In Europe Minié is pronounced *min-yea*. Americans, however, say *minnie*. Many modern muzzleloader shooters still use "minnie balls.")

Target rifles were changing too. As interest in long-range competition grew, rear sights evolved quickly. Traditional sights were some sort of small pyramid shape at the muzzle and a crude vee at the rear of the barrel, a few inches in front of the aiming eye. As the bullets, wads, powder, barrels and rifling for target shooting got more and more sophisticated the rear sight was moved farther and farther back— from the barrel to the receiver and then behind the action, just an inch or so in front of the eye. (The farther apart the front and rear sights, the more precise the aim can be.) The sight itself became a disk with a fine hole (known as an aperture or peep) centered in it that could move up and down on a calibrated frame called a vernier. This was capable of very precise adjustment for elevation, to compensate for the drop of the bullet at long ranges.

Target rifles also got precision front sights that could be adjusted sideways, to move the impact of the bullet right or left. This would compensate for a steady wind pushing the bullet aside.

Rear sights got most of the attention since that's where the shooter's eye is, but one of the challenges of shooting open sights is the size of the front sight. At long range the dot or pin of a front sight covers up a lot of the target, which makes precise shooting difficult, but making the sight smaller makes it harder to see. This is another area where lots of shooting experience makes all the difference.

Military rifles stayed with barrel-mounted rear sights until World War I (1914–1918), when Britain and the United States adopted versions of the same bolt-action rifle with an aperture (peep) sight on its receiver. From then on, both countries, and many others, put peep sights on military rifles. (The aperture in these sights, the aiming hole, was not as small as the one on a target sight.) It was thought that a soldier could get his "sight picture" more quickly than with the traditional barrel-mounted vee sight. That is, it was faster on target.

Scopes

Gunsights with glass lenses go back at least as far as 17th Century Germany. Telescopic sights, which magnify the target, became available in the US in the 1840s. They were used by snipers on both sides in the American Civil War (1861–1865), but they were too cumbersome and fragile for general combat duty. That began to change only in the 1970s, when Britain put an optical sight on its main battle rifle, the L1A1. Now it's common to see things like the ACOG, the Advanced Combat Optical Gunsight, on American military rifles too.

An Advanced Combat Optical Gunsight, which not only magnifies the target but also draws the shooter's eye to it quickly. It proved so valuable in Iraq that the Marines decided that "every rifle and every carbine in the Marine Corps inventory will have an ACOG optic."

A front sight for long-range shooting matches. The bead, inside the hood, could be changed for different targets; the bubble level was to keep the rifle from canting to one side or the other, which would throw the bullet off; and the shooter could adjust the bead horizontally to compensate for wind. These sights are too complicated for hunting or warfare, even sniping.

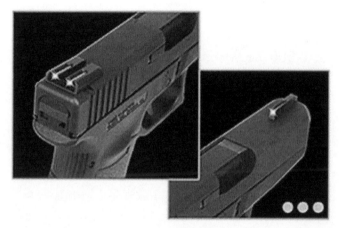

TRUGLO handgun sights with glow-in-the-dark tritium dots that are visible even at night. Line up the front bead between the two dots at the rear sight and squeeze. These can be put on many pistols.

After World War II (1941–1945) "scopes" surged in popularity for target shooting and for hunting. The diameter of scope tubes was standardized, along with how they were mounted on rifles and handguns, and since then scopes have been improved in about every imaginable way. Scopes are easier to use than open "iron" sights and, naturally, they are a tremendous help to shooters with vision problems. In addition to making the target look a lot closer, they're now available with built-in features that were just science fiction a generation ago: rangefinders, night-vision capability, reticles (cross-

hairs) that light up, even digital cameras. And now there are the so-called red-dots: optical sights that create a lighted red dot in the center of the tube. The shooter simply puts the dot on the target and fires. Some red-dot sights magnify, many do not. Some rely on battery power; some use sunlight to make the dot glow. There are green ones too, and triangles instead of dots.

Battery-powered laser sights are something different again. They project their aiming dot—it's the end of the laser beam—right onto the target. But their range is limited, so they're useful only for close-in shooting.

Over the past 150 years iron sights have not changed as much as optical sights have. Match-grade aperture sights are now fabricated on com-

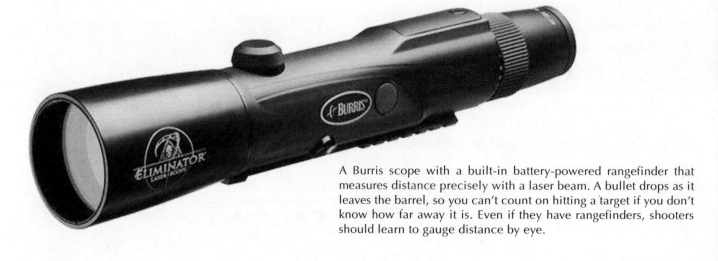

A Burris scope with a built-in battery-powered rangefinder that measures distance precisely with a laser beam. A bullet drops as it leaves the barrel, so you can't count on hitting a target if you don't know how far away it is. Even if they have rangefinders, shooters should learn to gauge distance by eye.

puter-controlled machinery and are the most precise of their type ever made, but a target shooter from the Leech Cup match at Creedmoor in 1874 (see "Competition") would recognize them instantly and know how to use them. They are still found on target rifles used at 1,000 yards and they are also on super-accurate pellet guns used at 10.9 yards—that's 10 meters, the distance at which Olympic air rifle and air pistol competition is shot.

Are You a Marksman?

Today, when almost everyone shoots rifles with scopes that make the target look closer (and sometimes even indicate the range, so you know how to compensate for the bullet's drop), it's easy to forget how accurate an expert can be without them. Later on we'll tell you about Billy Dixon and his true shot at the Battle of Adobe Walls. Dixon was an Indian fighter, buffalo hunter and cavalry scout—a plainsman who pretty much lived with a rifle in his hands. He had learned how to take into account distance, crosswinds, heat mirages, the size of his front sight bead and so on in his aiming. His famous shot was so unusual that it's still remembered today, but by about 1860 marksmen in America and Europe were competing in long-range shooting matches at distances of up to 1,100 yards, nearly two-thirds of a mile.

During the American Civil War Confederate marksmen armed with super-accurate British Whitworth rifles that had been smuggled past the Union naval blockade reportedly killed a few Union officers at long range. At least some of these rifles had scopes on them. One of the most famous shots of that time was made on May 9, 1864, when Sgt. Grace of the 4th Georgia Infantry killed Union Gen. John Sedgwick at a distance that was reported to be anywhere from 800 to 1,000 yards.

On the other side of the war, to qualify as one of Col. Hiram Berdan's Union Army sharpshooters, a man had to be able to put 10 consecutive shots "from the shoulder"—not firing off a fixed support—into a 10-inch circle at 200 yards with iron sights. Next time you're out with your .22 rifle or BB gun, see if you can safely sight on

George Swenson

Highly accurate muzzleloading Whitworth rifles with both iron sights, for quick shooting, on top of their barrels and scopes mounted alongside the barrels for more precise aiming. These were made in England and used by Confederate snipers during the American Civil War.

something that far away (with your gun unloaded). If you have to pace off the distance, figure one giant step is a yard. Impressive, isn't it? Some of Berdan's men used scopes, but the point is that they already were deadly without them.

Iron, optical and electronic sights all have their advantages and disadvantages, but none of them can make up for poor shooting. New shooters should learn the basics with iron sights and then those skills will transfer to scopes and dots. It's like learning to drive a car with a manual transmission and a clutch. You may never have to do it again, but it's nice to know how—and it makes you a better driver, and shooter.

Snipers: Then & Now

Sharpshooters as The Tip of the Spear

During WWI, not only was the German bolt-action Model 98 Mauser sniper rifle more effective than what the Allied forces had, but German snipers also started out better trained.

The modern sniper is a marvel. Every piece of his gear (we know of no women snipers today) seems to have been built for just one purpose, and he is a highly trained specialist. A sniper team—a shooter, one or more spotters and sometimes, especially in city fighting, a protective platoon—can pin down an entire enemy unit or throw a curtain of deadly accurate covering fire over a friendly unit.

Everyone's got the sniper bug now and the word gets tossed around like "assault rifle." It's applied to almost any kind of unseen shooter, including a juvenile delinquent with a pellet gun on a freeway overpass. And then there are terms like "countersniper" and "designated marksman."

We'll get back to them, but in the meantime let's stick with this definition: A sniper is a soldier or a police officer who specializes in shooting from a concealed position and over longer ranges than normal, often with a specially designed or modified rifle.

A sniper is skilled in marksmanship, camouflage and fieldcraft. Military snipers also have to be experts in infiltration (sneaking into enemy positions), reconnaissance and observation.

Snipers have become the "tip of the spear" in today's desert and urban warfare, but for most of our fighting history snipers got very little official attention. During the Revolutionary War some Americans earned a reputation as sharpshooters by picking off "redcoats," especially officers, under conditions that astonished the British. But these weren't true snipers; they were experienced woodsmen with accurate, long-barreled hunting rifles. Ordinary infantry muskets firing round balls were hardly long-range weapons. It wasn't until the 1850s, when conical bullets and rifled barrels became standard, that regular soldiers had guns capable of real accuracy. The telescopic sight appeared about then too.

Sniping with scope-equipped rifles may have begun in the Crimean War (1853–1856) in eastern

A WWI Springfield Model 1903 bolt-action sniper rifle with a crude Warner & Swasey scope and an extended magazine borrowed from a BAR, a Browning Automatic Rifle.

Europe. Ten years later, as mentioned, both sides in the American Civil War had snipers equipped with scoped rifles.

By the 1890s the effective range of army rifles—now bolt-action repeaters—had once again greatly increased, thanks to smokeless powder and jacketed, pointed bullets. Then, in late 1899, war broke out in South Africa, where British troops faced rebellious settlers called Boers. Like the American colonists of more than a century earlier, the Boers were mostly farmers and a lot of them were experienced hunters. In response Lord Lovat, the chief of Scotland's Clan Fraser, raised companies of what he called Scouts, men who were also hunters and riflemen. They brought their ghillie suits, the bushy camouflage clothing they used for

Roza Shanina, here holding a Mosin-Nagant Model 91/30 rifle with a 3.5X PU "universal" scope, was just 16 years old when she joined the Russian Army during WWII. As a sniper, she killed 75 German soldiers before she herself was killed on January 28, 1945.

hunting in the heather at home in the Scottish Highlands. This was the first known military use of the ghillie suit.

The British won, but at great cost: 20,000 killed, 22,000 wounded and, because of how they treated Boer prisoners, a huge blow to their international respect. The Lovat Scouts became the British Army's first true sniper unit.

Back home in Europe the Great War broke out just a few years later, in 1914. It's said that "Generals always fight the previous war" and this was especially true then, in what later became known as World War I. Allied military leaders were confused by all sorts of new challenges, ranging from machine guns and tanks to trench warfare, poison gas and lots of snipers. Their enemies, the Germans, were much better prepared for the war. They had, for example, built 15,000 scope-sighted Mauser bolt-action rifles and requisitioned many more hunting rifles, also with scopes, and trained soldiers to use them. These German snipers dominated the early part of the war. England and later the United States, when it joined the war, had to cobble together sniper rifles and training programs as best they could. (The Lovat Scouts were experienced hunters who were recruited into the army but still had to be trained as snipers.)

Wars eventually end and WWI was predicted to be the last big one, "the war to end all wars." Just as after the Revolution and the Civil War, national defense became low priorities in America. And so, when the next global conflict began—World War II this time, in 1939—once again the United States had no ready sniper program or sniper rifle. The US Marine Corps hurriedly picked the Model 1903A1 Springfield with an 8X Unertl scope; the US Army chose a different version of the Springfield as its sniper rifle and put ordinary Weaver and Lyman hunting scopes on them. By the end of the war the new semi-automatic M1 Garand rifle was also being fitted with scopes. But low-power civilian sights weren't right for long-range shooting.

In November 1939, two months after WWII began, the Russian (or Soviet) Red Army invaded Finland in what was called the Winter War. The Russians outnumbered the Finns by at least three to one, but the Finns resisted furiously. (A joke went around Finland: "We are so few and they are so many. How will we bury them all?") One Finnish sniper, Simo Häyhä, nicknamed "White Death," killed 505 Russian soldiers with his rifle. (He killed another 200 at close range with a submachine gun.) Camouflaged in white winter gear, Häyhä used a basic service rifle, without a scope, and tricks like putting snow in his mouth so that his breath wouldn't give away his position.

Häyhä was a perfect example of a sniper. Pure shooting skill is about 20 percent of what it takes, with the rest being patience, discipline, observation and the ability to use cover and estimate range and wind.

Some Russian snipers became famous in World War II as well, including a number of women who fought against the Germans.

The White Death of WWII, Simo Häyhä, with his Finnish M28 Mosin rifle. Häyhä was wounded on March 6, 1940, which means he racked up his incredible body count in less than a year. He recovered and lived a quiet life until 2002.

Lyudmila Pavlichenko, History Student & Sniper

In the mountains and canyons quiet as a deer,
down in the forest knowing no fear,
lift up your sights, down comes a Hun.
Three hundred Nazis felled by your gun.

From "Miss Pavlichenko," a 1946 Woody Guthrie song

Before dawn on June 22, 1941, in World War II, three million German soldiers set off on Operation Barbarossa—the code name for their invasion of Soviet Russia. With hundreds of thousands of airplanes, trucks, tanks, cars and motorcycles, the Germans fanned out toward Leningrad in the north and Moscow and Kiev in the east. Adolf Hitler, Germany's *Führer*, was mindful that when Napoleon's Grand Army of France had attacked Russia, 129 years earlier, savage winter weather and the vastness of the country had become its greatest obstacles. Hitler's plan was to move quickly in a summer *blitzkrieg*, "lightning war," and take over by autumn at the latest.

But history wasn't lost on Joseph Stalin either. The Russian leader knew that if he could slow the German advance, at all costs and by any means, he would trap the enemy far from home, where fuel, ammunition, food, shelter and even warm clothing would become scarce.

Lyudmila Pavlichenko in a publicity photo probably taken when she was a sniper instructor (and that's not a Mosin-Nagant). The story goes that when she enlisted, the recruiting officer, taken with her fashionable appearance, tried to sign her up as a nurse. She produced a marksmanship certificate from her shooting club and insisted she be allowed to carry a rifle and fight.

This was the largest military invasion ever and it became a titanic struggle between two of history's most brutal rulers, men who casually sacrificed many millions of their own citizens.

Hitler's forces started out well equipped and, in the field anyway, well led, but the blitzkrieg failed. Like the Finns in their Winter War two years earlier, now the Russians had their backs to the wall. They fought for their families and for their homeland as well as their lives. What Hitler thought would be a four-month campaign instead lasted four years, and when it ended Germany had lost not just Operation Barbarossa but the entire war. No one can say how WWII would have gone for Britain and America if the Soviet Union—Russia and the neighboring countries it had taken over—hadn't tied down and finally beaten such a large part of Hitler's forces.

The entire Russian population suffered terribly. Nowhere else in the world were women sent to fight in the front lines, but Stalin was happy to have women fly fighter planes and bombers, drive tanks and operate machine guns, and possibly as many as 1,800 Russian women went into combat as snipers. Soviet Maj. Gen. Morozov believed that women could be superior marksmen because "a woman's

hand is more sensitive than a man's. Therefore when a woman is shooting, her finger pulls the trigger more smoothly and purposefully."

In 1941 Lyudmila Pavlichenko was a 24-year-old history student at Kiev University in Ukraine, southern Russia. She also belonged to the *Osoaviakhim*, the Society for Facilitating Defense, Aviation and Chemical Construction—like America's Civil Defense or Britain's Home Guard—where she'd learned hang-gliding and parachuting, among other skills, and she already knew how to shoot. When the Germans arrived, in late June, she was a student intern in Odessa, a city on the Black Sea 250 miles south of Kiev. She joined a volunteer "destroyer squad" to shoot German paratroopers. Her unit was merged into the regular army and Lyudmila was assigned as a sniper to the 2nd Company, 2nd Battalion of the 54th Infantry Regiment of the V.I. Chapayev Division (the 25th Rifles, named in honor of Vasiliy Chapayev, a hero of the Russian Civil War) of the Soviet Independent Maritime Army.

In the two-month siege of Odessa, between 40,000 and 60,000 Russians were killed, wounded or went missing. German casualties numbered 93,000; Lyudmila killed 187 of them.

In October 1941 Lyudmila was among 350,000 soldiers and civilians evacuated from Odessa by ships of the Russian Navy. She was promoted to sergeant and sent to Sevastopol, another Black Sea port. In December the Germans attacked that city. There, over the next six months, Sgt. Pavlichenko scored 122 more kills. Her method was to pick a spot where she could ambush Germans, move in at three o'clock in the morning with food, water and cartridges, and stay there, hidden, for as long as two days.

Soviet snipers operated as two-person teams—a shooter and a spotter—but, unlike the way other armies did it, they took turns. Once the spotter confirmed and recorded a kill, she or he would swap binoculars for rifle and become the shooter. However, maybe because her skills were so exceptional, it appears that Lyudmila had a permanent spotter. Her final total of 309 "Hitlerites" (along with, reportedly, two unscored "test shots" on Romanian soldiers fighting with the Germans) included 36 especially high-value targets: enemy snipers. One of them was carrying a notebook that indicated he'd killed 400 British soldiers at the Battle of Dunkirk in May 1940.

Imagine the Allied lives—Russian, British, American, Canadian, Australian and others—Lyudmila may have saved.

In June 1942 Lyudmila was wounded for the fourth time, by mortar shrapnel, and again evacuated, this time by submarine. (One of her earlier injuries came when she fell out of a tree, pretending she'd been shot in order to escape three Germans who were stalking her.) By now she was a star of Russian newspapers and propaganda—not only was she extraordinarily effective against the enemy, she was also an example of "heroic Soviet womanhood"—and her fame had reached beyond Russia. The International Congress of Students Against War invited her to speak to school groups in America. Then Eleanor Roosevelt, the wife of American President Franklin D. Roosevelt, arranged for her to tour the country.

With the blessings of the Soviet government, from August into November 1942 Jr. Lt. Pavlichenko (with another sniper, a man, and a Soviet government "youth representative") traveled across Britain, the United States and Canada to tell people how hard Russians were fighting their common enemy, Germany, and to appeal for help. You can see her on YouTube and read translations of her speeches on the Internet.

Everywhere she went she was mobbed as "the Russian heroine." At the age of 26 Lyudmila

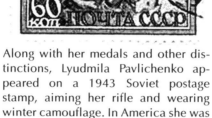

Along with her medals and other distinctions, Lyudmila Pavlichenko appeared on a 1943 Soviet postage stamp, aiming her rifle and wearing winter camouflage. In America she was the subject of an educational card that came in packages of chewing gum.

became the first Soviet citizen to be received by President Roosevelt at the White House. She met Americans of all sorts, from ordinary people to movie stars such as Charlie Chaplin and Paul Robeson. In Central Park, New York City Mayor LaGuardia introduced her to a crowd of 100,000 eager listeners. In Madison Square Garden workers from the Colt factory presented her with an engraved Model 1911 .45 pistol.

As a member of an entire society fighting for its existence, she was sometimes exasperated with Americans and their comfortable lives far from the carnage in Europe and Asia. In the September 28, 1942, issue of *Time* Magazine she shared some of her thoughts about American women:

"I am amazed at the kind of questions put to me by women press correspondents in Washington . . . They asked me silly questions such as do I use powder and rouge and nail polish and do I curl my hair. One reporter even criticized the length of the skirt of my uniform, saying that in America women wear shorter skirts, and besides my uniform made me look fat. This made me very angry. I wear my uniform with honor. It has the Order of Lenin on it. It has been covered with blood in battle . . . ."

When Lyudmila returned home, she was assigned to train other snipers. She was declared a Hero of the Soviet Union, her nation's highest award. After the war ended, in 1945, Lyudmila finished her studies at Kiev University and then worked as a research historian for the Soviet Navy.

Her service was never forgotten. Eleanor Roosevelt visited her in Moscow in 1957. When she died, in 1974 at the age of 58, retired Maj. Lyudmila Pavlichenko was buried in Moscow's Novodevichy Cemetery alongside many other famous Russians—composers, scientists, authors, soldiers, statesmen and leaders.

As a fresh enlistee she had been eager to shoot Germans. But when the crosshairs of her scope first settled on a living human target, she said she couldn't squeeze the trigger. That changed when a young Russian soldier near her was shot. "He was such a nice, happy boy . . . . After that, nothing could stop me." And nothing did. Pavlichenko became one of the most effective snipers of all time.

She was lucky to have survived. Nearly three-quarters of all the female Red Army snipers in WWII died in combat.

1.3 Shots, One Kill

Only five years after World War II ended Communist North Korea invaded democratic South Korea, in 1950. The US military and its allies went to the rescue. The Korean landscape sometimes let snipers see their enemy at very long distances, so it was here that the fearsome .50 BMG round was used for sniping for the first time. The "rifles" were Browning M2 heavy machine guns fitted with Unertl 8X scopes and set up for single fire.

In the early 1960s the United States found itself fighting Communist forces in Asia again, this time in Vietnam. The US Army had set up a sniper school in 1955, after Korea, but the program had to be reinvented almost completely because Vietnam's jungles were so different from Korea's mountains.

During the Vietnam War the US Marines began to get serious about their sniper-training program. This is Sgt. Carlos Hathcock shooting a bolt-action Winchester Model 70 with a heavy target barrel and a high-powered (for the time) scope. The North Vietnamese Army called him "White Feather" and promised $30,000 to anyone who killed him, but he survived the war.

(Remember what we said about armies always being prepared for the previous war?) The Marines handed the job to Capt. Jim Land. The Corps already had a supply of Winchester Model 70 hunting rifles with the 8X Unertl scopes, which were being used as match rifles, but Land started the process that finally led to the 7.62x51mm M40 sniper rifle, built on a Remington Model 700 action.

Some of this gear couldn't stand the rain and heat of the jungle and many different rifles, cartridges and scopes were tested. While their equipment could have been better, two Marine snipers, Carlos Hathcock and Chuck Mahwhinney, became famous in Vietnam. Hathcock's book *Marine Sniper: 93 Confirmed Kills* is a good read for anyone who wants to understand the challenges they faced.

One of the problems with snipers is that military commanders traditionally didn't know what to do with them. Detailed planning and logistics are necessary for units of troops—not to mention for coordinating artillery, ships, aircraft or armor—but not for a few lone-wolf dudes who prowl through the bush with rifles and face paint. Yet their spectacular results made snipers impossible for the brass to ignore. According to the US Department of Defense, it took an average of *50,000* rounds to kill one enemy soldier in Vietnam in battle. American snipers, on the other hand, killed an enemy with every 1.3 rounds they fired. That amounted to $23,000 per kill for the average infantryman versus 17¢ for the sniper.

After Vietnam defense officials figured the next war would be fought with tanks against the

Soviet Union in Europe, or maybe with airborne volleys of nuclear missiles. Wrong again. Instead our military faced (once again—see "Killer Apps") highly motivated Muslim warriors, this time in the deserts of Iraq and the mountains of Afghanistan. They had neither airplanes nor tanks nor formal battle units, just a strong will to fight, an endless supply of improvised explosive devices and the ability to fade into the civilian population. If this is the future, special-operations forces and especially snipers will play huge roles in wars to come.

The State of the Sniper's Art

The Secret Service has "countersnipers" who defend against threats. These are the shooters on top of buildings when the President makes a public appearance. They don't stalk other snipers. (The German-versus-Russian sniper duel in the movie *Enemy at the Gates* may have been made up by the Russians to boost morale.) Carlos Hathcock did have a couple of one-on-one encounters with North Vietnamese shooters, but that was before the USMC sniper program had a plan or rules. If two snipers duel, which one is the countersniper? Today the question is: If an enemy sniper is causing trouble, how should he be dealt with? Artillery or a helicopter or drone strike?

A "designated marksman" is a soldier trained to shoot at longer ranges than his squad mates and armed with a DMR (Designated Marksman Rifle), which is usually capable of automatic fire. He's part of an infantry platoon, like a machine-gunner, not a single specialist.

Some police officers carry rifles in their patrol cars. The best information we can find is that these rifles are used at an average range of about 35 yards, while a police sniper's typical shot is about 70 yards—at, for example, someone holding a knife to a hostage's throat in a house across the street.

Civilian interest in long-range military-style shooting has grown tremendously, and along with it the market for sniper gear. Today's sniper (and sniper wanna-be) has a dizzying array of special rifles to choose from. There are bolt-action and semi-automatic "platforms" in calibers ranging

Times, training and weapons have changed a lot. The US Army rates this semi-automatic .50-caliber Barrett M107 effective at nearly twice the range (1,500 meters) of its .308 sniper rifles (800 meters). Snipers often reach much farther with the .50, though. See the empty case in the air?

Department of Defense

from 5.56mm to .50 BMG, with finely tuned ammunition for each. The sniper also has night-vision scopes, laser rangefinders and palm computers to help determine his "firing solutions"—how to set a scope to compensate for bullet drop, wind, temperature, barometric pressure and other variables, even the earth's rotation while the bullet is in flight.

The days of the wood-stocked .30-06 sniper rifle with a 2½X Lyman Alaskan scope are long gone. Gone too are the days when snipers were treated as afterthoughts. Today they can stand off at incredible distances and launch API (Armor Piercing Incendiary) rounds from a .50-caliber Barrett M107 or coordinate with other teams to identify and take out an HVT (High Value Target).

Carlos Hathcock used fieldcraft to move through the jungle. Navy SEAL Chris Kyle was the top sniper from the Iraq and Afghanistan wars, with 150 confirmed kills. Kyle's fieldcraft

The British Army's Model L115A3 in .338 Lapua Magnum. This is the type of rifle used by Cpl. Craig Harrison to kill two enemies in Afghanistan at a range of more than a mile and a half.

didn't involve jungles or deserts; often he put himself deep into the shadows of city neighborhoods.

Kyle's longest kill was 2,100 yards with a .338 Lapua Magnum. That's 1.2 miles. Hathcock's longest in Vietnam was 2,000 yards with a .50 BMG. The combat record now belongs to Cpl. Craig Harrison of England's Household Cavalry regiment. In November 2009 Harrison used an L115A3 rifle in .338 Lapua Magnum to drop two Taliban machine gunners in Helmand Province, Afghanistan, at a range of 2,707 yards—2.47 kilometers, or 1.53 miles. Incredible.

You'll Put Your Eye Out!

BB Guns, Pellet Guns, Paintball & Airsoft

Yes, you just might, if you're not careful. Put your eye out, that is—yours or more likely someone else's. Or worse. Three weeks before this was written, a boy in California died almost instantly when a pellet fired at very close range got past his ribs and went into his heart. It was an accident, but he's still dead, and his friend who was holding the air pistol will remember this awful thing for the rest of his life.

Here is the problem with guns that fire "only" BBs or pellets instead of "real bullets": It's too easy to treat them like toys. Even a small-caliber firearm (powered by gunpowder) makes a loud *crack!* when it goes off, and this gets our attention and respect. A pellet gun (powered by compressed air or carbon dioxide) just goes pop! But what's important isn't the noise; it's the energy of the projectile.

A BB is a plain round ball; a pellet is cylindrical, precisely shaped for accuracy and with either a pointed or flat nose for hunting or target shooting.

Most air rifles in the United States are either .22 or .177 caliber. A .22-caliber pellet for hunting small game and shooting pests like rats typically weighs only about 15 grains (0.034 ounces, or the weight of a paper clip), but it's traveling at 600 to 850 feet per second (fps) or more when it leaves the gun. That's 410 to 580 miles per hour. Anything that moves carries energy with it, and that energy is transferred to whatever it hits. Energy comes from both mass (weight) and velocity (speed), so something light moving fast can have as much energy as something that's much heavier but traveling more slowly.

The energy of any projectile (whether it's a bullet, an arrow, a snowball or an airgun pellet) can

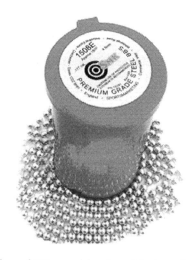

Firepower-brand BBs—gold colored but made of hard steel. They'll ricochet like crazy off a hard surface.

Hollowpoint .177-caliber BSA pellets designed for hunting—that is, for penetration and killing.

be measured in foot-pounds. Energy can do work. One foot-pound is a measure of the energy needed to move a one-pound mass one foot. Get a one-pound can of something from the kitchen and raise it 12 inches. Nothing to it, right?

But a .22-caliber pellet at 850 feet per second creates about 22 foot-pounds of energy. Now lift a stack of 22 one-pound cans and think of that much energy being applied by a pellet instead of your hand.

Pellets fired from this Sheridan Blue Streak air rifle severely dented the steel sheet and went right through the wooden board.

Steve Helsley

A .177-caliber target pellet has less mass (usually 7 to 11 grains), but if it's fired by a similar blast of compressed air or other gas, it travels much faster—up to 1,200 fps. As a result, it delivers just about the same amount of energy.

(These velocities are measured at the gun's muzzle, the end of the barrel. As a pellet travels downrange from there, air resistance makes it steadily lose velocity and gravity pulls it toward the ground. If it hits something before then, its energy will be less than it was when it left the gun because it has slowed down. Its mass won't have changed, though.)

At point-blank range, almost any air-rifle pellet will punch through a one-inch-thick wooden board. Fired across your living room and into bare skin, it will go anywhere from four to eight inches deep in human tissue. A bone will stop it, with lots of pain—but an eye will hardly slow it down at all, and the pellet may go through the back of the eye socket and into the brain.

They're not toys. And there is a more complete explanation of energy in "Hollywood & Newton's Third Law," in "How Far & How Hard."

Air Guns in History

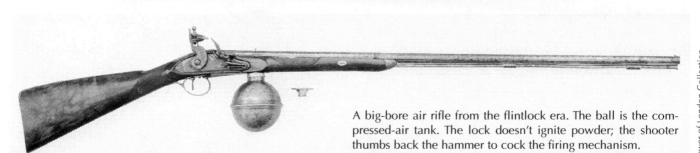

A big-bore air rifle from the flintlock era. The ball is the compressed-air tank. The lock doesn't ignite powder; the shooter thumbs back the hammer to cock the firing mechanism.

Tower of London Collection

Guns powered by blasts of air instead of gunpowder are not new. The first one probably appeared in Germany around 1560. Three hundred and forty years later, in London, Sherlock Holmes narrowly missed death at the hands of an assassin armed with a near-silent air rifle. Holmes was a fictional detective, but large-caliber air rifles capable of killing humans at a distance were real.

In America the best-known historic air rifle is the Girandoni that may have been Lewis and Clark's "secret weapon" on their expedition across the American wilderness from 1804 to 1806. According to the National Firearms Museum, in Fairfax, Virginia, that rifle might be the single most important gun in our history.

An Italian named Bartolomeo Girandoni invented the air rifle that bears his name in the 1770s. It was used by the Austrian Army from 1780 until about 1815, mostly against Napoleon Bonaparte's French Republican forces, which

National Firearms Museum

Lewis & Clark's "secret weapon" was a Girandoni rifle. Here's one with its buttstock air tank detached (right). There is no gunpowder to ignite, so the hammer is only a cocking mechanism; the shooter pulls it back until it clicks into a notch, which arms the air valve and sets the trigger. The loading lever is on the left side of the action, where the shooter's thumb can reach it.

were then trying to conquer all of Europe. As you know, most firearms at that time were single-shots that had to be loaded from the muzzle by pushing gunpowder, wadding and a lead ball down the barrel with a ramrod. In favorable conditions a trained infantryman could load and fire his musket three or four times in a minute. Muskets were smoothbores—no rifling—so they were horribly inaccurate. They also made clouds of dirty white smoke, and the military versions recoiled horribly.

The Girandoni must have seemed miraculous by comparison. No smoke, less recoil and, thanks to its rifled barrel, impressive accuracy. Even more amazing was that it had a tubular magazine next to its barrel that could hold 20 to 30 rounds, and it could be fired as fast as the shooter could flick the loading lever, cock the hammer with his thumb and aim. It threw a heavy lead ball (.46 to .51 caliber, which is about a half-inch diameter, depending on the gun) at around 800 fps—enough to kill at a hundred yards or more.

There were problems, though. The rifle's buttstock—hollow, made of metal and covered with leather—was the tank that held the compressed air. An Austrian soldier was issued three of these. A

full load of air could fire 30 to 40 shots before the power began to drop off noticeably. Then the empty tank had to be unscrewed from the rifle and a fresh one put on. Each soldier got a hand pump to refill the tanks, which could take an exhausting 1,500 strokes. Keeping that much pressurized air bottled up with the primitive materials of the day was difficult too, so there was a lot of leakage.

Technologically, it was years ahead of its time, but the Girandoni was too expensive and impractical to be a reliable military weapon. However, this didn't stop some well-to-do hunters and, in the case of Meriwether Lewis and William Clark, gentlemen explorers from making good use of it. In the journal of their trip, the air rifle is reportedly mentioned 39 times, and on the very first page of his own diary Lewis describes it as a "wonderment to the crowd."

Whenever their Corps of Discovery met an Indian band, Lewis and Clark and their officers (there were never more than 38 people in the company, including Sacajawea, the teen-age Shoshone girl who was their interpreter) dressed up in their military uniforms and put on a shooting demonstration—with the air rifle. It seems the Indians were always impressed with this powerful, accurate and, above all, rapid-firing weapon. Perhaps assuming that each of the Whites had one of these deadly rifles, they let the party continue onward. Had the expedition been wiped out and the Indians seized the company's powder and shot, pistols, rifles, muskets, shotguns, blunderbusses and one swivel cannon, American and possibly even European history could have developed very differently.

BB Guns: 'It's a Daisy!'

By 1900 smokeless gunpowder and many other advancements had made firearms so much more effective that air-powered guns all but disappeared. With one exception.

In 1888 the Plymouth Iron Windmill Manufacturing Company, in Michigan, came up with a cheap air gun as a giveaway for the farmers who were its customers. It was a big hit—in the slang of those days, "a daisy." The name stuck, and within a few years the Daisy Manufacturing Company was born and windmill production stopped. Daisy BB guns spread all over the world, even to China, which for a while accounted for almost one-third of the company's overseas business.

There's a story that the Daisy's resemblance to a real rifle worried the Chinese government. The Daisy salesman offered the seat of his pants as a target to prove that the gun wasn't harmful. We don't know what the range was, but we do notice that he didn't face the gun. He probably was wearing a suit too. Had he been bare-assed this would have been a genuine "pain in the butt."

For many shooters in America, their first gun was a Daisy. This is the classic BB gun, different from a pellet gun because it fires round balls. BB (from "ball bearing") shot was originally for shotgun shells, and Daisy settled on it because it was a useful size and also cheap and plentiful. BB shot is supposed to be .180-caliber, but birdshot isn't made to the same strict size tolerances that bullets are, and variations meant it didn't always fit in an air gun. So around 1905 Daisy began to make its own BBs, carefully sized. This solved the fit problem and also gave Daisy a new product to sell.

At first BBs were soft lead coated with copper or zinc. Today, though, they're made of coated steel, which offers one big advantage and one big disadvantage.

Modern BB guns are .177-caliber smoothbores, with no rifling in the barrels. BBs themselves are only .171 to .173 inch in diameter, so a BB would just roll out of the barrel if the gun were tilted downward. Daisy solved this problem by putting a magnet in the piston that drives the BB—a magnet strong enough to hold the steel BB in place but not strong enough to hold back its launch. This magnetic feature is the advantage of steel.

The disadvantage is that steel, being much harder than lead, doesn't deform and slow down or stop when it hits a hard surface; it bounces off and keeps going. These ricochets are part of what makes even cheap, low-power, spring-air (see below) BB guns dangerous.

So they're still not toys.

The days when a kid could wander the neighborhood plinking with a BB gun (knocking down toy soldiers or protecting mom's laundry from birds) are all but gone. But BB guns are still important when it comes to learning to shoot. A Daisy can be important in other ways too, as this note from a grownup friend about his BB gun indicates: "I've stood nose-to-nose with Cape buffalo, I've ridden a good mountain horse in the Rockies, I've dived with sharks, but I've never been as excited as I was when I opened that long, slim box on that Christmas morning 53 years ago!"

Possibly the rarest of all Daisy BB guns is this double-barreled Model 104 from the 1940s.

Pellet Guns: Spring-Air, Pneumatic & CO₂

There are three basic kinds of air guns. The first two, spring-air and pneumatic, are powered by air compressed by the shooter. Most BB guns are spring-air, or single-stroke, types: Cocking the action compresses a spring, which when it's released (by pulling the trigger) pushes a piston into a chamber with a tiny vent at its other end, creating the blast of air that shoves another piston that shoves the BB down the barrel.

A high-powered Gamo Whisper spring-air rifle that fires .177-caliber pellets at 1,200 feet per second. The barrel is hinged at the end of the stock; "breaking" it opens the breech so you can load a pellet. This also cocks the action.

Most lever-action air guns have springs soft enough for kids to compress, so they fire a BB at only about 275 fps. Some full-size adult spring-air guns, however, are true rifles that shoot .177 or .22 pellets at 600 fps or more. The barrels of these guns are hinged at the end of the stock, and "breaking" the barrel (cranking it downward) cocks the spring and exposes the breech so you can load a pellet into the barrel.

This .177-caliber Benjamin air rifle can fire pellets at up to 800 fps, depending on how many times you pump the handle under the barrel.

Pneumatic air guns don't have springs. By pumping the action with a lever or handle, the shooter raises the pressure in the air cylinder inside, which powers the piston that fires the BB or pellet. More

Feinwerkbau's super-sophisticated single-shot Model 800, a $3,000 Olympic-class single-shot target rifle. Its pre-filled air tank (under the barrel) fires .177-caliber pellets at 570 fps.

pumping increases the air pressure and thus the velocity of the round. There are also PCP, (pre-charged pneumatic), air guns that are powered by pressurized air reservoirs—just like the old Girandoni.

The third kind of air gun is powered by compressed CO_2, or carbon dioxide. This saves having to pump, but it means buying the cylinders. Even the small 12-gram cylinders that fit into a pistol grip have enough charge to fire dozens of rounds, usually at velocities of 400 fps or

Crosman's 18-shot semi-automatic .177-caliber C11 Tactical BB pistol is good for up to 550 fps. This one has a "suppressor," an accessory rail and an aiming laser. The replaceable CO_2 cartridge is in the grip.

more. If you put the gun away before using up the charge, this leaves it able to be fired. And eventually the leftover gas will leak out and be wasted.

Some gas-powered guns—Paintball guns, for example—have large built-in cylinders that last much longer and can be refilled.

As mentioned, serious air guns pretty much disappeared early in the 1900s. But after World War II things changed again. In 1950 the National Rifle Association established a Junior Qualification

TV personality Eva Shockey with a big, tough wild boar she killed in Texas with one shot from a .25-caliber Benjamin Marauder air rifle. Air guns are only now getting back to the sort of power output they were capable of two centuries ago.

Course for air rifles as a way to teach firearms safety. In Europe, where laws about owning firearms were becoming more and more restrictive, air guns became especially popular. And then, in 1984, air guns entered Olympic competition. As a result of all of this, the velocity, accuracy and sophistication of air guns have increased tremendously. So have their prices. Daisy still sells a lot of inexpensive spring-air BB guns, but now it's also possible to spend thousands of dollars on a target rifle that will put match-grade .177 pellets into the same hole all day long at 10 meters.

They're all good. Still not toys, though.

Shooting BB Guns & Air Rifles

• **Why:** Any BB gun is a great way to learn to shoot and to learn good safety habits. Regardless of what type of rifle you move on to—whether it's a Chipmunk .22, a Patriot Ordnance P-415, a Barrett .50, a Westley Richards .470 Nitro Express or a Remington .30-06, the basics are the same.

• **Where:** Your basement. The attic. A spare room. The back yard. Anywhere that you have more than 20 feet of range and a back wall that won't let BBs or pellets fly onward.

• **Aiming:** Adult pellet rifles may have fine scopes or Olympic-quality open sights, but BB guns generally have crude post-and-vee sights. Experience will show you where your gun shoots (high, low, left, right), and then you just compensate. Shoot with both eyes open so you have a better view of the target. You also may glimpse the BB in flight.

• **Targets:** A cardboard box stuffed with crumpled newspapers. Tape a bull's-eye or picture to the box, or hang something appropriate in front of it and use the box as a backstop.

• **Avoid:** Metal targets that make steel BBs or pellets ricochet; also things made of glass that might shatter (or make the round ricochet).

• **Safety – Yours:** You don't need hearing protection with air guns, but you should wear shooting glasses in case of ricochets or if somehow your gun develops a leak that blows air or gas back into your face.

• **Safety – Theirs:** Don't shoot at your friends. Or enemies. Cats and dogs are not fair game either; want to explain to the neighbors how you blinded or killed their pet?

• **Uh-oh:** How'd that BB-size hole in the basement window get there? Good luck blaming it on your little brother; better to get out in front of this and confess before your parents see it. Then they'll be impressed instead of ticked off (we hope).

• **The Bottom Line:** No air gun is a toy unless it fires NERF balls. (NERF, by the way, stands for Non-Expanding Recreational Foam.)

Paintball: Is This the Dark Side?

You're probably wondering, *What about Airsoft and Paintball? Aren't those air guns?* Yes, they are, and here you'll see why we put them in a different section.

As you know, adults have a tendency to see problems where kids don't. Sometimes this is bogus, and sometimes it's a matter of opinion, but often it's the result of painful experience. So while you may think Paintball and Airsoft are fantastic because they're like stepping into a video game, this is exactly why a lot of experienced shooters worry about Paintball and Airsoft. Allow us to explain . . . .

First the background: Hard-skinned balls of wet paint to be used as markers (mostly by foresters and ranchers to identify certain trees and livestock) have been around since the 1950s. At first they contained paint, but this was replaced by dye that washes off. Modern paintballs are nontoxic, biodegradable, food-grade gelatin, like bath-oil beads. They are around .69 caliber, almost three-quarters of an inch in diameter, but they weigh only about one gram, or 15 grains. Regulation Paintball guns fire them at about 300 fps and, since they're large compared to a BB or a .177 or .22 pellet, they slow down quickly. A paintball bursts on impact, so it won't penetrate flesh, but it does leave a welt on bare skin and will destroy an eye.

Like pellets and BBs, paintballs are propelled by compressed air or CO_2. The guns may be pump-action types, which have to be re-cocked between shots, or self-loading semi-automatics or even fully automatic machine guns. Some Paintball guns have hoppers that hold a lot of ammunition and large gas reservoirs so shooting can go on and on. The gun barrels are generally short, and forget about precision sights or well-aimed fire. Most Paintball players rely on "spray and pray" shooting.

The Daisy company made the first paintball gun, a CO_2-powered bolt-action pistol called the

These days, Paintball is played by about 10 million people in the US alone. The trouble is that Paintball (just like Airsoft) can teach dangerous firearms handling, and the guns can be mistaken for the "real" thing.

Splotchmaker, in 1970. But this was for commercial use (those ranchers and foresters); Paintball the game didn't arrive for another 11 years.

Paintball Is Born

To settle an argument about survival instincts—whether someone who worked in an office in the city was still as sharp a predator as someone who lived on the land and hunted—a friend of ours named Charles Gaines, a writer living in New Hampshire, organized a contest.

On June 27, 1981, he and 11 other guys walked into a hundred-acre section of woods at different points. Each of them was wearing camouflage and goggles and carrying a compass, a supply of paintballs and CO_2 cartridges, and an industrial-grade Nel-spot 007 paintball pistol. (These were actually Splotchmaker guns, made by Daisy for the Nelson Paint Company.) Each man also had a map showing four places in the woods where a dozen flags hung. The goal was to reach home base with four different flags and without having been shot by another player.

Everyone thought the game was tremendously exciting. The winner was a professional forester—the only player who never fired a shot and who was never even seen by anyone else.

As it happened, along with Gaines there were three other writers in that first game. One of them, another friend of ours named Bob Jones, wrote a story about it called "Survival" for *Sports Illustrated*. Then the other two wrote it up also, for *Time* and *Sports Afield*. Suddenly people all over the country wanted to play. Gaines and his friends cre-

ated a company called the National Survival Game, wrote a rulebook and began to sell Nel-spot guns and gear. The first commercial playing field opened in 1982, in Rochester, New York. In 1983 the first National Survival Game championship was held, with a cash purse of $14,000.

The craze was on. Competing leagues and team play were created, the name changed to Paintball (with a capital P), and more and more companies got involved, supplying high-performance guns and all sorts of gear, from face masks and body armor to special clothes and footwear. Paintball has become a global game, played indoors and out, informally or with referees and rules and sometimes with professional players, to capture objectives or reenact famous battles. Supposedly about 10 million people, mostly males between the ages of 12 and 24, now play Paintball in the US.

Airsoft: More Dark Side?

Airsoft guns are much more sophisticated and real-looking than Paintball markers. They fire a 6mm (.236-caliber) plastic BB from a smoothbore barrel at about 300 to 600 fps, depending on the type of gun and limits set by law or game rules. Airsoft began in Japan, where owning firearms is all but impossible, and then spread to Europe and the United States. Airsoft skirmishing has become a competitor to Paintball and requires the same sort of closed-off area for "combat."

There are four kinds of Airsoft guns: single-shot spring-powered types that have to be cocked manually; repeaters powered by CO_2 cartridges; guns fired by "green gas," which is basically propane with a small amount of silicone oil added for lubrication; and guns operated by built-in electric motors. The motor drives a piston that compresses air to blow the BB out of the barrel. Electric

Airsoft machine guns can fire up to 900 plastic BBs a minute.

About every type of tactical firearm—from pistols to submachine guns and assault rifles, combat shotguns, sniper rifles, even grenade launchers and heavy machine guns—is available as an Airsoft replica. (Some of these cost thousands of dollars.) You can't tell most of them from the real thing until you pick them up, and this is both their great attraction and their fatal flaw. A lot of Airsoft guns look like real guns that are illegal to own.

In the United States Airsoft guns have high-visibility orange tips on their barrels to set them apart from firearms, but some owners remove the tips. Some European countries require Airsoft guns to be made of see-through plastic or painted in ridiculous colors for the same reason—but a few genuine firearms are also available in colors like pink. Britain has strict laws governing replica firearms that apply to many Airsoft guns. Airsoft clubs and fields everywhere have their own rules about how to carry and handle the guns.

None of this, however, changes the fact that, to the general public, these things look frighteningly real. There have been some awful cases where police officers felt forced to shoot kids fooling around with what turned out to be Airsoft "toys." A lot of firearms experts think Airsoft guns are the worst of both worlds: useless as guns but so realistic that they can create very dangerous situations.

Like Paintball, Airsoft can also teach deadly firearms handling. One of the first rules of shooting is to never point a gun at something or someone you're not willing to destroy. Any kid who plays "Call of Duty" and has an Airsoft Heckler &

Koch MP-5 replica can learn everything wrong in a very short time.

Most Paintball and Airsoft players grow up, move on to other hobbies and never handle real guns. Many real shooters, on the other hand, never play these games. They're scared by them and the lessons they can teach.

If you absolutely have to have a Magpul Masada or a Barrett, wait till you can get the genuine article. And in the meantime learn how to shoot for real, well and safely. If you have fantasies about "special ops" and being a covert warrior, wait till you're old enough to enlist in the military. And then let's see if you have the right stuff.

The Echo1 USA full-size Gatling-type "Minigun" is one of those Airsoft models that look like real guns that people generally can't own. It weighs 33 pounds, fires thousands of pellets per minute and is driven by an electric motor with a separate power pack. It costs about $3,500.

Safety First

It's Easy to Be a Safe Shooter

The 15 Commandments of Gun Safety

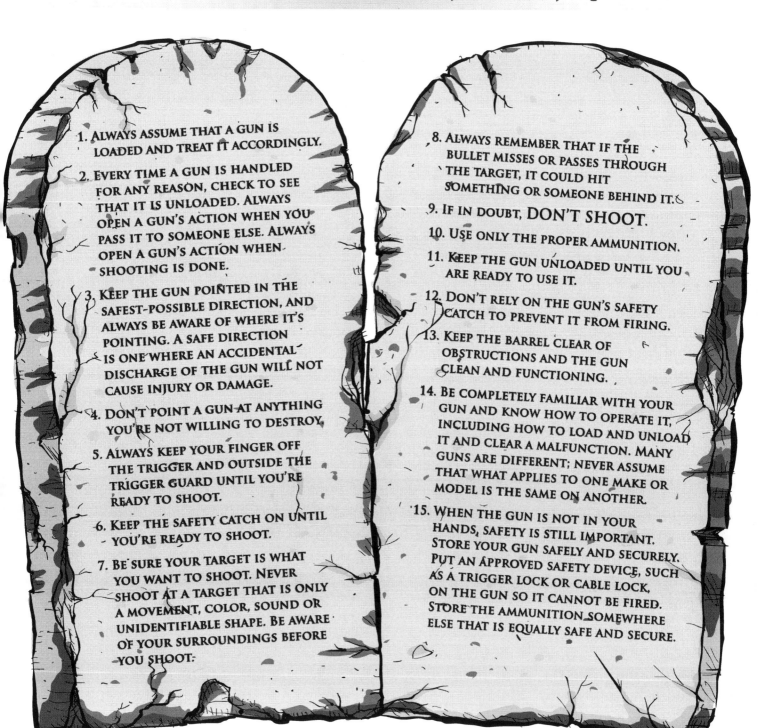

1. ALWAYS ASSUME THAT A GUN IS LOADED AND TREAT IT ACCORDINGLY.

2. EVERY TIME A GUN IS HANDLED FOR ANY REASON, CHECK TO SEE THAT IT IS UNLOADED. ALWAYS OPEN A GUN'S ACTION WHEN YOU PASS IT TO SOMEONE ELSE. ALWAYS OPEN A GUN'S ACTION WHEN SHOOTING IS DONE.

3. KEEP THE GUN POINTED IN THE SAFEST-POSSIBLE DIRECTION, AND ALWAYS BE AWARE OF WHERE IT'S POINTING. A SAFE DIRECTION IS ONE WHERE AN ACCIDENTAL DISCHARGE OF THE GUN WILL NOT CAUSE INJURY OR DAMAGE.

4. DON'T POINT A GUN AT ANYTHING YOU'RE NOT WILLING TO DESTROY.

5. ALWAYS KEEP YOUR FINGER OFF THE TRIGGER AND OUTSIDE THE TRIGGER GUARD UNTIL YOU'RE READY TO SHOOT.

6. KEEP THE SAFETY CATCH ON UNTIL YOU'RE READY TO SHOOT.

7. BE SURE YOUR TARGET IS WHAT YOU WANT TO SHOOT. NEVER SHOOT AT A TARGET THAT IS ONLY A MOVEMENT, COLOR, SOUND OR UNIDENTIFIABLE SHAPE. BE AWARE OF YOUR SURROUNDINGS BEFORE YOU SHOOT.

8. ALWAYS REMEMBER THAT IF THE BULLET MISSES OR PASSES THROUGH THE TARGET, IT COULD HIT SOMETHING OR SOMEONE BEHIND IT.

9. IF IN DOUBT, DON'T SHOOT.

10. USE ONLY THE PROPER AMMUNITION.

11. KEEP THE GUN UNLOADED UNTIL YOU ARE READY TO USE IT.

12. DON'T RELY ON THE GUN'S SAFETY CATCH TO PREVENT IT FROM FIRING.

13. KEEP THE BARREL CLEAR OF OBSTRUCTIONS AND THE GUN CLEAN AND FUNCTIONING.

14. BE COMPLETELY FAMILIAR WITH YOUR GUN AND KNOW HOW TO OPERATE IT, INCLUDING HOW TO LOAD AND UNLOAD IT AND CLEAR A MALFUNCTION. MANY GUNS ARE DIFFERENT; NEVER ASSUME THAT WHAT APPLIES TO ONE MAKE OR MODEL IS THE SAME ON ANOTHER.

15. WHEN THE GUN IS NOT IN YOUR HANDS, SAFETY IS STILL IMPORTANT. STORE YOUR GUN SAFELY AND SECURELY. PUT AN APPROVED SAFETY DEVICE, SUCH AS A TRIGGER LOCK OR CABLE LOCK, ON THE GUN SO IT CANNOT BE FIRED. STORE THE AMMUNITION SOMEWHERE ELSE THAT IS EQUALLY SAFE AND SECURE.

The 'Law of Three'

ccidents with guns can have awful conse-quences that change lives in an instant. Handling guns properly is neither com-plicated nor difficult. You just have to learn a few common-sense rules. Once you've programmed these rules into your subconscious mind so that they're habits, accidents with guns will be extremely rare—and when they do happen, their consequenc-es should be minor.

Accidents often turn out to be the result of three smaller mistakes, all building on each other. It seems to be true for all sorts of things, whether it's riding your bicycle, slicing a sandwich for lunch or shooting.

Think about it. You jump on your bike, fly down the street, cross over to a friend's house and get flat-tened by a car. Mistake No. 1: You weren't looking. Mistake No. 2: You were going too fast. Mistake No. 3: You didn't signal your turn. If you hadn't made any one of these three mistakes, the accident likely wouldn't have happened. You would have seen the car in time, or the driver would have seen you.

Here's how the "Law of Three" can apply to shooting:

On a pheasant hunt one of your authors got shot with a 12-gauge gun. His shooting glasses saved his eyes and maybe his life, and some pellets were slowed down by his heavy vest, but it took a surgeon hours to dig pellets out of his face, upper

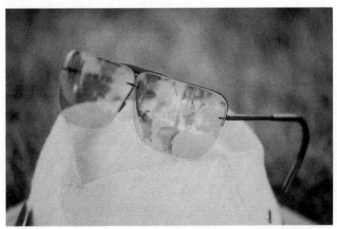

The author's Ranger shooting glasses, covered with blood that dripped down from pellets that hit his forehead. One lens stopped several 12-gauge shot meant for pheasants.

body and right hand and arm. The man who shot him—accidentally, of course—made three mistakes: First, his gun was still loaded when the group was done hunting and standing around chatting. Second, he fired low. And third, he failed to see the author standing beyond the bird that he was trying to kill, which suddenly appeared out of nowhere. (See Commandments 1, 3, 7 and 8.) Had the shooter not made just one of these errors, the author wouldn't have pellets in his chest still today, 20 years later. The ones that are too deep to remove.

Some True-Life Stories

ere's an accident that was the fault of one of your authors. He was about 14 at the time and preparing to open fire with his .22 rifle on a woodchuck that was raiding the vegetable garden. He stood just inside the kitchen, holding the rifle pointing straight up, and pumped a cartridge into the chamber. The plan was to ease

the screen door open, slide the barrel out, aim and shoot. What happened was that the rifle went off the instant the round was chambered, and the bullet blew a nasty gouge in the wooden doorframe.

He made two mistakes: He had his finger on the trigger when he closed the gun's action; and the safety wasn't on. (You could also say that he

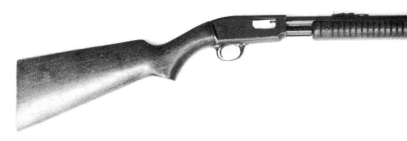

A Model 61 Winchester pump-action .22 like the one that put a hole in the author's kitchen-door frame. One good habit saved the day; a third mistake could have caused a serious problem.

shouldn't have loaded the gun in the house. There are times when it has to be done, but protecting vegetables isn't one of them.)

This scared the hell out of everyone, especially the author, and caused some damage. But he made just two mistakes, and one safety habit saved the day: He was pointing the rifle in a safe direction. Otherwise someone could have been shot.

Sometimes guns just malfunction. Once in Africa the same author and a Professional Hunter were getting out of their Land Rover. As he slid out the door, the PH reached back to get a shotgun from the rack behind the seats. The moment he grabbed it, the gun went off, blowing a hole in the roof of the safari car. The man hadn't touched the trigger; the gun was worn out and needed to be set right by a gunsmith. Again, the good news is that it was pointing straight up when it went off.

Some guns, particularly certain old ones (or new ones made on old designs), have features that can make accidents more likely. In "Killer Apps" we'll tell you about one of them: the Colt Single

Action Army revolver. It was called a six-shooter because it had chambers for six rounds in its cylinder. However, since the point of the hammer could rest directly on the cartridge primer, people quickly learned to keep only five of the chambers loaded and to carry the gun with the empty chamber under the hammer. Otherwise, if something hit the hammer or the gun fell—slipped out of its holster or was dropped—and landed on its hammer, the impact could fire a cartridge. Six-gun fans traditionally stuck a rolled-up $10 bill into one chamber; this prevented a mistake and provided some reserve cash.

Do not think, though, that if you're only going to make one or two mistakes, nothing bad will happen. Instead, build up so many good safety habits that when you do screw up, there are layers of protection that prevent something truly awful.

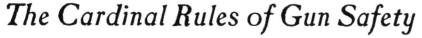

The Cardinal Rules of Gun Safety

1. **Always assume a gun is loaded.**
2. **Never load a gun until it's time to use it.**
3. **Never point it at anything you don't wish to destroy.**
4. **Keep your finger off the trigger until you're ready to destroy your target.**

If you learn these simple habits, then if you happen to trip and fall with a gun in your hands or something else goes wrong, you'll just feel clumsy and scared for a moment instead of guilty for the rest of your life. Or injured, paralyzed or dead.

What About the Safety Catch?

ou can't trust a safety catch. Safety catches are switches that slide, levers that pivot or buttons to push before a shot can be fired. Whatever its shape and wherever it is on the gun, the safety catch locks the trigger.

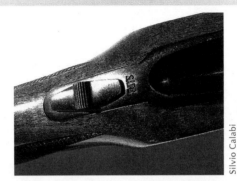

The safety catch on this single-shot rifle is atop the stock and just behind the action, where the shooter's thumb can slide it on and off. The word "safe" indicates the catch is engaged and the gun is safe—but don't count on it absolutely.

But in most firearms that's all it does; the action itself, which is cocked and ready to fire, is not locked. So dropping the gun or even just accidentally banging it into something—a rock or a tree, for example—might jar the action so that it fires the round in the chamber without the trigger doing anything.

Some safeties come on automatically when you close the action. Most, however, have to be switched on manually. Some specialized competition guns don't even have a safety catch—they're loaded and cocked only when they're about to be fired, and they're used only in highly controlled situations.

One of your authors once hunted with a rifle that seemed to have a mind of its own. Two or three times a day he found that the safety had mysteriously slid to the off position, even though it didn't seem loose and he didn't think he'd scraped it against anything. Since he was sometimes crawling through brush with the rifle on his back, a twig could have found its way into the trigger guard and given him a nasty surprise.

A safety catch is not foolproof. It's just one of those layers of protection that add up to help prevent accidents. Here are some others:
• Don't chamber a round until you expect to shoot.
• Don't cock the gun until then, either.
• When you do load and cock, make sure the safety catch is engaged. (It's not foolproof, but that's what it's for.)
• Keep the gun pointed in a safe direction.
• When it's time to aim and fire, bring the gun up so that it doesn't swing across another person, or a vehicle, or your dog or anything else you wouldn't want to shoot.

It Didn't Go Off!

ou squeezed the trigger, but instead of a loud *bang!* you got only a dry *click!* Now what?

First you'll wonder: Is there really a cartridge in the chamber?

Do not immediately open the action to look. This would be like running up to check on a cherry bomb that hasn't exploded yet. You may have a "hang fire"—a round that hasn't detonated yet, even though the hammer fell. (That's the click you heard.) Hang fires were common enough back in muzzleloading days that the term has survived till now, when even non-shooters use it to mean an unexpected and usually unpleasant delay. (It's in "Talking the Talk.")

Don't do anything just yet. If it's a shotgun or rifle, you can take it off of your shoulder—but keep a good grip on the gun and point it in a safe direction (at the ground, usually). Wait. If the gun doesn't go off within 30 seconds, you'll know it wasn't just a delayed reaction due to some odd malfunction in the primer or powder. Now it's no longer a hang fire; it's a misfire. Still keeping the gun pointed safely, open the action.

Chances are good that there's no cartridge in the chamber. If there is one, eject it and look at the base: If the primer has a dimple in it, it was hit by the firing pin. So what happened? Maybe the primer was bad. (This is extremely rare in modern, factory-made ammunition, but it's not impossible.) Maybe the firing pin was a few thousandths of an inch too short or the mainspring was just a little bit too weak to deliver a consistent whack. This is rare also, at least in new guns, but it's fairly common in vintage guns that may be showing the effects of a century or more of use.

Put that cartridge in a different pocket and carry on. If the gun fails to fire again, there's a problem. Stop shooting. It's time for a qualified gunsmith to figure out what's wrong.

How NOT to Hold a Gun

Even when a gun is unloaded, uncocked and completely safe and its action is open, muzzle control—meaning where the gun is pointing—is still important.

It's not enough to tell yourself, *Right, the gun can't fire, so it's OK to wave it around in any old direction*, because it's too easy to forget the details. *(Did I really unload?)*

The only way to build up proper safety habits is to treat *every* gun as though it were loaded all the time, no exceptions. The bottom line: Never point even an *empty* gun at anything you wouldn't want to shoot. This includes your own foot or hand as well as people, cars, buildings or whatever or whomever.

"It's OK, I don't need this foot—or my hands." This shows very poor muzzle safety, and the shotgun actions are closed too! What if the guns are loaded?

Left: More bad muzzle control. What's in the line of fire? This side-by-side shotgun should be pointed at the ground—and its action should be open! *Right:* One reason bird hunters like double guns is that the actions can be opened, which lets everyone around know that the gun is completely safe, even with cartridges still in the chambers. Here the gun muzzles are pointing at the ground too.

I Found a Gun!

If you find a gun at home, even if it's something a family member brought home long ago and it's in your attic or basement, assume it's loaded. Don't touch it. Leave the area. Tell your parents or another responsible adult.

If you're at a friend's house, get out of there and go home. Tell your parents or another responsible adult.

A gun found in the street or some other public place could have been used in a crime. Don't touch it. Call 9-1-1 on your cell phone, and tell the dispatcher what you found. The dispatcher will ask where you are and will send the police.

When they arrive, don't pick up the gun! The cops will think they're being confronted by someone holding a firearm.

If you find a gun in the woods, don't touch that either. But there may be an injured hunter nearby. Look and listen. Call 9-1-1, and follow the dispatcher's instructions. You might have to wait for the police or a game warden to arrive.

Don't take a chance with what seems to be a lost or abandoned gun. Leave it alone, and tell one of your parents or another responsible adult about it.

Things We Never Forget

We never forget accidental discharges or other close calls with guns. The author whose .22 went off in the kitchen remembers it like it happened last week, not 50 years ago. "The silence in the house afterward was deafening. And I've never loaded a gun, *any* gun, in the house, *any* house, since."

Another one of us had two accidental discharges with .22s: "I shot my parents' car. I was

emptying the magazine by pumping the rounds through the action, and I put my finger on the trigger—dumb, dumb, dumb.

"Even worse, though, was that I once shot a hole in my pants when attempting a fast draw with my .22 revolver. My parents never found out about that one. Scared the crap out of me. It could have gone into my leg. *Really* dumb."

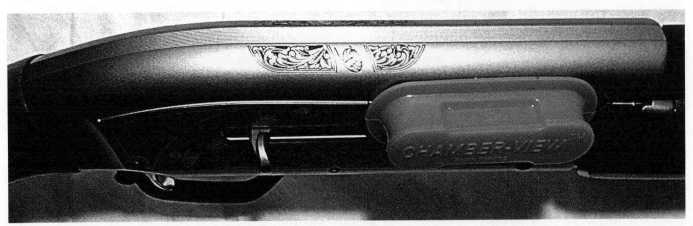

This is a soft-plastic Chamber-View plug made to go in the ejection port of a semi-auto or pump-action shotgun. You can't tell in this photo, but it's bright orange and therefore a highly visible indication that the gun is safe because its action is open.

Serious First Aid

f you or anyone gets shot or otherwise seriously hurt, don't panic. Call 9-1-1. If you can, leave the phone on for instructions or to tell the emergency operator what's going on. Then:

1. Make sure that all guns are unloaded or in a secure place.

2. Stay where you are unless it's not safe.

3. Now you have to act quickly because time is critical. The victim could lose consciousness or die if he or she loses too much blood. Find the injury and see how badly it's bleeding. There may be two wounds: one where the bullet went in and another where it came out again. Put a compress (your T-shirt, coat, bandana, whatever) over the wound and press firmly to try to stop the blood loss. If the gunshot is in an arm or leg, raise it above the level of the victim's heart and apply a tourniquet—your belt, a gun sling, a piece of clothing, whatever. Don't worry about whether the compress or tourniquet is sterile; just stop the bleeding.

4. Don't let the victim eat or drink anything.

5. In addition to blood loss, remember the ABCs of emergency care. A = airway: Make the victim comfortable so that his airway (mouth, nose, throat) is open so he can breathe. B = breathing: Make sure the victim is breathing. C = circulation: Check for a pulse either at a wrist or the side of the throat. If the airway is open but the victim isn't breathing and you can't feel a pulse, start CPR (chest compressions). The 9-1-1 operator should be able to help you with this.

6. If you're outdoors, keep the victim warm. Hypothermia, or cold, can also lead to death.

With most gunshot wounds, getting the victim to a hospital is critical. Reaching a 9-1-1 operator as soon as possible improves the chances of survival.

It isn't just gunshots either. A gun that somehow blows up can cause serious injuries too. This is very rare and almost always preventable, but it can happen if the barrel gets plugged or if the wrong ammunition is used. Read "Keeping Guns Clean & Safe."

Dumb Things

What NOT to Do with Guns

Guns at School

This one is really simple: Don't do it. Or, to put it another way, *Are you crazy?*

Sure, we all want to show our cool stuff to our friends, and what's cooler than a gun and being able to shoot it well? You may be a responsible person and already an experienced shooter with a good understanding of safety—but most of your friends in school are not. You can't risk one of them grabbing or sneaking the gun away from you. And don't even think about swearing them to secrecy. No kid (and few adults) can keep that kind of secret.

It's like that unwritten rule in the movies: If a gun shows up on the screen, you know that somehow, sooner or later, it's going to be used. Same thing in school—and if it isn't used, it will be talked about. Then you'll be in real trouble with the police, not just the principal and your family. The federal Gun-Free School Zones Act of 1990 and 1996 prohibit firearms on and within 1,000 feet of any private or public school property, kindergarten through 12th grade, except in the possession of a police officer, a licensed school security guard or someone who is authorized by the state to carry a gun.

Bring a gun to school, even if it's in a locked case in a car, and you'll be in trouble with the police, not just with the principal, your teachers and your family—and that's if nothing bad happens with it, like one of your friends "borrowing" it.

If you're lucky, you'll only be expelled for a while. You probably will lose your gun and your shooting privileges, and you could be charged with a crime.

The federal law applies to firearms, but state or local laws may include BB and pellet guns, Airsoft and Paintball guns, and in some cases even toy guns.

Even if you're old enough to have a driver's license, and you drive yourself to school, and it's hunting season and you're planning to go sit in your duck blind that afternoon—you still will be in violation of the law, even if your gun is in a locked case in the locked trunk. Go home after classes end and get your gun and gear, and then go hunting.

Some high schools still have organized, supervised shooting teams, usually for smallbore-rifle or for sporting clays, trap or skeet competition. (If your school does, you should get involved.) These schools have plenty of rules and regulations covering every aspect of this, and the guns probably aren't even kept at school.

The Gun-Free School Zones Acts do not apply to colleges and universities, which have their own policies about firearms on campus. These are spelled out on each school's Website.

Ammunition in a Fire

It usually goes like this: You're at the lake or camping, and everyone is sitting around the fire. Someone's been shooting and has a pocketful of leftover .22s or some such. And then some idiot says, "Hey, I wonder what would happen if . . . ."

If you don't stop him (it's always "him"; girls don't do this stuff) and he really does toss the ammo into the fire, here's what you can expect: First, never mind what you once saw in a movie; the cartridges won't do what they would in a gun. But they will explode. It'll take a few seconds for them to overheat, and then *pop! pop! pop!*

Because the detonations aren't enclosed in a gun barrel and the bullets aren't directed by a barrel, the bullets won't do any damage. No, this time it's the casings that are dangerous. The force of the explosions will burst the brass cases, which can send hot fragments of metal flying in all directions like shrapnel.

With .22 rimfire ammunition, this is *probably* not going to be dangerous, but it's unpredictable and a genuinely stupid thing to do. And if more powerful cartridges, like any sort of .30-caliber rifle ammunition, wind up in a fire, the shrapnel is just about guaranteed to be hazardous.

Line of Bore vs. Line of Sight

Take a good look at any rifle that has a telescopic sight on it. See how the scope sits well above the barrel? This means that where the bullet comes out is that much below where you're looking. We know someone who tore up his pickup truck because he forgot this. He was resting his Mini-14 on the fender, taking aim at a coyote. The first shot missed; it made an odd noise too. But the rifle was an autoloader and the coyote was still there, so he kept his eye glued to the scope and fired again. This time he picked up his head to check on that awful metallic noise. Turns out he'd fired two .223 rounds into the hood where it rose up in front of his rifle's muzzle. But in looking through the scope, all he could see was a clear line of sight to the coyote.

A bullet doesn't travel in a straight line. It arcs downward under the pull of gravity. (Remember trajectory?) To hit a distant target, the sights of a

See how high that sight sits above the barrel? Until the bullet from this AR-15 is some distance downrange, its path will be as much as three or four inches below what the shooter is looking at through the scope.

rifle have to direct the barrel upward so the bullet can rise along its arc and then drop into the target. When a bullet is 20 yards or more downrange, it has climbed far enough to clear anything that might be in line with the muzzle but doesn't stand high enough to be seen in the scope.

Shooting a Lock

e see this on TV and in the movies all the time and read about it in crime novels: A locked door stands between the hero and a kidnapped child (or a ticking bomb, a mad scientist, a suffering puppy, whatever). Time is running out, and there's no key—what to do? Hero pulls out his or her handgun and fires a round into the door. Ta-da! The padlock drops off its hasp, or the door springs open.

Nope, sorry, no way. If anything, firing a handgun bullet into a lock will just jam it so that not even the key will open it. And pumping more rounds into the lock usually just makes things worse.

A direct hit at close range from a powerful rifle or shotgun may completely demolish a padlock or blow a deadbolt right through the door—but you don't want to be nearby. Flying bits of the lock or the bullet or slug can cause nasty injuries, and the round may carry on to inflict even more damage farther away.

Well-equipped soldiers and police officers may have special door-breaching shotgun cartridges. These fire so-called frangible loads that dump their energy on impact and then fall apart and become harmless. The "operator" also shoots into the door around the lock, not directly at the lock—and then follows up with a hefty kick from a booted foot.

In general, a sledgehammer or a battering ram, not a bullet, is the best way to defeat a locked door. But even that may take some time to get through a thick wooden door in a solid frame with heavy-duty hinges and latches.

What Goes Up Must Come Down

e see it all the time on TV: Crowds, usually in the Middle East, firing guns into the air. Haven't you wondered where those bullets come down again? Harmlessly, out in some desert maybe?

Maybe not. When Saddam Hussein's sons were finally cornered and killed, on July 22, 2003, during the Iraq War, more than 20 other people were reported killed by bullets fired into the air in celebration.

A bullet fired up at a very steep angle travels until its energy is gone, and then it stops moving upward and falls back to earth. On the return trip the bullet is no longer propelled by gunpowder; it's being pulled downward by gravity. In a vacuum the bullet would hit the ground with the same energy that it left the gun, but in our atmosphere it is affected by air resistance, which slows it down considerably but not enough to be harmless.

Every falling object has a terminal velocity, the speed at which the acceleration of gravity is cancelled out by the resistance of the air. Terminal velocity depends on the size, shape and mass of the object. A human body leaving a plane without a parachute eventually hits the ground at about 120 mph, or 176 fps, no matter whether it falls 1,500 feet or 15 miles. A 7.62mm bullet from an AK-47 or a 9mm pistol bullet both reach terminal velocities of around 300 fps (if they're traveling point-first and not tumbling in the air). A bullet can puncture human skin at only 150 fps, and at 200 fps it can penetrate the skull.

It probably won't surprise you to learn that three-quarters of the victims of bullets falling randomly out of the sky get hit in the head. One-third of them are killed.

Unfortunately, even a bullet fired perfectly straight up won't come down and hit the idiot who fired it. Depending on caliber and velocity, it could travel two miles into the sky, where wind will push it one way or another and the earth will rotate during the time it's in the air (which could be almost a minute). So if anyone gets hurt, it's always some innocent bystander who's usually far away and unaware of danger.

A bullet launched upward at a shallower angle—less than about 45 degrees above horizontal—is still carrying some of the energy with which it was fired when it reaches the ground, so it's moving faster than if it were falling only under the pull of gravity and will hit harder.

These accidents don't happen only as a result of reckless "vertical marksmanship." Just before Christmas 2011, a man in Ohio who went to clean his muzzleloading rifle accidentally fired it into the air when it turned out to be loaded. The bullet came down a mile and a half away, where it hit a 15-year-old Amish girl returning home from a party in the head and killed her. Her brother found her in the road after the horse brought her buggy back empty.

When movie cowboys ride into town firing their guns into the air, they're shooting blanks. When a Navy ship fires a 21-gun salute, it's shooting blanks. (But even the blast and the wad from a blank are dangerous if you're standing too close.) If you fire a gun, accidentally or on purpose, without aiming it at a target, make sure it's pointed at the ground—not up into the sky.

And if you're a squirrel hunter, think about this the next time you shoot up into a tree: If you miss the squirrel and the tree, where will your bullet go? Even a tiny 37-grain .22 hollowpoint can travel nearly a mile.

Firing guns into the air on special occasions isn't like setting off fireworks in your backyard. Those bullets have to come down somewhere, and when they do they can kill. This doesn't happen only in the Middle East. In the words of Detroit Police Chief Ralph Godbee Jr., speaking about celebratory gunfire, "Guns don't kill people, morons do."

Accidents with Guns (and First Aid)

If you read this book carefully and stick to the rules and common sense, you won't accidentally shoot yourself or someone else. We also cover the two most common shooting-related injuries, which are hearing loss and getting things in our eyes. (Read about protecting your eyes and ears in "Armor All.") But there are other ways to get hurt with a gun.

You can, for example, pinch your thumb or fingers in the action. You'd have to be fairly clumsy to do this, but it's possible, especially if you're in a hurry or if you're not familiar with a certain kind of gun. Normally you can feel a pinch as you begin to close the bolt or lever or whatever, and then naturally you stop. Semi-automatics, though, slam shut hard when you hit the release button, so be extra careful there. Keep your fingers away from the moving parts.

You also can catch a finger under an outside hammer, which you'll find on most revolvers, some pistols and some older (or old-style) rifles and shotguns. This can draw blood, especially on a long gun with a powerful mainspring or on a revolver that has its firing pin on the hammer. Be careful.

"Watch what you're doing, Marine!" These Vietnam-era recruits handling the Model 1911 pistol learned, among other things, where not to put their fingers. The slide on any type of semi-automatic slams open and shut hard enough to cause injury. They're wearing ear and eye protection too.

Steve Helsley

How not to hold a pistol. This shooter's left thumb is about to get whacked as the slide slams backward and the action cycles when the shot is fired. A two-handed grip is excellent so long as hands and fingers lie below the working parts of the gun.

Steve Helsley

How not to hold a revolver. The left-hand fingers will be stung by hot gas, powder granules and even bits of lead escaping between the cylinder and the barrel. A two-handed grip is excellent so long as hands and fingers lie below or behind the working parts of the gun.

Recoil can hurt you too, if you aren't holding the gun properly or if it goes off accidentally before you're ready. This may produce a bruise or possibly a sore wrist or a split lip. A big pistol might hurt the web of your hand, between your thumb and trigger finger. If a scoped rifle slips off of your shoulder as you fire, the scope may catch you above the eye. The result might be a bruise, a headache or even a cut that bleeds.

YouTube has plenty of videos of people losing their grip on hard-kicking guns and getting smacked in the face, but a lot of these seem to be unsuspecting novices who were set up by their "friends." Severe recoil is no joke; it may not cause a direct injury, but it can shock you enough to make you flinch when you go to shoot again. Flinching is an involuntary and uncontrollable reaction that comes just as you pull the trigger—your body is saying, No way! This makes it impossible to hit anything, and getting rid of the habit of flinching can take a long time.

(This is one reason that new or young shooters should start with .22 rimfires; you learn to shoot without having to worry about recoil. Then, once you've learned how to hold a gun properly, you can move up to bigger calibers. Getting a little bigger yourself helps too. There's more about recoil in the following chapter.)

The accidents or mistakes we've just listed usually result in bruises and swelling and/or lacerations or cuts. Unless a cut bleeds heavily, these injuries are not life-threatening. Even so, if you get hurt, your concentration will be affected and you won't enjoy what you're doing as much. Stop shooting, unload, take a break and go home. Tell your parents what happened, and show them the injury.

If no one is home, you may need to clean and disinfect a cut yourself and then stick a Band-Aid over it. If you have a bruise or swelling, cool it down with some ice in a plastic bag. Don't put the bag directly on the spot, though—wrap it in a washcloth or towel first. When a parent gets home, show and tell. He or she will decide what more needs to be done, if anything.

Too much recoil can ruin your shooting and even mess up your face. If a hard-kicking rifle slips off your shoulder, you may get "scope-eye," which is a cut or bruise on your forehead. The stock has to be long enough to put some distance between your face and the scope for safety. This hunter is sighting in his rifle before a safari. He should be wearing those earmuffs!

Silvio Calabi

How Far & How Hard

Bullet Travel & What Happens When They Hit

Billy Dixon's 5.3 Seconds

In 1872, Dodge City, Kansas, was the last stop on the Atchison, Topeka and Santa Fe Railway and the hub of professional buffalo hunting. Something like 1½ million bison hides were shipped out of Dodge between 1872 and 1878. As buffalo became scarce in that area, some hunters ventured south into Texas. This was dangerous; the Indians in that region—Comanche, Kiowa and Cheyenne—were angry about white intrusions, and the US Army couldn't provide much protection.

In what is now Hutchinson County, Texas, the tiny town of Adobe Walls had been set up to serve hunters. It had a hide buyer's house, a blacksmith shop, a general store, a saloon and an outhouse. On the morning of June 27, 1874, there were 29 buffalo hunters, skinners and residents in town when at least 200 Indians attacked. Fighting lasted most of the day. Despite the Kiowa medicine man's bulletproofing spells, the attackers suffered heavy losses. Not yet ready to quit, on the second day, June 28, the Indians carried out hit-and-run skirmishes and probing actions.

Buffalo hunter Billy Dixon's long shot with iron sights at the Battle of Adobe Walls made him famous. A modern sniper can reach much farther, but only with a big scope and a special rifle and ammunition. This photo is from Dixon's wife Olive's book, *The Life of Billy Dixon*.

On day three the town's defenders spotted a group of about 15 Indian warriors sitting on their horses in plain sight on a bluff east of Adobe Walls. Maybe they were discussing tactics. Clearly they thought they were at a safe distance. One of the hide hunters decided that they were an inviting target. His name was Billy Dixon, and he was particularly skilled in long-range shooting.

His weapon was a Sharps, the legendary single-shot rifle. To those who bragged that Winchester was the gun that won the West, Sharps men always replied that theirs was the gun that made the West safe for Winchester.

Sharps percussion breechloaders had served in the American Civil War (1861–1865), and by 1874 they were being chambered for some of the most powerful cartridges available. The rifle in Dixon's hands was probably a .50-90—that is, a .50-caliber bullet of about 475 grains in front of a charge of 90 or more grains of black powder. Primitive scopes were available by then, but Billy didn't have one.

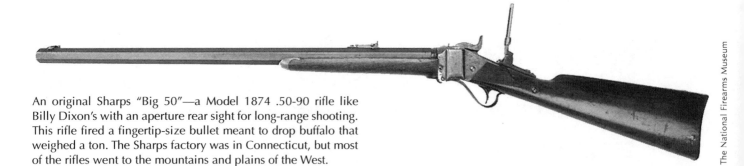

An original Sharps "Big 50"—a Model 1874 .50-90 rifle like Billy Dixon's with an aperture rear sight for long-range shooting. This rifle fired a fingertip-size bullet meant to drop buffalo that weighed a ton. The Sharps factory was in Connecticut, but most of the rifles went to the mountains and plains of the West.

The National Firearms Museum

He took careful aim at a barely visible target and fired. The heavy bullet began its leisurely journey toward the unsuspecting warriors. Its mortar-like trajectory arced it close to a hundred feet above Dixon's line of sight. It's unlikely that the Indians heard the shot or saw the puff of smoke, but suddenly one of them fell off of his horse.

This was unaccountably strong medicine. The Indians decided they had urgent business elsewhere, and the Battle of Adobe Walls was over.

The fate of the ineffectual Kiowa medicine man is unknown, but Billy Dixon and his Sharps passed into history. Later a group of Army surveyors determined that the distance of the shot was 1,538 yards, or seven-eighths of a mile.

Eighteen seventy-four turned out to be a good year for both Billy Dixon and Sharps. Dixon was hired as a scout for the Army and went on to earn the Medal of Honor at the Battle of Buffalo Wallow on September 12. And two weeks later, at the Creedmoor range, in New York, Americans with Sharps and Remington rifles narrowly defeated Ireland's famous team of marksmen to win an international long-range shooting championship.

Dixon's fame lives on. He may have been the inspiration for Matt Quigley, Tom Selleck's Sharps-shooting cowboy character in the movie *Quigley Down Under*.

Long-Range Shooting Tests

A century later, in a newsletter article about Dixon, a forensic scientist questioned whether a Sharps could even send a bullet that far. He must have missed class the day that maximum range was covered.

Way back in October and November 1879, the US Army conducted long-range shooting trials on the beach at Sandy Hook, New Jersey. Two .45-caliber "trapdoor" Springfield service rifles were tested with different bullet weights and charges along with a British Army .577/.450 Martini-Henry rifle at 2,500, 3,200 and 3,500 yards. One of the Springfields and the British rifle wouldn't

reach 3,500 yards. The other Springfield, firing a 500-grain bullet ahead of 80 grains of powder and with different rifling in its barrel, achieved the maximum distance: 3,680 yards, or 2.09 miles. This was more than one mile farther than Billy Dixon's famous shot at Adobe Walls.

A stopwatch and the newly invented telephone were used to determine that the flight time of that bullet was just about 21 seconds. Perhaps even more surprising was that, at maximum range, the bullet could still penetrate a one-inch-thick pine board.

Forensic scientists are an inquisitive bunch. In the early 1990s several of them decided to apply

20th Century technology to the Billy Dixon shot. They took a new .50-caliber Sharps believed to be similar to what Dixon used to the Yuma Proving Ground, in Arizona. The US military tests all sorts of artillery, mortars and missiles inside Yuma's 1,300 square miles of desert.

With the barrel of the Sharps tilted upward at 32 degrees above horizontal, the best angle for maximum range, a 450-grain bullet propelled by 100 grains of powder went 2,585 yards. Then a 675-grain bullet backed by 90 grains of powder landed 3,600 yards downrange. (The heavier bullet had more momentum, even with a bit less powder behind it.)

A few years later a man named M.L. McPherson published a story in *Precision Shooting* Magazine about his attempt to replicate the Dixon shot. He set up a single life-size horse-and-rider target at 1,538 yards. (Remember that Dixon was shooting at a group of riders, not just one; his overall target was larger.) McPherson fired 130 rounds at the target with a new .40-caliber Sharps and hit it 13 times. He calculated the flight time of the bullet at 5.3 seconds.

Bullets can travel a very long way and are still capable of causing serious damage and injury when they get there. You may have seen the warning printed on many boxes of .22 Long Rifle ammunition: "RANGE ONE MILE BE CAREFUL." Believe it.

Maximum Ranges

Cartridge	Bullet Weight (grains)	Muzzle Velocity (feet per second)	Maximum Range (yards)	(miles)
.22 Long Rifle	40	1,350	1,600	0.90
.357 Magnum	158	1,430	2,350	1.34
.45 ACP	230	850	1,800	1.03
.223 Remington	50	3,300	3,600	2.04
.243 Winchester	100	3,070	4,000	2.27
.30-06 Springfield	152	2,800	3,500	1.99
.375 H&H Magnum	270	2,740	4,500	2.56

Shot Size	Diameter (inches)			
12-gauge slug	0.645	1,500	1,420	0.80
.410 slug	0.380	1,600	850	0.48
0 buckshot	0.32	1,100	704	0.40
No. 2	0.15	1,100	330	0.19
No. 5	0.12	1,100	264	0.15
No. 7½	0.095	1,100	209	0.12

At the Yuma Proving Ground

ne of your authors was lucky enough to be able to test-fire his own .30-caliber prairie-dog rifle at Yuma.

The particular range to which he was assigned was 30 kilometers (18.6 miles) long. The rifle was mounted in a special cradle in front of a control room filled with computers and other instruments and surrounded by thick armor plate. Alongside the rifle was an ultra-sensitive Doppler radar system.

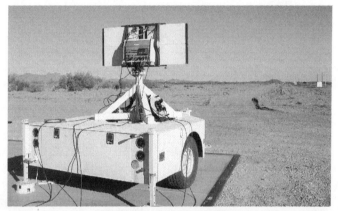

The computerized Doppler tracking radar that followed the flight of the .30-caliber bullet. Normally it tracks artillery shells that weigh as much as 100 pounds or more.

A voice from the control room asked for the bullet weight (220 grains), the ballistic coefficient of the bullet (0.629) and its muzzle velocity (3,020 fps). After some programming and calculating, the control room announced that maximum range would result from elevating the rifle muzzle to 32 degrees.

The staffer who was managing the operation said that they were more experienced in tracking "big bullets"—like the ones fired from tanks—so he predicted that the radar would be able to follow the tiny projectile for about 1,000 yards; beyond that the bullet's trajectory would be calculated by computer.

With the radar elevated for tracking, the control room gave the 5-4-3-2-1 countdown, and

the bullet was on its way. A blue light on the radar module flashed to indicate that something was happening, but the screen didn't move . . . and then, after what seemed like forever, it slowly began to return to horizontal as it followed the arc of the bullet downward. A few minutes of data-crunching followed, and then the control room announced that radar had been able to track the bullet fully 5,500 yards downrange, at which point it was still 900 yards above the ground. Three more rounds were fired to confirm. The final data showed a flight time of 34 to 35 seconds and a maximum range of between 6,500 and 6,600 yards. That's 3¾ miles.

The cradle holding the author's .30-8mm Remington Magnum rifle came off a 1970s Soviet tank. The apparatus is elevated for maximum range and the rifle is ready to fire.

This is why a shooter has to be aware of what lies *behind* a target. (Number 8 of The 15 Commandments of Gun Safety: "Always remember that if the bullet misses or passes through the target, it could hit something or someone behind it." Or if it ricochets off and continues.) Think about what's above your target too. In this case the author's bullets arced almost *one mile up* as they traveled downrange. This is one reason why small aircraft have to detour around the Yuma Proving Ground.

Ricochets & Bouncebacks

It's all too easy to skip or bounce a bullet off of a hard surface or even off of a surface that doesn't seem hard at all. This is called a ricochet, and it can happen when you least expect it.

It's generally true that the shallower the angle at which the bullet hits a surface, the more likely a ricochet becomes. But this doesn't mean that if you shoot at something hard at a high angle nothing will happen. If you fired a bullet squarely into a slab of rock, for example, fragments of stone could bounce back in all sorts of unpredictable directions. A bullet that hits a mild steel plate seems to turn itself inside-out and may bounce right back toward the shooter. However, target plates of an especially hard steel called T1 make even metal-jacketed bullets blow up on impact, so they can't ricochet or bounce.

In "You'll Put Your Eye Out!" we told you that many years ago the Daisy company replaced its lead BBs with steel. Unlike soft lead, when a steel BB hits a hard surface, it bounces off and keeps going. These ricochets are part of what makes even low-powered BB guns dangerous.

If you've ever skipped flat stones across a pond, you already have a good idea of what happens when you fire a bullet—or a shotgun pellet or a BB—at water at a low angle: It bounces off and keeps going. Aim the gun at a higher angle, and the bullet is likely to just dig into the water and come to a quick stop (just as you do when you belly-flop into a swimming pool.)

It's unpredictable, though. The potential for ricochet depends on many factors beyond just the angle of the hit, including the surface itself and the speed and material of the bullet and even its shape. A bullet can ricochet off a grassy lawn if the conditions are just right.

The military sometimes puts ricochets to good use. In the days of sailing ships, gunners

Steve Helsley

Bouncebacks and ricochets can be serious. This copper-jacketed .470 Nitro Express bullet hit the steel plate and not only turned itself inside-out, but part of it also bounced straight back to where the shooter was standing, 50 yards away. Luckily, no one was hurt. This was the wrong kind of steel to use as a target. BBs and air gun pellets can do this too.

extended the ranges of their cannons by skipping the balls across the water into an enemy's hull. Today it's possible to bounce a bomb into the mouth of a cave by dropping it from an airplane at a certain speed and distance above the ground. There are stories of snipers ricocheting bullets off of walls or ledges into buildings.

None of this is terribly useful to us, though. For us the possibility of ricochets and bouncebacks is just one more good reason to be aware of what lies beyond our target when we fire a gun. It is also one more really good reason to wear shooting glasses.

Hollywood & Newton's Third Law

Have you ever heard Clint Eastwood's famous line in the movie *Dirty Harry*? "This is a .44 Magnum, the most powerful handgun in the world, and would blow your head clean off."

The .44 Magnum is no longer the most powerful handgun in the world (now the .500 S&W Magnum is), but it can generate more than 1,000 foot-pounds of energy at the muzzle. A 12-gauge shotgun produces about twice that. No wonder, then, when you see a bad dude get whacked with a sawed-off double-barrel in the movies, he's blown right off the porch or through a window. That's a ton of punch—*two* tons, if both barrels are touched off together! Awesome power, wouldn't you say? And the mighty .45 Colt, with its hefty 230-grain bullet, will flatten a person with just a hit in the arm. The old-time cowboys' big .44 Special will knock a horse right off of its feet.

Dirty Harry's handgun (which very few cops carried even when cops had revolvers, because it's too big and heavy and hard to shoot): a Smith & Wesson Model 29 .44 Magnum that generates more than 1,000 foot-pounds of muzzle energy. More than enough to knock a bad dude off his feet, right?

Well, no, they won't. None of these things can happen.

"Knockdown power" is a widely accepted, near-sacred belief. It is also wrong. If in school you have already been introduced to Sir Isaac Newton (1642–1727), you know that this English scientist had something to say on the matter. His Third Law of Motion states: "For every action, there is an opposite and equal reaction." That is, for every force, there is a counterforce that is equal in size and opposite in direction. Punch your fist into the wall. Your fist exerts a force on the wall, but the wall exerts an equal force back onto your fist. Ouch!

When a rifle or handgun launches a bullet, the bullet exerts an equal push backward. But even the most powerful cartridges, such as the .50 BMG or a .700 Nitro Express, firing the biggest bullets, don't knock down the shooter.

An inexperienced shooter or one who is caught by surprise might drop such a gun or stagger or even fall down in fright, but she won't be pushed to the ground by the recoil. Watch an expert fire one of these cannons: She'll sway backward slightly, and the rifle's muzzle will lift a foot or so, but that's it. (See "Recoil Doesn't Have to Hurt," at the end of this chapter.)

Now let's follow this bullet downrange, keeping Newton's Third Law in mind. When the bullet hits something, whether it's a tree or a target plate or a body, it meets pushback that's equal to the force of its impact. (Like the wall on your fist.)

We've already established that the first reaction, the one when the bullet was fired, wasn't enough to knock down the shooter, so how can the bullet knock down a person it hits? Much less pick him off his feet and slam him into a wall?

For a bullet's impact to knock someone over, the recoil of the shot would have to knock over the shooter. This doesn't happen even in the movies, or the good guys would go flying too. If the recoil doesn't do this to the shooter, the bullet won't have the energy to do it to someone downrange. Even worse, the recoil felt by the shooter is actually greater than the bullet impact because of the added push of the gas in the detonating cartridge.

Still don't believe it? In 1962 the editors of *American Rifleman*, the technical magazine of the National Rifle Association, tested this another way. In a sort of antique *Mythbusters* episode, they put the knock-down question to the test.

It turns out that when a bullet strikes an object, the force it exerts on the object lasts just slightly longer than one millisecond (one one-thousandth of a second), no matter whether the bullet penetrates or just splats on the surface. This will blow up a watermelon or go deep into human or animal tissue, but will it shove an object backward, even if nearly all of the energy is delivered to its surface?

To demonstrate, the NRA put a 175-pound wooden mannequin on a free-rolling platform as a target. The dummy moved easily with just the touch of a fingertip. Shooting it with a .22 Long Rifle moved it ¹⁄₁₆ inch. A hit from a .38 Special revolver rolled it ³⁄₁₆ inch. A 230-grain .45 ACP (Automatic Colt Pistol) bullet moved it all of a half-inch. Finally they got out a .30-06 rifle and fired a 150-grain bullet at 2,900 fps. This is far, far more powerful than Dirty Harry's .44 Magnum; in the movies it would have blasted the victim halfway to next week. In real life it shoved the dummy backward just 2¼ inches.

1 175-lb. manikin was mounted on free-rolling platform to show the motion caused by the bullet impact

2 For firing, figure was placed on smooth side of Masonite sheet for easiest movement. Camera was aligned with figure and a marker (see arrow) to record displacement, which was measured

BEGINNER'S DIGEST

It is occasionally stated that the impact of a bullet can knock a man or an animal down.

This idea should be distinguished from 'stopping power', which means the ability to kill or make helpless. Bullets achieve their intended effect by interfering with life functions, and a bullet has stopping power if it does this immediately so that the animal collapses or at least cannot move. 'Knockdown' implies that the animal is thrown violently to the ground.

Such an action can indeed be seen in the case of a very small animal such as a ground squirrel, or even a woodchuck weighing a few pounds. In larger animals, a semblance of this might be given by a convulsive muscular movement. Experienced hunters, however, would not credit such a real effect in an animal the size of a whitetail deer or larger, having often observed that after the first hit which makes the animal

KNOCKDOWN

insensible to pain or shock, there is no visible effect of further hits. When men are hit by small arms fire in combat, they are not knocked down.

Nor would the so-called knockdown effect be given credence by any engineer acquainted with the quantities involved. There is indeed a large momentary force, at the instant of striking, which damages the target. Such damage often has been illustrated in photographs of bullets striking gelatin blocks. The bullet energy is expended in this way and not in moving the target.

The .45 ACP is a comparatively heavy pistol cartridge, firing a 230-gr. bullet at 800 feet per second (f.p.s.). When brought to rest in 6″ of travel in a target, the bullet exerts an average force of about 800 lbs. The total time, however, is only slightly over .001 second, much too short to move a heavy target very much. A target weighing 175 lbs., even if it were entirely free of any frictional contact with the ground, would be given by this impact a velocity of less than 2 inches per second, which is hardly noticeable.

For comparison, this velocity also would be produced by a push of about ½ lb. lasting one second.

The 150-gr. bullet of the commercial .30-'06 hunting load has a muzzle

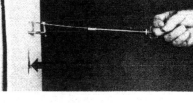

3 After the firings, freedom of movement was rechecked with trigger scale pulling on screw hook in figure's back. Figure required only 1 lb. pull to move. Hole indicated by arrow was made by .45 bullet which missed lead plate — this impact caused less movement and was not counted. Back sheet was loosened by bullet striking interior lead plate, showing momentary impact force

velocity of 2970 f.p.s. Striking and remaining in a target with a penetration of 6″ it develops an average force of about 5800 lbs. during about .0003 second. A 175-lb. target moving with perfect freedom would be given a speed of about 4 inches per second. A push of only 2 lbs. lasting for one second would do the same.

Gun recoil, with which all shooters are familiar, provides another way of looking at this matter. The recoil impulse involved in bringing the bullet up to speed is equal to that on the target in stopping it, except that the gun recoil is always heavier by the reaction from accelerating the powder gases also.

To make the movement clearly visible, THE AMERICAN RIFLEMAN con-

structed a wooden dummy of approximately the height and outline of a man. It was mounted on a platform rolling on sealed ball bearings of very good quality. Lead plates within the figure brought its weight to 175 lbs. and stopped the bullets. The figure moved freely at the push of a fingertip.

Impact of a .22 long rifle standard-velocity bullet caused the figure to roll back ¹⁄₁₆″, an amount barely visible. The .38 Special factory bullet moved the figure ³⁄₁₆″; the .45 M1911 Service bullet moved it ½″; and the .30-'06 commercial 150-gr. bullet moved it 2¼″. These give a good idea of the comparative movement from impact of different bullets, and of the smallness of the movement throughout. ∎

The *American Rifleman* story showing the 175-pound test dummy on its free-rolling platform. Even a solid hit with a .30-06 bullet, three times more powerful than a .44 Magnum, moved the dummy just 2¼ inches.

Stopping Power

We've been talking about "knockdown," a force that is different from "stopping power," which is how that force affects whatever has been hit.

Stopping power is a vague term too, but it has practical meaning. When a bullet hits an animal or person, it usually, as a doctor might say, "interrupts the life functions." It penetrates skin and tissue and may cut blood vessels, muscles and tendons and break bones. A bullet that snaps an animal's spine

of factors. It doesn't even have to be a large bullet. This is stopping power, and it's the reason a relatively tiny bullet can kill so massive an animal as a rhino or an elephant.

A bullet doesn't necessarily have to go deep, either. A .600 Nitro slug might not penetrate a charging elephant's thick skull, but the impact on the animal's forehead may stun it and make it drop to its knees. It's been stopped, literally, but not killed. The hunter has to follow up with a fatal shot, or the beast will regain its senses and be a nuisance again. (According to big-game veterans, this won't work with a light bullet, which has relatively little shocking power and has to penetrate to a critical organ to be effective.)

So stopping power is not an overwhelmingly fast or heavy bullet; it's a well-placed one.

And, no matter what, a bullet or shotgun blast can't throw its victim up against a wall or even push him to the ground.

Hollywood is never bothered by such details. Six-shot revolvers fire 20 times without reloading, cowboys shoot Indians from galloping horses, action heroes leap from one building to another while accurately firing pistols in each hand, and Dirty Harry's .44 puts bad guys into orbit. Hope we didn't ruin it for you, but now you know.

Brad Fitzpatrick Outdoors

Stopping an animal with a bullet isn't always the same thing as killing it, and where a bullet is put is more important than how powerful it is. To practice for hunting really big game in Africa, this hunter is firing a double-barreled rifle at a realistic elephant target at the Safari Shooting School in Texas. (Where is his eye and ear protection?)

usually drops the animal in its tracks. (The animal may even look like it was flipped over onto its side, but that's the effect of gravity plus where or how it was standing.) A bullet into the brain, heart or lungs will also stop an animal, either near-instantly or within some minutes, depending on a whole raft

Knockdown Force

ere's yet another way to come at it: Imagine being charged by a rhinoceros. The beast weighs three tons. But you're facing it with a .600 Nitro Express firing a massive 900-grain bullet that generates 8,400 foot-pounds of energy at the muzzle. Three tons is only 6,000 pounds—you've got the rhino covered. Hey, they don't call these things "stopping rifles" for nothing!

Well, again, no. The force required to stop the beast has to be equal to its own momentum. This is easy to calculate: Its mass (in pounds divided by 32.2) multiplied by its velocity (in feet per second). If Mr. Rhino is coming at 15 mph, that's 22 fps, so the formula is (6,000 ÷ 32.2) × 22 = 4,099 foot-pound-seconds.

Now let's figure out the momentum of the bullet, which would have to be the same or more in order to stop the rhino—that is, to completely cancel its forward rush. The 900-grain bullet has a muzzle velocity of 2,050 fps, so let's say Mr. Rhino is close enough that the bullet's velocity has dropped to an even 2,000 fps by the time the two collide. Nine hundred grains equals 0.1285 pounds, so momentum becomes (0.1285 ÷ 32.2) × 2,000 = 7.9 foot-pound-seconds.

Still feeling confident about knocking the rhino on his butt?

We know that a bullet's energy comes from both its mass and its velocity and that something light and fast can make as much energy as something that's heavier but traveling more slowly. So let's see how fast your .600 bullet would have to be traveling to generate enough momentum to counteract the rhino: If we divide the bullet's mass (0.1285 pounds) into 4,099 foot-pound-seconds, the pounds cancel out and we get . . . 31,898 fps!

That's eight times faster than the hottest cartridges yet made, and they fire tiny 50-grain bullets, not fingertip-size .600 slugs.

Even if it were possible to drive a bullet that fast without destroying the rifle, the recoil would of course knock you backward too—Newton's Third Law and all that.

A big bull rhino that weighs three tons and charges at 15 miles per hour has much more momentum than a bullet can generate, so the hunter has to "interrupt its life functions" instead.

Recoil Doesn't Have to Hurt

ow you know that recoil is the "opposite and equal reaction" to launching a bullet or a load of shotgun pellets down the barrel of a gun. The science of recoil gets astonishingly complicated, but for the average shooter it boils down to this: The heavier the projectile and the faster it's going to travel, the more force has to be applied to it—and more force (in the same gun) means greater pushback. This is why newcomers should begin shooting with nothing more powerful than a .22 rimfire. A bullet that weighs only 29 to 40 grains leaving the muzzle of a gun somewhere between about 900 and 1,500 fps (depending on the ammunition) just can't create much recoil.

According to Newton's Third Law, however, even a little .22 cartridge has to generate *some* recoil—but if it's fired in a rifle that weighs five or six pounds, the effect is almost unnoticeable. You'll hear the *crack!* of the shot and you'll feel the rifle move slightly, but that's all. The mass of the gun absorbs most of the energy. A .22 handgun will jump slightly more because it's lighter, but that's all.

An air gun that shoots a BB or a pellet at anywhere from about 275 to 1,500 fps usually generates even less recoil, but many spring-air guns react more noticeably when they're fired than a .22 rifle does. But what we feel isn't the recoil of the pellet being launched; it's the sudden release of the piston that compresses the air—but this is very slight too.

Recoil is often a beginner's worst fear. Firing a big gun can be shockingly loud and violent, and, yes, it can hurt. Severe recoil is no joke. Even if it doesn't cause a bruise or a cut, it can lead to flinching, jerking the trigger or just closing your eyes. You can't shoot accurately if you do any of these things.

But it's all in our heads. Hunters are never aware of recoil when they shoot at game, even with big guns. They're so focused on the target that everything else is blocked out. (This is true for police officers and soldiers in combat too.) They don't even register the *boom!* of the shot—and yet often they hear the much lesser sound of the bullet hitting its target. When the same people fire the same guns at paper targets, they feel every kick and hear every shot.

Recoil affects shooters differently. Some are oblivious to it, and others, even big macho dudes, are almost terrified of it. The suddenness of the accompanying noise probably has something to do with this, as people usually think that suppressed guns don't kick as hard. (See "Silencers: Naughty or Nice?" in the chapter "Killer Apps.") Therefore, one easy way to reduce the effect of recoil is to wear hearing protectors. (Which you're going to do anyway, even with a .22, right?)

The way you hold a gun—ideally, with the buttstock tucked firmly into your shoulder and your face in the right place—also affects how you feel recoil. A shooting instructor or your mentor will show you how to do this.

If you shoot from the prone position, lying on the ground, your body can't move much and has to soak up most of the energy. Fire the same gun standing up, and you'll sway backward a bit at the shot while the muzzle of the gun rises upward. Much more comfortable! Also, when you're lying prone, the butt of the stock bears directly on the top of your collarbone instead of on the softer tissue in front of your shoulder, so the recoil is more jarring.

(You may fire your first shots with a rifle while sitting at a bench at a shooting range. For comfort, the seat and rifle, on its support, should be at the right height, and you'll need to protect your elbows from the bench, which may be made of concrete.)

Another way to reduce the impact of recoil is to make sure the gun fits. (A gun with a stock that's too long or short or shaped wrong for you seems to kick harder, and it can bruise your cheek or shoulder and upper arm.) Even so, a thick and squishy pad on the butt of the stock helps. So does shooting only a few rounds at a time to get used to it.

Self-loading guns kick less, because the mechanism of the action absorbs some of the recoil energy. So does the weight of a gun. The hardest-kicking gun that most people ever en- counter is the common 12-gauge shotgun. We'll talk about this more in "Cool Guns 4 U," but now we'll answer another common question on the subject: Since recoil makes a gun move, why doesn't it throw a bullet off-target?

If the gun was weightless but the bullet was not, and if it was fired in a vacuum, recoil would affect the gun just about instantly. But in the real world, thanks to inertia, time and other factors, a bullet has left the barrel before recoil begins to push the gun significantly. (Otherwise we'd never hit anything we were aiming at.)

Serious recoil can take the fun out of shoot- ing, but you don't need to subject yourself to it. You can stay with .22s—rimfire or centerfire—or you can move to more powerful guns only gradu- ally, learning to handle them in stages and keep- ing in mind all of the factors we've mentioned here. Growing a bit in the meantime helps too.

This brave young shooter has just touched off a Smith & Wesson .500 Magnum, currently the most powerful production handgun. Her eyes are closed and the tremendous recoil has ripped the revolver out of her support hand, but she has not lost control—the gun didn't hit her face and she hasn't dropped it. (After this, we hope she said, "Well, that was interesting. Now let me have my .22 back.") The shape, thickness and material of a handgun's grip has a lot to do with how comfortable it is—or isn't—to shoot, and a long, heavy barrel helps resist upward flip.

Katherine Smith

Armor All

Protecting Your Ears, Eyes & Other Body Parts

We're not telling you to wear ballistic armor whenever you go out to blow up tin cans with your .22. No, the main thing here is to protect yourself against two kinds of incidental injury—one that otherwise *will* happen every time you fire a gun (or are near someone who does) and another that *can* happen any time you're shooting or are around shooting. You can protect yourself easily in both cases; you just have to remember to do it.

Ears

A lot of shooters, particularly older ones who didn't wear hearing protection when they were kids, think everyone around them is just mumbling all the time. Many shooters also have tinnitus, a high-pitched buzzing in their ears that never goes away. We can make up for some hearing loss with hearing aids, but they're expensive and annoying. This kind of tinnitus can't be cured or gotten rid of, and it's really unpleasant.

The very best way to protect your hearing is with foam ear plugs worn underneath earmuffs. Some people think ear defenders aren't needed while shooting smallbore guns like .22s or .17s—but you know better.

The good news is that both problems can easily be prevented by wearing some kind of hearing protection when we shoot. The goal is to prevent the sonic blast of a too-loud sound wave from reaching the sensitive micro-hairs inside our ears that enable us to hear. No one is immune to hearing damage, so it's not a matter of if, but when and how much. And once the damage is done, the ear can't heal itself or be repaired.

A .22 makes a sharp *crack!* when it goes off, but it's not a huge noise. No big deal, you say. True, maybe, for a few shots. But over a year how many times do you hear it? And then we graduate to bigger guns that make more noise, and we start shooting sporting clays or practical pistol, or hunting. Remember: The damage adds up. Our ears don't "rest" when we're not shooting and then start fresh again.

If you've watched shooting competitions or demonstrations, you've already noticed that almost *everyone* wears earmuffs. Most of them also have plugs in their ears under the muffs. This doesn't interfere with shooting; in fact the reduction in noise helps them concentrate, for better scores, in addition to protecting their hearing. As we pointed out earlier, it also seems to reduce the effect of any recoil.

It's hunters who really have a problem. They need to hear what's going on around them—the sounds of a bird dog's bell, a deer tiptoeing through leaves, the snort of a buffalo. Many hunters figure that they're not going to fire their guns often so they can get by with naked ears. It's sort of true; a deer hunter might shoot just once or twice in an entire season (or not at all, if she strikes out). Again, though, the damage adds up, and just one blast from a rifle can cause damage.

The best solution for hunters is expensive: custom-fitted electronic plugs that allow normal sounds to enter the ear but that instantly shut down when they detect a noise that's too loud. (These plugs are often some hideous color like neon orange, because the owner lost her first pair when she put them down somewhere and walked off without them.)

The next-best thing is dirt-cheap: foam plugs that you squash in your fingers and stick into your ears. They expand to fill any ear canal, no matter how oddly shaped, and they block the worst noise of a gunshot. Some hunters put these things halfway into their ears, so they can hear, and then jam them all the way in when it's time to shoot. This is helpful—if you remember and if you have time. Every gunshop and shooting range gives away packets of these things.

Target shooters—and here we mean everyone who uses a gun in a situation where they can control when they fire—should wear foam plugs, over-the-ear muffs specifically meant for shooting or both. (Or use a suppressor—read "Silencers: Naughty or Nice?" in the chapter "Killer Apps.") Make sure the earpieces, or temples, of your shooting glasses don't ruin the seal of the muffs around your ears.

If you're watching someone shoot and you don't have your ear defenders with you, stick your fingers into your ears.

It isn't just shooting, either. If you're next to someone on the bus and you can hear the music they're listening to in their earbuds, it's too loud. Even if they don't notice it yet, they're losing hearing and lowering the threshold for more damage. They are that much closer to permanent loss.

Everyone, not just shooters, is exposed to noise that's too loud. Leaf blowers, lawn mowers and chainsaws will do damage; so will dance clubs and rock concerts, certain motorcycles and just about every airplane engine, if you're too close. These noises may not be as momentarily loud as a gunshot, but they go on for much longer.

Pay attention to what you're hearing. If running the mower or the snow blower is your job, wear the ear protection you use for shooting.

Eyes

Losing part of your hearing is bad enough, but an eye? It doesn't take much to injure or destroy an eye, either. Even worse, something could not only destroy your eye but also penetrate the back of your eye socket and enter your brain. (We went over this in "You'll Put Your Eye Out!")

It isn't just a ricochet, either, or a misdirected shotgun pellet. Hot gunpowder gas can come back at your face. (Percussion and flintlock guns and even modern revolvers are prone to this.) Autoloading guns eject empty cartridge cases with considerable force. Shooting clay pigeons creates shards of broken targets that fly around. Hunters dodge twigs and brush. Guns can explode and fling bits of shrapnel like grenades. Let's not even mention BBs, air-gun pellets or paintballs.

And finally, like good sunglasses, shooting glasses should also filter out ultraviolet rays of sunlight. Protecting your eyes while shooting is not merely a good idea, it's essential.

Just as with ears and hearing, the solution is simple: safety glasses or goggles (or helmet visors, if you insist on Paintball or Airsoft). There are three different sets of standards for impact resistance in eyeglasses. You can find them easily on the Internet, if you like to wade through legal and technical jargon, but all you really need to know is that you should wear high-quality shooting glasses.

Different lens colors can help you see targets better in different light conditions, but protecting your eyes from bits of clay pigeons, twigs, brush and even shot pellets is much more important than helping you shoot well. And that means choosing the right lens material.

Beretta

Don't rely on ordinary sunglasses or your own eyeglasses to stop a shotgun pellet or a bit of shrapnel. They might stop it, but they might not, either. And then your eye may have to deal with not only the pellet or whatever but also jagged bits of broken lens.

Impact-resistant glass is heavy. The best shooting lenses are plastic: CR39, Polycarbonate or Trivex. Polycarbonate was invented in the 1970s for aircraft windshields and military pilots' helmet visors. Trivex is newer, is just as strong but thinner and lighter, and has better optical qualities. Both materials block ultraviolet rays too. They are softer than glass and need scratch-resistant coatings. The lenses also have to be mounted in a tough frame; impact-resistant lenses aren't much use if they pop out of their frames when they're hit.

If you wear glasses anyway, you can find shooting glasses that fit over them. Wraparound lenses offer more side protection, but the extra curvature of the lenses may cause some distortion. The parts of the frame that go back to your ears are called the temples. We like cable-style temples, the ones that wrap around your ear. They stay on better.

Once you've decided on the frames and lens material, you can pick lens colors to enhance your aim. Shooting glasses often come with several sets of interchangeable lenses. Shooters who are looking for better contrast, to make their targets stand out, use yellow, orange or reddish lenses, depending on the target and the background and whether it's sunny or cloudy. Hunters usually want no shift in how they see colors, so they choose neutral gray lenses that reduce sunlight evenly, not just part of it. (Sunglasses, in other words, but impact-resistant ones.) On a gray day, gray lenses may be too dark; in that case pop in the clear ones.

Try them all and see which ones you like. Make sure you get them mounted right in the frames, so they don't come out just when you might need them the most.

Other Body Parts

Many shooters wear thin, close-fitting gloves. Such gloves give decent trigger feel, and they don't make you any more clumsy when it comes to reloading. They do, however, protect your hands from hot barrels (somewhat). On a cold day they're warm, on a hot day they soak up some sweat, and in both cases they can improve your grip on a gun. Some shooting gloves have pads on the palms that help absorb recoil. Some shooters wear thicker gloves on their non-trigger hand.

Hats are always good. They help protect your head and face from the flying junk that glasses are

meant to ward off. Also, just keeping the sun out of your eyes can improve your shooting.

You'll see shooting shirts and jackets with patches sewn onto the shoulders. These may not soak up much recoil, but they can help you bring a rifle or shotgun to your shoulder in a nice, smooth mount that won't snag on pockets, buttons, straps, seams or wrinkles in the fabric.

A shock-absorbing, gel-foam recoil pad that straps to your shoulder can help you get used to a harder-recoiling gun. Browning's Reactar Shooting Harness has adjustable elastic straps and a hook-and-loop patch to stay snugly in place, and it fits right- and left-handed shooters of nearly all sizes.

Some companies offer recoil pads that strap onto your shoulder or fit into a pocket on a shirt. If they stay in place, they do absorb some kick. (They can be removed for washing too.) They are most useful if you get a chance to put a few rounds through an unfamiliar and hard-recoiling gun. If we worked for a gun company as a tester and fired lots of rounds through big-bore guns, we'd wear them.

Beretta

Shooting gloves should fit snugly so you can hold and work the gun and feel the trigger. They can also protect your hands from a hot barrel.

Bulletproof Vests: Really?

Well, maybe. You can almost answer this question yourself if you think about it: Body armor *will* resist a bullet, depending on the mass, shape and velocity of the bullet and on what sort of armor we're talking about. An undershirt that will trap a blunt-nosed, 115-grain 9mm slug generating less than 400 foot-pounds of energy is no defense against a 661-grain .50-caliber bullet that's still making 10,000 foot-pounds a hundred yards downrange.

It's the same with vehicles. Sure, the warlord's Land Cruiser has multi-layer Lexan windows, hardened ballistic-steel body panels, anti-mine plates underneath and puncture-proof, run-flat tires, so his enemies can fire all the AK and maybe even 12.7mm they've got at him—but a hundred-pound Hellfire missile from a Reaper drone will put him and his Toyota out of business in a single awful blast of heat, smoke and flame.

Rather than bullet-*proof*, it's better to think of ballistic armor as bullet-*resistant*. Also, the bullet has to hit the armor in the first place, and no one is covered from head to toe. Military and police vests help protect the heart, lungs and torso and sometimes the crotch and back of the neck, but hands, arms, shoulders, throat, face and head, not to mention the legs and feet, are exposed.

When special squads raid a big drug lab or other criminal enterprise, they wear impact-resistant goggles and helmets, gloves, knee and elbow pads, lace-up boots with steel toe caps and insoles and, over their battle dress, bulky Type III ballistic vests. They're following the basic rule of body armor: Protect yourself against the sort of weapon that you're carrying yourself or that you expect to face. In these cases the cops usually go in with 9mm submachine guns and possibly 12-gauge shotguns, with pistols as backups. There will be several marksmen waiting outside with rifles too.

No body armor provides complete protection against every threat. Look at this SWAT warrior dressed for work: Even with a helmet and the add-on panels over his crotch, shoulders, neck and throat, he's still very exposed. Add more protection and he'd lose more mobility. There's always a trade-off.

Along with a couple of pit bulls or Rottweilers, the villains inside might have pistols (9mm, .40 S&W, .45 ACP), submachine guns (9mm, .45 ACP), maybe shotguns and AR (5.56x45mm) or AK (7.62x39mm) rifles. If they have time, they might even put on the same kinds of vests.

Type III is the armor of choice here because the US National Institute of Justice (NIJ) certifies it against the 7.62mm NATO round—a 147-grain FMJ (full metal jacket) bullet launched at 2,780 fps. In other words, something a bit hotter than what the other team is likely to be shooting.

There are five more standard categories of body armor. Three are rated for handgun calibers: Type IIA (withstands up to .40 S&W), Type II (up to .357 Magnum) and Type IIIA (.44 Magnum). The remaining two, including Type III, are for rifles. Type IV is supposed to stop an armor-piercing 166-grain bullet fired at 2,880 fps—a .30-06 round. The NIJ will also test special armor meant to counter higher threat levels.

The armor may be flexible—some combination of woven fibers such as Kevlar and nylon—or hard, with plates of steel, titanium or a ceramic such as boron or silicon carbide. A Type IIA vest is light and bendy enough to be worn under a shirt, but as the level of protection increases, the garment gets heavier, thicker and more awkward until finally no one wants to wear it any more. And then it does no good at all.

Stopping a bullet is excellent, but getting hit with a round that doesn't penetrate can still hurt—a lot sometimes. The transmitted energy creates the "backface signature," which is determined by shooting at armor mounted on modeling clay and then measuring the indent of the bullet. In its resistance ratings the National Institute of Justice allows for up to 44 millimeters of backface signature. That's 1¾ inches, more than enough to cause internal injuries, depending on where you're hit.

We might say, "A bulletproof vest may keep you out of the mortuary but not necessarily the hospital."

Kevlar & Rhino Hide

Reportedly, more than 3,000 American law-enforcement officers have been saved by body armor since Kevlar hit the market in the early 1970s. Kevlar is a light but super-strong synthetic fiber that was invented at the DuPont chemical company in 1965. Strands or sheets of Kevlar are now in everything from skis to tires to boats, as well as all sorts of protective helmets and clothing, even hunting vests that will stop birdshot. Before Kevlar, fiberglass, aluminum, nylon and ceramics were used in body armor.

Armor in the form of thick leather surely goes back to prehistory. The ancient Chinese used turtle shells and rhino hide and then bronze plates sewn onto leather.

Mounted knights, the heavy cavalry of medieval Europe and Britain, wore elaborate suits of steel-plate armor. Plate was far too expensive for foot soldiers; they wore mail armor, fine links of iron woven together. Crossbow bolts and arrows from powerful longbows could punch right through chainmail and sometimes (depending on range, the power of the bow and the type of arrowhead, the arrow's angle of impact, the thickness and quality of the steel, and other things) even plate armor. Knights began putting mail under their plate. No matter how good the armor, though, the problem of coverage never went away; there were always gaps or weak spots where something sharp could get in.

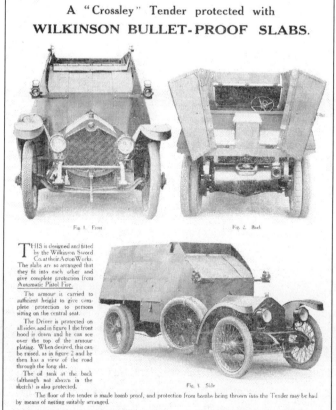

Just like a medieval knight's warhorse, this 1920s Crossley military vehicle was outfitted with overlapping armor plates, rated to stop "automatic pistol fire." But the more armor, the greater the weight and the slower the vehicle—or the horse.

Some knights wound up wearing close to a hundred pounds of steel and weaponry, so archers or pikemen would go after their horses—armored too, but not as completely. On foot a heavily armored man was clumsy and could be surrounded and overwhelmed, especially if his field of view was limited by a helmet visor meant to keep out arrows.

There's always a trade-off between coverage and mobility. The size and weight of armor has consequences too. Knights' warhorses had to be bred bigger and bigger to carry the load. In World War II Britain's Royal Air Force stopped issuing flak jackets (flak is anti-aircraft fire, so really these should have been called anti-flak jackets), because they were too bulky to wear in the Avro Lancaster bomber.

Firearms arrived on the battlefield in the 13th Century, but it was another 400 years before massed musket fire finally made suits of armor obsolete. To be effective after that, the steel had to be so thick that full suits were impossibly heavy. Steel vests, however, were used into the 1940s.

Hank Morgan, the hero of Mark Twain's 1889 sci-fi satire novel *A Connecticut Yankee in King Arthur's Court*, used 19th Century technology to take over 6th Century England. At the end Morgan, "the Boss," and a small band of young cadets use electricity and Gatling guns to wipe out an army of 30,000 knights.

The idea that old-fashioned armor couldn't stand up against modern guns is so common that in 1961 the National Rifle Association put it to the test. The staff of *American Rifleman*, the NRA magazine, got a genuine 17th Century breastplate, a steel vest weighing about eight pounds and a little more than an eighth of an inch thick, and shot at it from a distance of 24 feet. The results surprised them.

Blackpowder musket and pistol balls (.71 and .60 caliber) couldn't punch through. Then they shifted to modern handguns. Everything from .22 rimfire up through .357 Magnum, including metal-

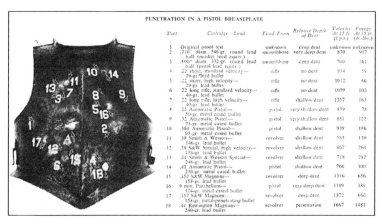

This must have been a fun test. Here is part of the *American Rifleman* Magazine story from October 1961, showing the results (including dents) of firing modern guns at a 300-year-old steel breastplate. The old armor turned out to be truly bulletproof—most of the time.

jacketed .45 ACP, at best only dented the steel. Not until they unleashed a .44 Magnum did a single round penetrate the vest.

A direct hit from a .30-caliber rifle would have wounded or killed the wearer, but this was so-called half proof or pistol armor. In the late 1600s thicker musket armor was called "full proof"; had the NRA found a good example of this to test, who knows what the results would have been?

When it comes to personal combat, it's been a many-centuries-long race between offense (stones to swords and arrows to bullets) and defense (leather to bronze to iron to steel to Kevlar). Some ancient cultures went with thickness and flexibility instead of strength and rigidity: The Aztecs of Mexico used quilted cotton, while in Asia highly effective body armor was made of layers of paper or silk.

Silk is marvelous stuff. In the blackpowder era people often put on silk when they went out to fight because the long, strong fibers could be removed from a gunshot wound more easily than wool or cotton. Now synthetic spider silk is being tested for bullet-resistance, and at least one company offers dressy-looking clothes that will stop a pistol bullet at point-blank range. The light, flexible, silky fabric is a closely guarded secret, but it seems to be a big step forward.

Shooting in Fashion

Functional Clothing Can Look Good Too

Women who shoot face the same challenges that bother women who take up any traditionally male activity, from playing hockey to motocross racing to fly-fishing. One of them is *Where do I find clothes that fit?* It's even harder for young girls, because they take smaller sizes.

Just about every kind of shooting has its own clothing. For plinking and most kinds of casual shooting with your BB gun or a .22, all you need is eye and ear protection and maybe a hat, along with whatever clothing the weather calls for. But for specialized shooting, things get more complicated. For example, competitors who shoot match rifles, whether at 10 meters or 1,000 yards, often wear heavy coats with straps and buckles to provide extra support in each shooting position— prone, kneeling, offhand (standing) and sometimes sitting.

Hunting clothes have to take into account not just ease of movement but also the weather and even safety. Upland bird hunters want a comfortable vest that holds cartridges and lets them mount the gun quickly and easily. Duck and goose hunters are usually out in the cold and wet, so they wrap up in water-

This is the National Championships season at Camp Perry, the "World Series" of target shooting. Between July 20 and Aug. 18, more than 3,000 entrants will have competed in scheduled rifle and pistol events on the Ohio shore of Lake Erie.

Pistol competitors included this dashingly-attired all-woman team from the Tonawandas Sportsmen's Club, Pendleton, N.Y., shown in practice. (Note all four .45 empties in the air.) They are (front to rear) Ellie Collins, Peggy Wendell, Rose Minko and Vicki Daigler. Mrs. Collins, a Master since 1971, when asked what special exercises she took to strengthen her arm and hand, replied: "Housework."
(Photo courtesy The Buffalo Courier Express)

American Rifleman

Times have changed, fortunately. Members of the Tonawandas Sportsmen's Club ladies team, of Pendleton, New York, fire their .45s at the 1974 national championships at Camp Perry, Ohio. Ear and eye protection might have clashed with their color-coordinated go-go boots, blazers, bell-bottoms and Aussie-style Panama hats.

Fashion & function: World champion mounted shooter Kenda Lenseigne, dressed and equipped for success in Cowboy Action competition. She helped design her six-guns (.45-caliber Cimarron Thunderstorms) and also her Safariland belt and holster rig. Kenda guides Justin, her shooting horse, with her left hand and shoots with her right, so one holster is set up for cross-draw.

John Beckett Photography

hunting clothing. For safety, hunters often have to wear some hunter-orange clothing—a hat, say, or a vest—which other hunters can see but that doesn't seem to bother most game animals. Hunters who want to hide from their game wear camouflage, but in some countries camouflage is illegal for anyone but the military. And so on and so forth.

As your interests develop and you head off into one or another kind of shooting, you'll get plugged into that world—you'll learn what works and what doesn't, from guns to gear to ammunition, and what people wear. The good news is that as more and more women get into shooting, more and more specialty clothing is being designed by women specifically to fit women—and to look good too. Fashion and function can go together very well. This kind of clothing is available from international brands such as Barbour, Beretta, Le Chameau, Browning, Eddie Bauer and Filson or small boutique companies with names like Pistols & Pumps, SHE Outdoor Apparel, Prois Hunting and MizMac Designs.

Style, function and proper fit are important, but what about answering the "call of nature" while you're in the field? Outdoor Comfort, in Tucson, Arizona, has come up with an alteration to long pants that it calls EZ2P. Sound it out and you'll understand. The company says it lets a woman PIP, or pee in peace.

proof fabrics. In the Deep South many hunters like snakeproof boots. At posh hunts in England and Europe and at the annual Safari Club International convention in the US, formal dinners that require ball gowns and tuxedos aren't uncommon. And so on and so forth.

Size, comfort, practicality and style aside, there are sometimes also legal requirements for

Silvio Calabi

Traditional British-style driven-bird shooting, where the guns wait for the birds to fly overhead, calls for a special wardrobe in addition to double-barreled guns. At the Cold Aston shoot in England's West Country, Martha Johnson from Alabama wears a tweed suit and high Wellington boots. Her shotgun is in the leather sleeve over her shoulder.

Terry Allen

Along with her double-barreled gun and springer spaniel Lil, upland bird hunter (and professional photographer and dog trainer) Christina Power-Agnew of Craney Hill Kennel is outfitted with brush pants; a water- and thorn-resistant waxed-cotton coat with bellows pockets (for cartridges, shooting glasses, gloves, dog whistle, etc.) and a zippered game pouch at the back; and a stylish but practical hat.

NRA Women's Network

Big-game hunting takes place in arctic cold or tropical heat and every climate inbetween. When this photo was taken, on a moose hunt in Newfoundland, Canada, Laura Wood was 95 years old and had been a hunter for 79 years. Her one-piece camo suit, made of soft fabric that is quiet in brush, can be unzipped for ventilation. In remote areas where other hunters are unlikely to be, high-viz hunter orange may not be required.

Bob Nikkel

Cyndee Nikkel from Colorado, a member of the Order of Edwardian Gunners, at a clays shoot in Maryland. Known as the Vintagers, members of the club dress in "vintage" gear and shoot "vintage" guns from Pre-WWI England. *Vintage* means from a certain period in time, and *Edwardian* refers to Edward VII, King of England from 1901–1910. While he was the Prince of Wales and waiting to inherit the throne from his mother, Queen Victoria, Edward made driven-bird shooting fashionable among Britain's aristocracy. One result of this was that fine handcrafted British doubles became the best shotguns in the world. Another was that these shooters wore a certain style of clothing. For women it was high-waisted, long skirts (often tweed) with high boots and feathered hats. When the Vintagers get together, the shooters and sometimes even the spectators dress in the Edwardian style, changing their outfits each day just as was done a century ago.

Along with visors and eye shields to keep them from being distracted, match shooters wear stiff, custom-fitted, adjustable coats and pants for stability. This is German gold-medalist Sonja Pfeilschifter competing in 10-meter Air Rifle in Bangkok, Thailand, in 2007. The square toes of her shoes help hold her steady in the kneeling position.

Elizabeth Lanier, left, and Sharon Paré show off what the well-dressed upland bird hunter wears in the American West—weather permitting, of course.

Sporting-clays competitor Vanessa Maiorino, at Dover Furnace Shooting Grounds, in New York, is wearing Beretta from head to toe (and shooting a Beretta over/under). Her shirt and cap and the matching piping on her navy-blue vest are hot pink.

Shooting at Stuff

Secrets of Becoming a Good Shot

Hey, you got a BB gun for your birthday. Great! What are you going to do with it?

If you've read "You'll Put Your Eye Out!" you know a lot about air guns already, including where to shoot them and what not to shoot with them. As you've seen, it's easy to set up a range for BB guns at home. You need just three things: a safe place to shoot, a backstop to trap the BBs and some targets.

Make that four things. You also need permission from your parents. Read this section and the next four (down through "The Law") carefully and completely yourself, and then show them to one or both of your parents. When they're on board with the project, you may proceed.

Assuming you're not breaking the law somehow, the best place to shoot a BB gun is usually the basement of your house. Ideally you'll have at least 30 feet of range, although just 25 would be OK. If you can, set the backstop against a wall that doesn't have a window nearby. Basement walls are usually hard enough to make a BB bounce, so get someone to help you hang an old bed sheet behind the backstop to trap any stray shot.

If your house doesn't have a basement, does it have an attic with enough space? How about a room that your family will let you convert into a shooting range at least part of the time? This might work in a city apartment too. The hanging bed sheet should keep walls and windows safe.

The backstop is just a good-size cardboard box, like what a microwave oven or desktop computer comes in. (Everybody used to use TV boxes, but now TVs are flat-screens and the boxes aren't

If you can't find a big cardboard box, companies such as Beeman make pellet and BB traps that hold different targets and are safe for indoor shooting. The silhouettes jump when you hit them, but don't have to be reset. If the steel box deforms your BBs and pellets, you won't be able to reuse them.

always fat enough.) Fill it with wadded-up newspaper and tape it closed. The cardboard won't stop your BBs, but the newspaper will. You can just put the box on the floor or set it on top of another box or a pair of sawhorses or the like.

You can buy paper bull's-eye targets like the ones used in official competitions (like the Olympic 10-meter air-gun events) or targets with everything from squirrels to charging rhinos to terrorists on them. There are hundreds of different kinds and sizes available. There are even Websites with targets that you can download to your computer and print.

After you've shot up some of your ammunition, open the box and harvest the BBs. They won't be deformed, so you can use them again.

More Targets

Punching holes in paper can get boring. Then you start looking around for more interesting things to shoot at. Tin cans that jump when they're hit! Save these for shooting outdoors with your .22; you don't want BBs ricocheting around the basement.

When we were younger, we had three favorite targets. One was the red cardboard tube that BBs came in. It was about three inches long and a lot less than an inch in diameter. Hung on a string in front of the backstop, it jerked and swung around when hit. After a while, we could keep it swinging back and forth by hitting it at just the right place each time. BBs still come in tubes or small bottles; they're made of plastic, but this should still work.

DO-IT-YOURSELF

BULLET STOP

By GEORGE H. PADGINTON

A BULLET STOP which is most effective and can cost you very little, or nothing at all, can be had by acquiring a large section of any good solid log. Living in the vicinity of a sawmill makes things a bit easier, though you can cut out your own if you wish.

The cross section of the log should be large enough to accommodate the size of the paper target you wish to shoot at. After placement, the log should be firmly secured or wedged in position so that the force of bullets impacting upon it will not dislodge it. The firing must be done into the end grain of the log so that the bullets will follow the grain and become entrapped in the wood fibers. Be careful, too, to shoot roughly at right angles to the log.

This type of stop is not recommended for high power rifle or pistol ammunition. Large caliber, medium range pistol ammo may be used, but it causes a more rapid deterioration of the log than if just .22 cal. rimfire ammo were used. After one end of the log has been shot out and become impacted with lead, it can be turned end for end, giving a fresh shooting surface. I've found that this is a good inexpensive bullet trap.

The September 1957 issue of *Guns* Magazine suggested the end of a log as a cheap and easy bullet stop. It's still a good idea, at least until the wood has been shot to shreds.

Another favorite: Necco candy wafers. They're about the size of a quarter and break with a nice puff when hit by a BB—kind of like a mini-clay pigeon, except obviously you can't throw them in the basement. Instead, stick them to your backstop with some folded-over Scotch Tape.

The best targets, though, were little plastic figurines like toy soldiers. First we lined them up in front of the backstop box. Pretty soon we were hiding the "enemy soldiers" behind "barricades" and toy trucks and so on.

Some adults have gotten completely carried away with this urban-warfare game. They set up elaborate miniature street scenes, with buildings and vehicles, "innocent civilians" and "enemy snipers." Instead of BB guns they use match-quality air rifles with scopes and scale their shooting distances to the size of the figurines. Hitting a three-inch figure 75 feet away is like shooting a six-foot person at a range of 600 yards.

You can do the arithmetic yourself. Convert everything to inches first, then do a simple ratio calculation. (A six-foot, or 72-inch, human at 200 yards looks like a three-inch toy soldier at 25 feet. Your mom or dad probably has a 25-foot tape measure you can borrow.) Then go for it—hostage situations, countersniper fire, street-by-street squad actions, air extractions. You can shoot offhand or from a rest, lying down behind a barricade, against a timer, whatever. All it takes is imagination.

Whatever angles you shoot at or targets or obstacles you set up, keep the 15 Commandments (see "Safety First") in mind. Even with a BB gun, always be aware of what's behind your target and of the possibility of damage or ricochet.

NOT Shooting Indoors

By the time one of your authors was 15, he had an arsenal of four firearms plus a Daisy air rifle and a Plainsman CO_2 pistol. Still too young to drive himself to a shooting range, he set up a range in the basement. He took the cardboard box a television came in, stuffed it with newspaper and taped targets to it. Then he blazed away with his single-shot Stevens Favorite and an H&R revolver, both .22s, indoors. (Not recommended. See below.)

Most kids have a friend who their parents don't like. Naturally, it was that very friend who the author invited over to do some shooting one day when both of his parents were out. Everything went fine for a while. Then the friend loaded and cocked the Stevens, pointed it straight up and *bang*!

"It was like having an ice cube pass through an artery into my heart.

"Luckily, no one was home. We ran upstairs to look. The bullet had passed through the hardwood floor and the carpet over it, just missed the dining room table and went into the plaster ceiling. Trying to flatten the bump in the floor didn't work. Covering the hole in the ceiling was out of the question. All we could do was wait.

Practice targets come in about every imaginable shape and style. This one is life-size; the whitetail deer's vital areas are drawn in, for scoring hits, but the shooter can't see the lines at normal hunting distances. Every hunter owes it to the game to practice and practice for a clean kill.

"Dad was home for about 20 minutes before he spotted the hole in the ceiling. A full and immediate confession minimized the long-term problems. Until Dad patched the hole, though, whenever the heater came on, plaster dust floated around the room as a reminder of a very bad idea."

Firearms Indoors?

Almost always a bad idea, as you saw above. Unless you live in a very unusual house, you don't have the sort of walls and floors needed to stop a .22 bullet that's aimed the wrong way. Not to mention dealing with the noise and the powder fumes.

Also, as you know, pellet guns are generally much more powerful than BB guns, so to be on the safe side we're including them in the category of **Do Not Use Indoors**—even in the basement.

By the way, many towns and cities have zoning regulations about building an indoor shooting range, even for private use. Even if you can follow those rules, building a safe indoor range is expensive and probably impractical. It will be easier and better to join a licensed commercial range or gun club.

The Law

It is illegal to discharge a firearm in many towns and cities. Furthermore, while in this book we use "firearm" to mean a gun that fires a projectile by the action of an explosive (in other words, not an air or CO_2 gun), some towns and cities define a firearm like this: "any instrument used in the propulsion of pellets, shot, shells or bullets by action of gunpowder, compressed air or gas exploded or released within it." So shooting your BB gun outdoors may be illegal.

You might even be breaking the law by firing it indoors. Really. In many places it's illegal to fire a gun within a certain distance of a house or other building—usually 100 to 500 feet. Well, shooting inside the house is within that distance, so if your BB gun is considered a "firearm," you may be out of luck. Your parents will have to figure this out for you.

Adults sometimes use pellet guns to drive off pests like squirrels or crows that are getting into the attic or making a racket in the yard, but this may be illegal too, depending on the local definition of a firearm.

Even if the law doesn't forbid shooting an air gun in your community, going outside with a BB gun in your hands may freak out your neighbors. They may come over and ask you what you're up to or call your parents. Or they might just call the cops.

Your neighbors aren't necessarily over-reacting either. Considering the property damage and injuries to people and pets that even a BB gun can cause, they have a right to wonder whether you are a safe and responsible shooter.

'Practice Makes Perfect'

There are a lot of other old sayings that we can quote here too. Like "It takes 20 years to become an overnight success." Or "The continuous drip polishes the stone." Or even "Stick to your guns." The point of all of them is that, whether we're talking about playing the violin or shooting baskets or shooting a gun, there is no substitute for practice.

Kim Rhode, who won her first world skeet championship when she was 13 and earned an Olympic gold medal in doubles trap five days after her 17th birthday, fires 500 to a thousand rounds every time she goes out to practice. Which is almost every day of the week. Like all world-champion athletes, Kim has almost superhuman reflexes and hand-eye coordination. But if she didn't hone those natural abilities with constant practice, she'd be just a lucky shot, not an expert one.

Shooting practice means capping off rounds—a lot of them. But by itself, shooting doesn't do much more than give us an instinctive feel for the gun. This is very important, but if we shoot badly, doing it over and over just makes the bad habits stick harder.

Before you ask: Yes, it is possible to shoot badly and still hit the target. Just because you're crushing those Necco wafers with your Daisy doesn't necessarily mean you're an expert. If your technique is poor but you're hitting targets, just think how much better you'd be if your technique was good.

"Technique" is everything that we do in handling and firing a gun, from loading to taking aim, the let-off (trigger squeeze) and follow-through, plus our ingrained safety habits. Even the way we carry and hold a gun is part of our technique.

So how do you know if your technique needs work?

While you're shooting a BB gun in the basement, only two things really matter: safety and fun. Stick to the guidelines in this book and you'll be safe; if you love to shoot, you'll be having fun. When it's time to move outdoors or to a proper shooting range with a .22 rifle, your parents will have to get involved again. (We explain this in *The Gun Book for Parents*.) They will help you find a mentor: an experienced, grown-up shooter who'll help you in the next stages of shooting. Among other things, your mentor will help you develop techniques for the kinds of shooting you want to do.

American shooting star Kim Rhode is a world-class athlete blessed with awesome reflexes and skills, but she still has to hone them with constant practice. She was 17 when this photo was taken.

Your Mentor

Mentor was a veteran warrior in *The Odyssey*, that epic story from ancient Greece. Odysseus, the hero, asked Mentor to keep an eye on his son Telemachus while he, Odysseus, took off to fight in the Trojan War. With some help from the gods, Mentor did such a good job of teaching Telemachus and keeping him out of trouble that, more than 2,000 years later, we still call this kind of older, trusted counselor, teacher and friend a mentor.

Once you have a shooting mentor, think of us, through this book, as the mythological gods of shooting who are here to back him or her up.

Thanks to Odysseus—this is Sean Bean as Odysseus in the 2004 movie *Troy*—we have mentors today.

Dry-Firing & the Dime/Washer Exercise

This means shooting a gun without ammunition in it—when it's "dry," or unloaded. Or, as an army gunnery instructor might say, "to simulate the firing of live rounds with an empty weapon."

Dry-firing is an important part of shooting practice, and you should build *every* part of shooting into it: position, aiming, breathing and trigger squeeze, as well as safety habits. Without the bang and the recoil, dry-firing even helps prevent the involuntary flinching that can come from shooting too much gun. (In fact, someone who's never fired a gun should always do some supervised dry-firing first.)

The secret to good shooting is endless practice—while wearing the sort of gear you'd have on in the field. Military forces usually set up very realistic practice areas that copy the sort of combat conditions their soldiers will face.

The US Army and Marine Corps can turn total newbies into marksmen in a few weeks. It requires hours of live fire on the range and a lot of just handling their weapons and dry-firing them in different ways. There's even something called the Weaponeer,

a training device that looks, feels and "shoots" like an M16 rifle. It's linked to a computer that tells an instructor how the student is messing up and even prints out the "target" that the trainee "fired."

Here's something else the Army does that we can do too. It's called the Dime/Washer Exercise: With your rifle unloaded and cocked, and with a dime (or a washer) balanced on the receiver, aim at a target taped to the wall and *sque-e-e-eze* the trigger. If you can hold your aim and drop the hammer six times in a row without dropping the dime, you've mastered the smooth let-off. Do it from the standing, sitting and prone positions. Think of the trigger as the connection between your brain and your gun.

This is more difficult with guns like the Ruger 10/22, which has a rounded receiver, than it is with rifles that have flat tops, but difficult is better. (It might not even be possible with a gun that drops its hammer really hard.) The biggest drawback is that you can't do it alone; you need someone to place the dime after you've shouldered the rifle.

Ready for a real challenge? Try this with a pistol. And then with a double-action revolver, cycling it with the trigger.

Here is a critically important thing about dry-firing: The safety commandments are still in force. (Go back to "Safety First" and review.) Even though it's unloaded and you're just practicing, you must treat the gun as if it is loaded. Keep it pointed in a safe direction. Don't point it at anything you're not willing to shoot. Keep your finger outside the trigger guard until you're ready to shoot. Keep the safety on until you're ready to shoot. Be sure of your target and what's behind it. When you put the gun down or hand it to someone, open the action.

Yes, you're only dry-firing it and, no, it's not loaded. But what if it is? As shooting instructors like to say, "Guns are sneaky. They'll reload themselves when you're not looking."

OK, so it is definitely not loaded. You've double-checked and re-checked, and anyway the ammunition is still in the safe. But dry-firing is meant to help you build your shooting technique, and safety habits are core parts of shooting technique.

If you have snap caps, add loading, ejecting and reloading to your dry-fire exercises. Most shooters seem to forget this, but good technique means more than just aim-and-squeeze. Think about facing a charging Cape buffalo with an empty rifle: You have to grab your ammo, reload, mount, aim, fire and reload—quickly, smoothly *and* accurately. Make just one mistake, and the buff wins.

Another accuracy "secret" is to use a rest whenever possible. This student at SAAM (Sportsman's All-Weather, All-Terrain Marksmanship) school, at the FTW Ranch, in Texas, is shooting from an adjustable Bog-Pod.

Snap Caps

Snap caps are substitute rounds (no powder, no primer, no projectile) shaped like the ammunition for a particular gun. They're supposed to provide something for the firing pin to hit during dry-firing, so the gun's lockwork doesn't have to absorb this impact. It's a fine idea, but not all snap caps are made right. If what the firing pin hits is too hard, the pin can deform. The best snap caps have spring-loaded disks or plastic inserts in them that give a bit when hit by the firing pin and then rebound.

One of your authors had an ancient British Webley .455 revolver that he dry-fired endlessly until one day the cast-metal hammer just snapped in half. Many modern guns, though, can be dry-fired thousands of times without snap caps with no damage. The real benefit of snap caps then is to practice handling ammunition—loading, unloading, ejecting.

(If you're dry-firing a semi-automatic of some sort, you'll have to eject the "fired" snap cap manually. Speaking of semi-autos, Ruger says that its super-popular 10/22 rifle, our choice as a top fun gun, isn't hurt by dry-firing and doesn't need snap caps.)

These are snap caps for different shotgun bores, but dummy cartridges come in all gauges, calibers and styles. The good ones have special inserts that absorb the impact of the firing pin without damaging it.

So have at it. Just 20 minutes of practice, especially with the Dime/Washer Exercise, three times a week can make a huge difference in your shooting.

A big, red-flag caution: Don't confuse snaps caps and real cartridges. Whenever you load *anything* into the chamber of a gun, you must be fully aware of what you're doing.

Dry-Firing Shotguns

Shooting moving targets with a shotgun is generally harder than hitting something that's standing still with a rifle, so dry-firing can be even more helpful in wingshooting. Think about this: You have to hold, mount and fire the gun—while everything is in motion. To hit moving targets consistently, the gun has to be moving too.

What's more, a shotgun has to *keep* moving, even after the shot has been fired. That's the follow-through, and without it you'll shoot behind the target every time.

Mount the gun to your shoulder while your body swivels toward the bird. With both eyes on the target, catch up to the bird with the gun's barrel(s), swing past it on the line it's flying and pull the trigger. If everything comes together right, the gun shoots where your eyes are looking. Swinging the gun ahead of the bird creates the "lead" that's needed to intercept a moving target. (Like a quar-

terback who throws the ball to where the receiver will be—when the ball gets there.)

You can't learn wingshooting from a book any more than you can learn how to hit a golf ball by reading about it, but dry-firing is an excellent way to practice this swing-fire-and-follow-through movement. Instead of taping a bull's-eye on the wall, as you might for rifle or handgun dry-firing, pretend the bird is at the point where two walls and the ceiling meet, in a corner of the room. Face away from that point, and then smoothly turn toward it as you raise the gun to your shoulder. Find the line where one wall meets the ceiling, and follow it to the "bird." Swing to and past that point, pulling the trigger as you pass through it.

After you've made double-double sure the gun is empty, of course.

The Man with One Gun

Here's another old saying: "Beware the man with one gun." (Maybe we should say "the person" with one gun.) It refers to someone who uses the same gun for everything. Maybe he or she can't afford more than one, or maybe it's by choice, but the point is that they've gotten lethal with it through constant use.

Karamojo Bell, the Scottish ivory hunter who retired rich after "harvesting" close to 2,000 elephants in the early 1900s, became a crack shot partly because of his rifles. Bell used bolt-actions that weighed half as much as some of the double-barreled shoulder cannons that other elephant hunters carried. But they didn't really carry them; their gunbearers did and handed them over when it was

time to shoot. Bell's rifles never left his possession, and they were so light he didn't even have slings on them. They were always in his hands and he dry-fired them constantly. He also used them to shoot the hundreds of zebras, buffaloes, giraffes and other game needed to feed his work crews. Bell was "the man with one gun."

He had more than one, in fact, but they were all the same. Eventually they became extensions of his hands and eyes. Where good shots killed birds with shotguns at 45 yards, Bell could shoot birds out of the sky at a hundred yards with his rifles.

When we had only our .22 rifles to shoot, we were good too.

Hunting the Big Mouse

If your grand-father is a gun buff, he probably longs for the good old days, when a kid could put his .22 rifle across the handlebars of his bicycle and ride to school to shoot at the Junior Reserve Officer Train-ing Corps range. You could buy an Army-surplus .45 revolver through the mail for $15 and, for $189.50, a 20mm anti-tank cannon left over from World War II. Those were also the days when shooting rats at the dump was a cherished pastime.

After our planet's next mass-extinction event—you know, an asteroid impact followed by megatsunamis, global forest fires, toxic rains and a global ash cloud, then nuclear winter—three species will likely survive: the cockroach, the coyote and the rat. (Maybe the leop-ard too.) In ancient Rome the rat was *Mus maximus*, the big mouse, and people have been trying to exter-minate the big mouse since cave men invented the club. There are some 64 species of rats worldwide,

The next best thing to stalking real dump rats might be this nightmare Dar-kotic "splattering" target from Birchwood Casey. The fine print says "Any resemblance to real beings, living or dead, is purely coincidental."

and they don't just eat farm crops; in Europe they were blamed for spread-ing the plague, the Black Death of the 14th Century.

Now there's the Rat Chick Rescue and Advo-cacy Group, which specializes in "rat rescues" and find-ing them good "forever homes." From their Web-site: "The Rat: Always loving, always caring, al-ways misjudged."

Cuddly furballs? Maybe to a few people, but consider the unin-habited Italian is-land of Montecris-to (made famous in *The Count of Monte Cristo*). According to bi-ologists, it has one rat per square yard. Since it's four square miles in area, that's 12,390,400 rats. It would take 26 tons of poison pellets to rid the island of these rats—or you, a suppressed and scoped Ruger 10/22, and a lifetime supply of Long Rifle hollowpoints.

An early (circa 1814) English shooting book was called *Hanger To All Sportsmen*, and it included "The Rat Catching Secret." During the

American Revolution the author, Maj. Gen. George Hanger, was an aide to Sir Henry Clinton, commander of British forces in New York City. Hanger wrote that the rats in Sir Henry's headquarters were so thick that "he had been forced to have the bottom of the doors lined with tin, for they had nearly eaten through the door where he kept his papers." Using obviously exceptional ratting skills, Hanger reported that in one night he caught "very near three hundred."

That was during the flintlock era, when shooting rats was impractical. But help was on the way.

The rimfire cartridge appeared in the 1840s. This divinely inspired combination of lead, copper and propellant became major rat medicine with the introduction of the .22 Long Rifle round in the 1880s. (In the interest of truthiness, we must note that some historians feel the .22LR was put on earth for woodchucks, not rats, while others say gophers.) At the same time the growth of cities brought about the spread of dumps, also known as landfills. Whatever they were called, they became rat hunters' paradises, a virtual Serengeti teeming with game.

Ask your granddad about rat hunting, and he may tear up embarrassingly while recounting tales of prowling through abandoned refrigerators, bald tires and broken furniture as majestic gulls soared overhead looking for rotting fruit. It took supreme sneakiness to get within range of a feeding rat, and then keen eyes and steady hands to put a 37-grain hollowpoint into such a small target.

German and Russian snipers stalking each other through the ruins of Stalingrad in 1942, Mausers versus Mosin-Nagants, were hardly more stealthy. And what better training for hunting the wily whitetail deer in the forests of Minnesota or tracking the elusive sitatunga through the remote swamps of Zambia?

Ah, nature, red in tooth and claw. And we didn't even have to clean up afterward. The carcasses were already at the dump.

Some rat hunters rose to national prominence. (Probably.) The legendary Mike "Reloading Man" Ball may have been the Jeremiah Johnson of rat hunters. At the height of his career he would slip, at night, into the ricefields around a certain major airport. The landing lights of incoming airplanes lit up the reflective pink eyeballs of rats, giving away their locations, and soon a high-velocity lead pill was en route. (Try this today and see how long it takes a police tactical team to start hunting *you*.)

For a first date, one of your authors' fathers-in-law, a hopeless romantic, took his wife-to-be to the dump with a picnic lunch to shoot rats.

Rat hunting may have been the perfect shooting sport. It was close to home, dirt cheap, offered challenging targets and caused no harm to the environment and endangered no species. And every dump was a target-rich environment. But it is now mostly a memory. Alas, the habitat is being lost. Dumps now have roofs and are called recycling centers. Do rats even live in such sterile places?

He probably wasn't a rat hunter, but the German philosopher Goethe said it for all of us: "There is no past that we can bring back by longing for it." So sad.

Competition

Shooting Games: Ways to Test Your Skills

Make a snowball, and what are you going to do with it? Drop it on the ground? Feed it to the dog? No, you have to throw it at something, or someone. And what good is a basketball or a Frisbee if you can't throw it? What's a gun for other than to reach out and touch something? The enjoyment we get from shooting and from throwing things comes mostly from the satisfaction of being accurate, of hitting whatever we're aiming at. It's a skill, and skills are to be developed and then tested—which means competition.

This isn't always just fun and games, either. The peasants of medieval England were required to be skilled archers. In 1363 King Edward III declared that "every man in the country, if he be able-bodied, shall, upon holidays, make use, in his games, of bows and arrows . . . and so learn and practice archery." The point was to have expert marksmen ready whenever king and country needed soldiers.

It worked. For at least two centuries, until firearms took over the battlefield, the longbow kept England safe from invasion. And five centuries after Edward III's declaration, both Britain and the US created National Rifle Associations to train citizens to shoot in case the army needed them. Naturally, the training involved target shooting.

Today we call any sort of lopsided fight, where one side wipes out the other without much damage to themselves, a "turkey shoot." In Colonial

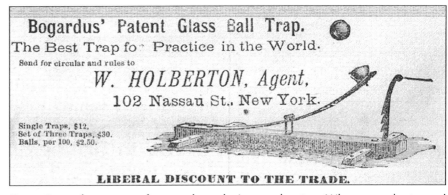

Capt. Bogardus was a famous boxed-pigeon shooter. When people turned against using live birds as targets, these spring-powered glass-ball launchers were invented. To try to be more realistic, the balls were sometimes filled with feathers—but they still weren't hard to hit.

America, though, a turkey shoot was a contest. Men and boys took turns shooting at a very small target: a turkey's head. The one who killed the turkey brought it home as his prize.

Now there are more kinds of organized target shooting than ever before involving about every sort of firearm available, from the guns of the Wild West to modern submachine guns, from short-range BB guns to long-range match rifles, and shotguns of every type.

Let's start with shotguns. The first wingshooting competitions used live pigeons. Today the most popular forms of target shooting with shotguns are trap, skeet and sporting clays, with targets called clay pigeons. Just as in other sports, there are leagues and championships and professionals. Most people, however, shoot clay pigeons just for fun or to practice for hunting.

Trapshooting

A man from Boston named Charles Portluck gets the credit for inventing trapshooting around 1866. At first, this meant shooting at glass balls launched by a catapult instead of live pigeons released from a trap. For realism, the balls could be filled with feathers that flew out in a puff when the ball was hit. But then in 1880 came the clay pigeon, a little disk that shatters when struck by a shot pellet. It flew much farther and faster than a glass globe and could be made to curve in the air (like a Frisbee). It didn't leave broken glass behind, either. Rules and regulations developed, and in 1900 trapshooting joined rifle and pistol matches as an event at the Olympic Games.

In modern trap clay pigeons are thrown from a small building, called the house, set into the ground facing away from the shooters. Five shooters stand in a row 16 yards behind the house. In turn each one calls for a target, which the trapper—the person operating the trap—launches. The clay streaks away, climbing at a shallow angle. The trap, or launcher, swings back and forth to vary the direction. The challenge is to break each clay before it gets out of range.

Each person takes five shots from each of five positions for a round of 25. Scorekeepers note the hits and misses. To do well in competition, shooters

The ideal shotgun target came along in 1880: the clay pigeon. Modern ones fly like Frisbees, shatter easily and come in different sizes and colors. They can be easy or fiendishly hard to hit, depending on how they're thrown.

usually have to break several hundred clays without a miss. It becomes a test of mental concentration and even physical stamina.

The five shooting stations and the house at a trap field. The angle varies, but the clays are always going away from the gun. Trap, skeet and sporting clays courses have electric machines to throw the targets; you can get an inexpensive hand thrower for use at home.

To make things interesting, there's also handicap trap, where competitors shoot from farther behind the trap house. There's doubles trap too, where two clays come out of the house at the same time going in different directions. Trapshooters use 12-gauge double-barreled guns or semi-autos loaded with two shells.

The hardest is International trap. Instead of just one machine, there's a line of 15 traps in the house (here called a bunker), each set at a different angle, and the clays are thrown much faster. The shooters also stand farther back. This is Olympic trap shooting.

The American ATA (Amateur Trapshooting Association) has special classes and categories for young shooters and even awards college scholarships to high-school trapshooters. High-school trapshooters? Why, yes. Minnesota, for example, has more than 100 schools with trapshooting teams and each year hosts the Minnesota State High School Clay Target Tournament.

What's available in your state?

Skeet Shooting

Skeet was meant to be like shooting upland gamebirds—grouse, woodcock and quail that flush from the ground and go rocketing off into the brush. The shooting is fast and fairly close.

The shooting positions, or stations, are in a semi-circle. At each end of this half-circle is a trap house. One is the high house and the other is the low house, and they are 42 yards apart. They throw their clays toward each other. High-house clays start at 10 feet off the ground and climb up to 15 feet; low-house clays reach the same height but are launched from three feet off the ground. Each house always throws its targets the same way and at the same speed, but as the shooter moves around the semi-circle, the angles of the clays change.

In trapshooting the birds are always going away from the gun; in skeet they cross in front of the gun.

Skeet shooters begin at station 1, at the high house. Station 7 is at the low house. The five stations in between are spaced evenly along the semi-circle. At each one the shooter gets some combination of singles and doubles that adds up to 22 targets. A double is one clay from each house thrown at the same time. This is trickier than a trap double because the birds are moving in opposite directions, so you have to swing the gun one way and then abruptly stop and go the other way to catch the second clay before it's out of range.

Station 8 is in the middle, directly between the two houses, and here the shooter takes two singles, one from each house. If he hasn't missed any so far, he shoots one more from the low house for a total of 25. Just as in trap, really good skeet shooters will miss just one or two out of a hundred targets.

Skeet was invented around 1915, also in Massachusetts. At first there were 12 stations in a complete circle around one trap house, in the center, and skeet was called "shooting around the clock." But this took up too much room, so the present layout was adopted. The man who made the game famous was William Harnden Foster, a bird hunter who was also the editor of two outdoor magazines. He wrote about the new shotgun game, and one of his readers (Gertrude Hurlbutt, of Dayton, Montana) won $100 by coming up with the winning name for it: "Skeet" (from the Scandinavian word for shoot: *skyte*).

It became tremendously popular. In World War II, American anti-aircraft gunners shot skeet as a way to learn how to hit fast-flying targets. Today there are skeet-shooting associations, tournaments and even a hall of fame. (Foster was the first member, naturally.) Serious skeet shooters use over/under shotguns in 12, 20 and 28 gauge and .410 bore. In 1968 skeet was added to the Olympic Games, where, like trap, it was made more difficult.

Skeet Field Layout

A skeet field, with its half-moon layout, eight shooting stations and high and low houses. Some shots are much harder than others, depending on where you are on the semi-circle. Station 8, on the line between the houses, takes a lot of practice, but then it's no longer so difficult.

Sporting Clays

Sporting clays is sometimes called golf with a shotgun because, just as there are different holes on a golf course, there are different stations on a sporting clays course. Each station presents clays in a way that imitates real gamebirds: "pheasants" flying fast directly away from the gun, "ducks" landing on or taking off from a pond in front of you, "quail" scattering in every direction, "doves" crossing fast, even "rabbits," which are clays rolled along the ground at high speed. There may be a dozen or more stations set in the woods or in the open, and at each one the shooter faces some combination of singles and doubles.

Clays can be thrown at all sorts of angles and speeds to all sorts of heights and distances. Clays come in different sizes and colors too. The traps, or launchers, can be on the ground or on towers, behind bushes or on hillsides. No two stations—or even two sporting clays courses—are the same. The operator also can change things around. A trap that was throwing full-size clays could be loaded with minis, which are lighter and faster and harder to hit, and aimed in a different direction.

The British set up the first sporting clays courses long ago, but for some reason the idea didn't catch on in the US until about 1980. Today sporting clays is one of the most popular shooting sports, and there are competitions at every level from local to international. Almost any kind of hunting shotgun can be used for sporting clays.

Birds in Boxes

Pigeons are strong, agile, fast flyers, with big wings and strong chest muscles. Long before there were clay pigeons, shooters used real ones to test their skills.

Competitive pigeon shooting began in England in the late 1700s. If using live animals for target practice seems cruel, remember that this was in a time and place when popular entertainment included fights to the death between dogs, bulls or bears and there was nothing that "the mob" enjoyed more than seeing criminals executed in public, usually by hanging. By comparison to these spectacles, shooting pigeons with expensive shotguns was a polite activity for gentlemen.

By 1812, when the first pigeon-shooting club, at London's Old Hats Tavern, was organized, rules regarding scoring, distances, shooting styles, guns and cartridges were being established. Other clubs quickly sprang up, and the sport spread across Britain and then to Europe and America.

Ernest Hemingway, the famous writer, shooting boxed pigeons at the club he belonged to in Cuba in about 1941. The shooting stations are set up as on a trap field; the bird boxes, or traps, are off to the right. Hemingway has fired his Winchester pumpgun once—you can see the empty shell in the air—and he's about to shoot again, to try to "anchor" the bird before it escapes over the penalty fence.

John F. Kennedy Library

It became an expensive game, with big prize money and big bets on the scores. Newspapers and magazines reported on the matches—and the disagreements, penalties, scandals and disgraces that went along with them. (Baseball, football and basketball were still in the future.)

Just as racing made automobiles better, pigeon-shooting competitions advanced the design of shotguns and ammunition, and makers whose products won tournaments bragged about it in their advertising.

The shooter stood facing a row of small boxes about 30 yards away called traps. Beyond the traps was a fence, inside which a shot pigeon had to fall in order to count.

When the shooter called for a bird, the trapper pulled a cord that opened one of the boxes. The pigeon inside would try to escape, and the gunner would try to kill it. To bring down a pigeon—launching itself off the ground at unpredictable angles, flying fast and dodging erratically—inside the fence

took skill. To win several matches of 10 birds in a row took skill, great concentration and some luck.

The first recorded American pigeon shoot took place in Ohio in 1831. As it had overseas, "trap shooting" spread rapidly. A famous competition in Kentucky in 1883 pitted professional sharpshooter "Doc" (William F.) Carver against Capt. A.H. (Adam Henry) Bogardus, the American and world pigeon champion. Carver outshot the captain 19 times in 25 matches. By this time pigeon tournaments in the United States were drawing huge crowds, and the winners became celebrities.

Pigeon shooting even made a one-time appearance at the Olympics, in the Paris games of 1900. But by then the public was turning against using live targets, and the clay pigeon took over.

They may now be called boxed-bird or flyer shoots, but live-pigeon matches are still held, mostly in Spain and parts of Latin America and at some private gun clubs in America.

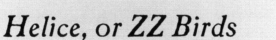

Helice, or ZZ Birds

Live pigeon shooting is so challenging that a humane version of it almost had to be invented. (Modern trap is the direct descendant of pigeon shooting, but it's nowhere near as interesting.) So a Belgian nobleman came up with a game called Helice (*hell-EECE*), which is French for "propeller." The targets, called ZZs (*zee-zees*), look like orange plastic helicopter rotors 11 inches across. Each one has a white cap in the center, between the two wings. The ZZ is spun up to high RPM (revolutions per minute) by an electric motor, and when it's released by the trapper, it flies off at crazy angles. The shooter has to hit it hard enough to knock the cap off before it crosses the penalty line—the fence that's 21 meters behind the traps.

Everything is arranged just as in pigeon shooting, with five or seven traps that are released at random when the shooter calls for a bird, and

Silvio Calabi

A shot-up ZZ from the Italian World Cup. The white cap has to be knocked off the rotor to score as a "kill." This can be even more challenging than shooting boxed pigeons, and of course it is a lot more humane.

the electric motor in each one constantly swings back and forth to change the launch angle. If anything, Helice is even more difficult than shooting live birds. It's about as expensive to shoot too, even though the targets aren't live and can be used over, because a human has to reload the traps by hand after every round.

Now let's leave shotguns and wingshooting and look at handgun competitions.

Fast Draw for Speed

Clyde Howell earned "the badge of the gun-slinger," a limp, from shooting himself in the leg while practicing fast draw. In a magazine story in 1959, Howell, who was one of the pioneers of this sport, said he'd been working on his fast draw for more than 25 years. It didn't become a national fascination, though, until the cowboy movie *High Noon* came out in 1952. The hero, played by Gary Cooper, saved the girl, Grace Kelley (who later became the real-life Princess of Monaco), and the entire town with his lightning-fast gunplay. Boys and girls of all ages took note. Then, in 1955, the TV Western *Gunsmoke* started its record-setting 20-year run on CBS.

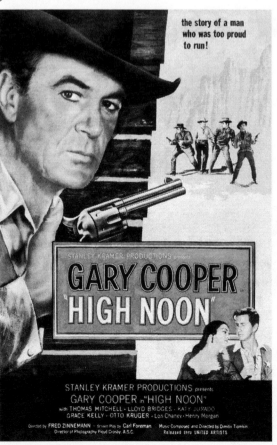

the story of a man who was too proud to run!

STANLEY KRAMER PRODUCTIONS presents

GARY COOPER "HIGH NOON"

STANLEY KRAMER PRODUCTIONS presents
GARY COOPER in "HIGH NOON"
with THOMAS MITCHELL · LLOYD BRIDGES · KATY JURADO
GRACE KELLY · OTTO KRUGER · Lon Chaney · Henry Morgan
Directed by FRED ZINNEMANN · Screen Play by Carl Foreman · Music Composed and Directed by Dimitri Tiomkin
Director of Photography Floyd Crosby, A.S.C.   Released thru UNITED ARTISTS

Each episode began with actor James Arness, playing Marshal Matt Dillon, squaring off against an outlaw on the main street of what was supposed to be Dodge City, Kansas, sometime after the Civil War. The show became a monster hit. Each week kids all over the country would test their reflexes in that opening sequence. (We always wondered how many TV screens wound up shattered by bullets.)

Marshal Dillon's adversary was played by a stuntman named Arvo Ojala, a genuine fast-draw expert who taught two generations of movie and TV actors how to handle guns. (He also invented the steel-lined safety holster, although too late to save Clyde Howell's leg.) Marshal Dillon was the hero, so naturally he won every time. Westerns had an unwritten code of rules that said the villains were always "back-shootin', no-good pole-cats" wearing black hats, and they always lost in the final showdown.

Such do-or-die confrontations with six-guns were pretty much historical nonsense, the product of Hollywood screenwriters' imaginations, but they touched something in the American soul. By the late 1950s 200,000 people were reportedly taking part in fast-draw competitions, including stars like Clint Eastwood, Jerry Lewis and Sammy Davis Jr. (Ask your parents.) Championship matches were held in Las Vegas. A man named Dee Woolem, one of the "cowboys" who staged shoot-outs for the crowd at Knott's Berry Farm, in California, became the top gun. He was clocked at 0.37 seconds to draw and fire his single-action revolver on a signal, and 0.12 seconds when he could draw on his own. It takes that long to blink your eye.

Fast Draw with Accuracy

Some people pooh-poohed fast draw because it was just about speed and ignored accuracy. It was getting dangerous too. In 1959, in its magazine *American Rifleman*, the National Rifle Association complained about the fast-draw "craze" and the "needless accidents" it led to: "Teen-agers and grown men, in all parts of the country, have become devotees of the fad with exaggerated zeal." The problem was that people were drilling themselves in the foot or leg while racing to "clear leather" with a loaded gun. The NRA wanted shooters to switch to blanks, wax bullets or even BB pistols.

But in Big Bear, California, a group headed by Jeff Cooper, a Marine WWII veteran and gun writer, went a different way. The group's "leather slap" events with live ammunition led to the formation of the South West Pistol League. The SWPL encouraged accurate fast-draw shooting by coming up with timed and scored pistol competitions that included running, climbing, crawling, quick reloading and shooting with the weak hand. Not only that, but instead of wheelguns, most competitors used Colt Model 1911-type semi-auto pistols that were carried cocked and locked. (See "Killer Apps.")

Old-school pistoleros feared bloody mayhem. Instead, SWPL competition led to dramatic advances in shooting techniques and handgun and holster design. Eventually Jeff Cooper was elected to the NRA's board of directors.

In the 1950s and '60s almost every cop carried a Smith & Wesson or Colt double-action revolver, and the FBI recommended the so-called combat crouch for close-in shooting. This began to change when an early Big Bear competitor, Los Angeles County Deputy Sheriff Jack Weaver, proved that standing upright and using two hands to shoot could be deadly quick and accurate. This became known as the Weaver Stance.

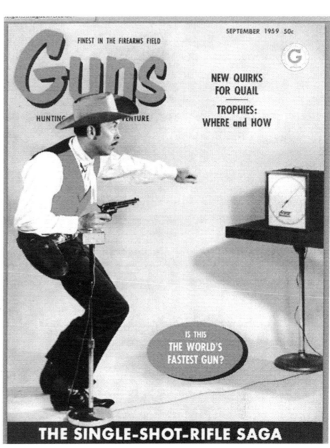

Fast-draw champion Dee Woolem on the September 1959 issue of *Guns* Magazine. He's not shooting a TV; that's a timer.

Armand Swenson, the pistolsmith to the SWPL and himself a competitor, was just as influential. Swenson customized Model 1911s to make them more accurate and reliable. He added safeties that worked for either the right or left hand, beveled the magazine wells so they could be reloaded faster, checkered the front straps for better grip, and came up with other features that are now standard on combat and self-defense pistols.

All of these advancements had a huge impact on police training and equipment. Today almost no cop carries a revolver, and hardly anyone even remembers the combat crouch.

Interest in combat pistol shooting spread beyond the United States. In 1976, in Columbia, Mis-

A fast-draw competitor lets it rip. Her right hand snatches the gun from the holster while her left slams across to fan back the hammer for the shot. A sound-activated timer measures her speed. Notice her eyes are closed and the shot doesn't seem to be aimed. She's firing special blanks.

souri, representatives from the SWPL and the Missouri Practical Pistol League sat down with shooters from Asia, Europe, Africa and New Zealand. The result was the International Practical Shooting Confederation (IPSC). The new group elected Jeff Cooper as its first president and adopted the SWPL motto: *Diligentia, Vis, Celeritas* (Accuracy, Power, Speed). The word "pistol" doesn't appear in the name because

the group anticipated that rifles and shotguns would someday be included in IPSC matches.

As competition heated up, IPSC guns and holsters got more and more specialized. The sights, extended magazines and compensators developed for these heavily modified "race guns" finally made them impractical for law-enforcement or normal self-defense use, so, in 1996, yet another group formed: IDPA, the International Defense Pistol Association. Later that group too added long-gun matches, but IDPA emphasizes "practical" guns and "real-life self-defense scenarios."

There are other organizations and matches that focus on "three gun" (pistol, rifle, shotgun) competition and even four-gun events that include submachine guns. You can watch many of the top competitors—such as Jerry Miculek, who once fired eight shots from a revolver on four targets, hitting each one twice, in 1.06 seconds—on YouTube.

Law-enforcement agencies and the NRA were slow to accept these new shooting sports, styles

A hardcore Bianchi Cup competitor working her tuned and tweaked "race gun," complete with some sort of optical sight, in a two-handed grip. The Bianchi Cup is the annual National Action Pistol Championship, the biggest handgun competition in the world, with $500,000 in prize money at stake. (Note the empty shell in the air and her wrist bands and eye & ear protection.)

Daniel Brenner

and gear. That changed in 1984 when the NRA became the sponsor of the Bianchi Cup, which is the National Action Pistol Championship. Today it is co-sponsored by MidwayUSA, the giant shooting-products supplier, and the Bianchi Cup calls itself the "most prestigious and richest shooting tournament in the World." It is held in Columbia, Missouri, where the IPSC was born.

Cowboy Action Shooting

eanwhile, the first fast-draw shooters, the ones interested in the Old West (or at least Hollywood's notion of the Old West) didn't die out. In 1981, in California, some of them started what they called cowboy action shooting. This led, a few years later, to the formation of SASS, the Single Action Shooting Society, which has grown

Cowboy Action "shootists" have fun. They give themselves Old West nicknames like Pistol Pete and Calamity Jane; compete with old (or old-style) rifles, shotguns and revolvers; and dress in costumes. This Winchester Model 1897 pumpgun fan is looking good—but notice the protective Oakleys and the earplugs and the empty shell in the air.

tremendously. Entire families take part. Members call themselves "shootists" and dress in Old West costumes; compete under Old West nicknames like Six-Gun Sam, Calamity Jane and (of course) Marshal Dillon; and use the sorts of rifles, revolvers and shotguns that were around in the 1800s. Some of the competitions involve shooting from horseback or even stagecoaches.

SASS chapters around the country get quite imaginative with their events. Here's a scenario created by the Rivanna Rangers (who are based in Virginia) that's supposed to be set near Roswell, New Mexico, where aliens allegedly crash-land their UFOs:

> **COWBOYS & ALIENS**
>
> Apache Country, New Mexico Territory: *A passel o' alien critters has appeared from th' sky with flyin' machines. They're eatin' the livestock and kidnappin' an' killin' folk. Th' aliens is big an' tough.*
>
> *The Rivanna Rangers have moved in a wagon full of guns and ammo to deal with the scourge. Buffalo rifles, 10-gauge shotguns with buck and ball, and heavy-loaded Colt .45s.*

Original fast draw is still around too, with hundreds of local, state and regional groups all over the globe. For safety, the World Fast Draw Association now limits competitors to wax bullets propelled by .22 blanks or shotshell primers; live ammunition is not allowed. Speed is still key, but competitors also have to put their (wax) bullets on a target, either a man-size silhouette or a balloon.

One of Jeff Cooper's students in the early days at Big Bear was the late Bob Munden. As a kid, Munden practiced shooting in a dump near his home. He competed in his first match with live ammunition when he was 11 years old. He went on to set 18 fast-draw records, including the fastest time for a self-start shot: .0175 second, or 17.5 milliseconds. You literally cannot see his hand move. That's much *faster* than the blink of an eye.

In 2009 and 2012 the world champion in Cowboy Mounted shooting (from a horse, that is) was a woman named Kenda Lenseigne. She's in the "Shooting in Fashion" chapter.

Long-Range Matches

The National Rifle Association of America was founded in 1871 by a group of military men who were disgusted by the poor marksmanship of soldiers during the Civil War (1861–1865). Their goal was to promote target shooting—to get civilians interested in it and to teach them how to do it. The thinking was that this would make the Army much more effective the next time America went to war and had to enlist new soldiers. One of the first things the NRA did was ask Congress for $25,000 to buy 70 acres of moorland on Long Island, near New York City, from a family named Creed and turn it into a shooting range. The American NRA's first Annual Matches were held at the new Creedmoor Range on October 8, 1873.

The British already had set up a National Rifle Association in 1859 for the same reason. Their soldiers had shot poorly in the Crimean War (1853–1856). Britain's NRA held its national matches at a place called Wimbledon Common, outside London. Rifle shooting became very popular. By the late 1870s, 2,500 shooters were gathering at Wimbledon for two weeks each year, and teams from Ireland, Scotland and England were competing for trophies.

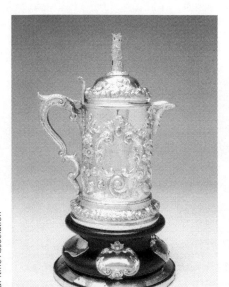

In 1873 Ireland won the team championship. The team captain, Arthur B. Leech, wrote a letter to the editor of the largest newspaper in the US, the *New York Herald*: "At the great meeting held annually at Wimbledon, a team of eight Irishmen, shooting with Irish-made rifles, this year beat the picked eights of England and Scotland. As the great American nation has long enjoyed a world-wide reputation for skill in rifle shooting, it occurs to me that the enclosed challenge from Irish riflemen, now the champions of Great Britain, might be accepted, and if so, a team would be organized to visit the United States in the summer of 1874."

The American NRA accepted the challenge. The match would be at Creedmoor. Each competitor would get 15 shots at 800, 900 and 1,000 yards. The Irish would use Rigby muzzleloading rifles, while Remington and Sharps would build breechloaders for the home team.

On September 26, the day of the event, a crowd of 8,000 people gathered to watch. At 800 yards the American team posted a score of 326 points to the Irish team's 317. The *New York Herald* and other newspapers telegraphed the scores to their offices in the city, where they were posted on public bulletin boards, and from there they were relayed to Ireland by cable.

Then it was time for lunch and speeches. Arthur Leech announced that he would like to leave a souvenir of his team's visit, a large and ornate silver tankard in the shape of an old Irish tower. It was inscribed: "Presented for Competition to the riflemen of America, by Arthur Blennerhassett Leech, Captain of the International Team of Riflemen, on the occasion of their visit to New York."

Competition resumed. At 900 yards, after each man's 15 shots, the score was Ireland 312, America 310. The Irish lead would have been greater, but one of the team's members blew it. J.K. Millner bull's-eyed his first shot at 900 yards—on

The Leech Cup, two feet tall and made of silver, was presented to "the riflemen of America" by Ireland's shooting team in 1874, at the Creedmoor Range, near New York City. The match drew tremendous public attention in the US and Britain. The American team won by just three points. Shooters still compete for the Leech Cup every year.

the wrong target, thus earning a zero. Total scores now were 636 for America, 629 for Ireland.

At 1,000 yards the Irish caught and then passed the Americans. The match came down to the last shot, by Col. Bodine of the United States. Bodine was about to sip a fizzy drink when the glass bottle exploded in his hand. In spite of the bleeding, he got into position and fired: bull's-eye! The Irish had won at that distance, 302 to 298, but they lost the overall match by just three points—931 to 934. America had won the Leech Cup.

Today at Wimbledon rifle shooting has been replaced by tennis. In America the Creedmoor Range is gone too, swallowed up by New York City. The NRA's National Matches are now shot at Camp Perry, in Ohio. (The British shoot at a place called Bisley.)

The Leech Cup, the oldest target-shooting trophy in the United States, is still hotly contested every year. The match is still fired at 1,000 yards, prone and unsupported, with open sights, but now it's 20 shots with bolt-action rifles, and the 800- and 900-yard stages are gone. The biggest change, though, is in the competitors. As it did in 1874, victory in the 2011 Leech Cup hung on the last shot. But the Irish and Americans of more than a century ago would have been shocked to hear that the winner was a woman. Nancy Tompkins of Arizona edged out the second-place finisher by one point.

Since 1995 Tompkins has won the Leech Cup an astounding seven times—losing it once to one of her daughters, Michelle, and in 2012 edging out her other daughter, Sherri, to do it.

Marksmanship runs in the Tompkins family. Michelle has taken home the Wimbledon Cup, another 1,000-yard shooting trophy, five times and won the National Long-Range Championship three times. Michelle's sister, Sherri Gallagher, was the World Long Range shooting champion in 2003 and was the NRA National Rifle Champion twice.

Sherri is a member of the US Army Marksmanship Unit, but shooting is just her hobby; her day job is jumping out of airplanes. Back in 2003,

Michael Molinaro

In 2012 Nancy Tompkins promised her dying mother that she would win the Leech Cup for her. She did. And whom did she beat? Daughter Sherri. Here Nancy and Sgt. Sherri Jo Gallagher celebrate Sherri's award as 2010's Army Soldier of the Year. Excellence shows in many ways!

when she won the world championship, she was invited to make a jump with the Army's Golden Knights Parachute Team—and as a result of that she wound up a member of the team.

Think of a sports dynasty, and Michael Jordan and the Chicago Bulls come to mind, or (for your dad) Vince Lombardi and the Green Bay Packers. In long-range shooting there's the Tompkins dynasty: Nancy, Michelle and Sherri. Together, their accomplishments with a target rifle would fill a separate book.

Mom started plinking with a .22 more than 40 years ago near Phoenix, Arizona, which happens to have some first-class shooting facilities, including a 1,000-yard range. Nancy loved to shoot, was lucky to find some great mentors and stayed with it. When her daughters came along, it was time to determine if there was a gene for accurate shooting. (It takes exceptional skill—and top equipment—to drop bullets consistently into a five-inch ring at almost six-tenths of a mile even with a scope, never mind iron sights.) By the time the girls were teenagers, they too were long-range high-power-rifle shooters—and Mom had some serious competition.

Nancy is proud of her daughters. "For all three of us," she said, "our shooting highlights have always been team matches—family teams, international teams, national teams and team matches with friends. Those are truly the most fun times that we have all experienced in shooting."

As we wrote at the beginning of this section, shooting is a skill, and skills are to be developed and then tested—which means competition. In King Edward III's day in England, shooting meant bows and arrows. Today, think of a kind of firearm or air gun, and chances are that there is an organized form of target shooting for it, complete with official targets, trophies, sponsors and a rulebook. Want to shoot military rifles at 1,000 yards? Air pistols at 10 meters? Rimfire .22s while you're skiing? (This is called biathlon—very interesting!) Pre-1896 blackpowder rifles at silhouettes of pigs, turkeys and rams? It's out there, along with much, much more, at every level from local clubs to college teams to national and international competition and the Olympic Games.

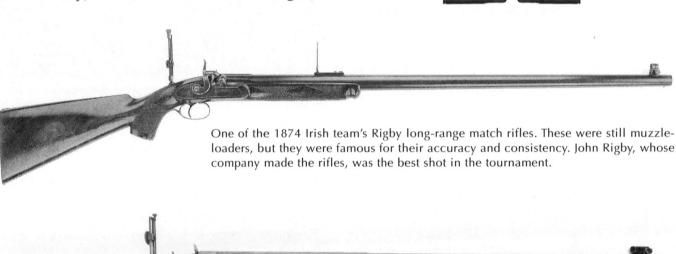

One of the 1874 Irish team's Rigby long-range match rifles. These were still muzzle-loaders, but they were famous for their accuracy and consistency. John Rigby, whose company made the rifles, was the best shot in the tournament.

The Yankee team that barely won the Leech Cup used breechloading cartridge rifles specially made for them by Sharps and Remington. This is a No. 1 Creedmoor model, one of the finest rifles Remington ever made.

Game: Animals & Birds

Taking Guns Afield for Hunting

A game animal is one that's hunted, either for its meat or as some kind of trophy. It's a wild animal, not a domesticated one we'd find in a pet store or on a farm. A cow is not a game animal; a Cape buffalo definitely is. A chicken

One of Africa's "Big Five," the Cape buffalo. *Not* a domestic animal; bad-tempered when disturbed, very dangerous when wounded. As Robert Ruark wrote in one of his hunting books, a Cape buffalo glares at you like you owe him money.

pecking in a barnyard is not fair game, but a ruffed grouse or a pheasant rocketing out of a thicket is. A hamster, no; a squirrel, yes.

There is small-game hunting and big-game hunting and then there is BIG-game hunting. In North America "big game" usually means deer. It's true that North America has much larger game animals than deer—elk and moose and the big northern bears, for example—but for most of us who hunt near home in the US and Canada, the whitetail or mule deer are our big game. (Along with wild pigs, which are spreading across America like a bad cold.) Some big-game hunters

travel to Africa to hunt the great variety of animals there, from kudu, eland and other antelopes to leopard, lion and Cape buffalo and even the biggest game of all: elephant. An African hunt is a safari, which is Swahili for "journey."

Theodore Roosevelt, our 26th president and an enthusiastic outdoorsman, was one of the early Americans to go on safari. Just 18 days after his term of office ended, early in 1909, he boarded a ship in Hoboken, New Jersey, en route to Mombasa, in what was then called British East Africa (Kenya and Uganda today; Africa

Kermit Roosevelt, age 19, with a lion he shot in East Africa with his famous father. Their expedition lasted 15 months and got Kermit out of his first year of college. His rifle is a lever-action Winchester Model 95 in .405 Winchester.

has, at last count, 59 different countries, counting islands). With him was his son Kermit, who'd gotten a break from his freshman year at Harvard to go with Dad, and four scientists. This was the beginning of a fantastic adventure that lasted 15 months, with nearly a full year in the field.

On the march across the African plains, the Roosevelt party's column of hunters, naturalists, trackers, gun-bearers, skinners, guards, grooms, horses, mules, wagons, camp staff and 200-plus porters stretched for more than a mile. The party's camps spread over acres. Roosevelt's tent flew the Stars & Stripes overhead. Eventually he and Kermit shot 17 lions, 11 elephants, 20 rhinos, 10 Cape buffaloes, 10 eland, nine giraffes, eight hippos and so on, down to four each of crocodiles and pythons. In all, the party collected more than 3,000 animals, even insects.

There was some complaining in American and British newspapers about the huge bag, but this was a scientific expedition charged by the Smithsonian Institution and the American Museum of Natural History with obtaining specimens for their collections. (Some of these animals are on display, in Washington, DC, and New York City, to this day.)

Theodore Roosevelt was an internationally acclaimed figure, so the world eagerly read the news reports of the expedition and his own stories, which he sent to the nearest telegraph office by messenger for publication at home in *Scribner's Magazine*. Roosevelt's book of his journey, *African Game Trails*, is still a terrific read today; back then it was a bestseller. People everywhere promised themselves that they too would someday explore exotic lands and face wild beasts.

This was more or less the beginning of the safari business, where men and women hire guides to take them hunting somewhere in Africa. From Roosevelt's day up into the 1970s, these guides were called white hunters. Then, as more and more African colonies broke away from their European masters and became independent countries, people began to get touchy about anything "white" as implying racism. Today, even though most of them are still white, they're known as PHs, or Professional Hunters. They're not all men any more either. In all the countries of Africa that allow hunting, they must pass tough exams in order to become licensed.

Hunting for Ivory

Big-game hunting in Africa is now mostly for the adventure of being in the bush and facing challenges that most people can only read about. There was a time, though, when it was possible to make a living by shooting elephants for their tusks. Before plastics were invented, ivory was used for a lot of things: buttons, hair pins and combs, drawer pulls and door knobs, billiard balls and piano keys, jewelry, trinkets and decorative items such as fancy pistol grips and umbrella handles. Ivory includes teeth from whales, walruses, wild pigs and a few other animals, but elephants were the prime source. A very big bull might carry 200 pounds or more of it. In the early years of the

20th Century a handful of white men spent months and even years at a time in the African bush hunting these tuskers. It was grueling, dirty, dangerous work, but it could make someone rich. And for a certain kind of person, it sure beat sitting at a desk.

One of them was Walter Dalrymple Maitland Bell, born in Scotland in 1880. From the moment he could read adventure novels, he yearned to hunt elephants. At about the age of 10, he tried to sell a pocket watch for a steamship ticket to East Africa, but the shopkeeper called the police, who returned him home. As generations of "problem" children have been, Bell was sent to boarding school. He got himself out by cracking a senior boy over the

Walter Dalrymple Maitland Bell, nicknamed Karamojo Bell, took a break from chasing elephants to be a British fighter pilot in World War I. His harvest of ivory made him a rich man, and his unusual life made him well known.

to become an ivory hunter. He was still only 22 then, so he had plenty of time.

This determination, not to mention unusual toughness and intelligence and a sense of humor, finally made him "Bell of Africa" (as one of his books was called, years later), the most famous and successful ivory hunter of all.

He sawed his first elephant skull in half to see exactly where and how big the brain was and how to slip a bullet past the bone that protected it. He peered into the gut cavity of a dead elephant while his trackers pushed spears in from the outside, to learn the angles to the vital organs. He realized that a small bullet could kill an elephant just as easily as a big one, if it was put in just the right spot.

Bolt-action .275-caliber rifles made on German Mauser actions by John Rigby & Co., in London, became his favorites. These were half the weight and one-third the price of the double-bar-

head with a cricket bat. His family went to Plan B: They packed him off to sea as a cabin boy. Bell jumped ship in New Zealand, and then worked his way home. He was still only 14, so his family sent him back to school, this time in Germany. Not for long. He escaped in an Eskimo kayak he built after reading a book about exploring the Arctic.

Bell was 16 by now. His family caved in and bought him a single-shot rifle and some ammunition and a ticket on a ship to East Africa. There he got a job hunting for meat to feed the work gangs that were building the railroad inland from the coast. No elephants, though. It took Bell six more years (and amazing adventures in the Yukon Gold Rush in Canada and the Boer War in South Africa)

Holt's Auctioneers

Karamojo Bell became famous partly because he hunted the largest land animals, elephants, with the sort of light rifles that other people used for deer. This is one of his guns: a Rigby .275 bolt-action. Bell is shown here in his 60s.

The largest pair of elephant tusks on record, 236 and 228 pounds. (Any tusks that weigh more than 100 pounds are rare.) The bull was shot in 1898 by an African slave with a blackpowder musket. An American ivory dealer paid about $5,000 for the tusks, equivalent to $120,000 today. They were never cut up for billiard balls or piano keys; these tusks are now in the Natural History Museum in London.

reled rifles that other elephant hunters used, and the ammunition was much cheaper too. (This was business. Costs had to be kept down!)

Bell became a crack shot, cool and quick under pressure. Like the professional buffalo hunters of the old American West, he also learned how to approach a herd and which elephants to kill first (and how to kill them) in order to drop as many big tuskers as possible before spooking the others.

One day on a bend in the Nile River in northeastern Uganda, shooting in a cold, hard rain and grass taller than he was—with a young native boy at his side with a backup rifle—Bell dropped 19 elephants in a row. Eleven lay so close to each other

that he could jump from one to the next without touching the ground.

This remote part of Africa was the home of the Karamojong tribe. Bell spent so much time there that he became known as Karamojo Bell. He hunted from 1902 until about 1920, with time out for trips back to civilization to sell ivory and buy supplies and occasional visits back to Scotland. He also served as a fighter pilot in the British Royal Air Force in World War I (1914–1918).

Bell killed somewhere between 1,700 and 2,000 elephants. This amounted to at least 145,000 pounds of ivory—almost 73 tons, which made him a millionaire. He was able to retire to an estate in Scotland, where his wife, Katie, was waiting, when he was only in his 40s.

Even before World War II (1939–45), shooting elephants for ivory was becoming more and more restricted, but the commercial sale of ivory

Retired NBA star Yao Ming uses his Facebook page and his popularity at home to try to convince fellow Chinese not to buy ivory carvings: "When the buying stops, the killing does too." Here he examines the carcass of an elephant poached for its ivory in northern Kenya.

Kristian Schmidt/WildAid

was banned worldwide only in 1990. This was meant to halt illegal elephant hunting, which had turned into an epidemic of unregulated killing. (Illegal hunting of any kind is called poaching.) The ban worked for a while, sort of, but now poaching has returned. In the Philippines and China especially, ivory is in huge demand for religious and art carvings, and as the value of ivory goes up, poaching has returned. Now even baby elephants are being slaughtered for their precious teeth.

Loss of habitat is also a critical problem. Human populations across southern Africa are ex-ploding, and each new highway, settlement, factory and dam chips away at game country. Even small farms can cause problems. When elephants find a new crop of maize where before there was forest or savannah, they gratefully wade in and eat. The farmer, naturally, objects and runs them off by banging pots and pans together to make a racket. After this happens a few times, elephants lose their fear and may turn on the farmer. Then they're called "problem" animals and often are shot by game wardens. It's a lose-lose situation.

People-Eaters of India

A few hunters make a specialty of wiping out genuine problem animals, especially the big cats that become man-eaters. The most famous of these hunters was a man named Jim Corbett, who was born in northern India in 1875. Between 1907 and 1940 he tracked down and killed something like 19 tigers and 14 leopards that likely had accounted for around 2,000 people.

Corbett was the son of a postmaster who had gone to India from Ireland. Until it became independent, in 1947, India was the largest colony in the British Empire (25 times bigger than England itself), and hundreds of thousands of people from England, Scotland, Ireland and Wales went to India to work. Many of them settled there and raised families.

Corbett grew up in a small town called Nainital, in the foothills of the Himalaya Range. He attended a local British school with other white children but had just as many native Indian friends, and he could speak Hindi as easily as English. From the beginning he loved hunting and fishing. He learned to shoot the old-fashioned way, first with a ratty old muzzleloader, and then, one cartridge at a time, with rifles and shotguns whose recoil belted him black and blue.

When he was 18, Corbett went to work for the Bengal and North Western Railway as a ship-ping manager. On his vacations he went back to Nainital, where he was making a name for himself as a hunter. In 1907 a government agent asked him to try to hunt down a man-eater, a tigress so notorious that the peasants thought she was a *shaitan*, an incarnation of the devil.

This particular devil came to India in 1902 when she was driven out of Nepal, where she'd already eaten some 200 people. Civilian and government hunters and even a unit of Gurkha troops went after her with no success. By the time Corbett was called in, she was taking a fresh victim every three to five days. When Corbett arrived in a tiny village called Pali, 30 miles from his hometown, he found it in a state of terror. No one dared step outside.

That evening Corbett sat under a tree, hoping the moon was bright enough to show him the tiger over his sights if she approached. With "teeth chattering, as much from fear as from cold," he sat out the long night and finally at dawn fell asleep with his head on his knees. Nothing. After a cup of tea and resolving never to do such a stupid thing again, Corbett told the headman that he would shoot some meat for the village. Three locals offered to guide him for *ghooral*, or small mountain goats. With a single-shot blackpowder army rifle,

Jim Corbett with a huge tiger known as the Bachelor of Powalgarh. India's peasants worshipped Corbett for saving them from deadly man-eating tigers and leopards.

Corbett killed three *ghooral* with three cartridges, shooting steeply uphill at 200 yards. Back at the village, Corbett's guides swore the range had been more than a mile, and, since the goats had rolled downhill almost into their laps, the Sahib's magic bullets even brought the animals to his feet! The Corbett legend was beginning to build.

Man-eating tigers are especially challenging to hunt, because they have learned human behavior. Corbett tracked this one for hours one day by following the trail of blood and body parts of a girl the tiger was carrying. Finally he decided to use hundreds of men, marching abreast with noisemakers through the forest, to drive the tiger off of the steep ridge where she lived.

The district *tahsildar*, an Indian official, insisted on backing him up with an ancient shotgun loaded with slugs. When the tiger appeared, Corbett fired his .500-caliber double-barreled rifle at her three times, at ranges from 300 to 30 yards. And then, with a wounded tiger just steps away, he was out of ammunition. He'd been overconfident; the third round had been his reserve.

Corbett grabbed the official's shotgun and turned to where the tiger crouched on a rock. He aimed at the animal's open mouth, 20 feet away, and fired. The tiger collapsed.

Corbett found the slug not in the cat's head but in its right paw; he could pluck it out with his fingers. Two bullets from his .500 were what had finally killed her. The jubilant natives lashed the carcass to stout poles and, forming a long line, passed the tiger hand-over-hand 1,000 feet up the steep ridge to where their village was.

In thanks, the lieutenant governor of the province presented Corbett with a new rifle. By coincidence, it was the same type of modern, light-weight rifle that Karamojo Bell used for his ivory hunting: a Rigby .275, built in England on a German bolt action.

Also like Bell, Corbett became a legend in his own lifetime and wrote a series of books about his adventures. They are still in print in India, where Corbett is regarded almost as a saint. His home, near Jim Corbett National Park, India's oldest wildlife reserve, is preserved as a memorial.

India's government once encouraged tiger hunting "to protect Indian men, women, and children from the savage creature" and even offered a bounty of 50 rupees for an adult tiger, with bonuses for certain man-eaters. India banned tiger hunting entirely in 1972 but, as with Africa's elephants (and so many other species), habitat loss due to human population growth has taken a terrible toll. The tiger, too, suffers from poaching; its organs are in high demand for bogus folk-medicine "cures." There were 60,000 tigers in India when Corbett was young; today the number is less than 2,000.

Wild Animals vs. Humans

Wild animals still kill humans in fairly large numbers, especially in the African and Indian countryside. Totals are hard to pin down, but it seems certain that more than 2,000 people are fatally drowned or trampled, gored, clawed or bitten every year around the world by hippos, crocodiles and alligators, lions, leopards, tigers, rhinos, buffaloes, elephants, bears, hyenas, wolves and so on. Poisonous snakes, insects and fish kill another 100,000 or more people annually. (But by far the most deadly "animal" of them all is the mosquito, carrier of malaria, yellow fever and dengue fever.) Except for crocs and gators, which grab humans to eat them—sometimes a big cat or bear will do this too—most of the attacks amount to an animal defending itself from what it sees as some kind of intrusion.

True cases of man-eating lions, leopards, tigers and bears have always been rare, but they still occur. Corbett found that Indian man-eaters were often cats that had been crippled somehow, maybe by porcupine quills, which limited them to feeding on slower, weaker prey such as people tending their farm fields. In Africa, however, at least at one time, man-eaters seemed to be healthy specimens. One theory is that lions learned to eat human flesh if they lived near the routes of the Arab slave caravans, which left a trail of dead and dying "merchandise" by the wayside for them to sample.

One of the notorious pair of mane-less lions that killed dozens of railroad workers at Tsavo, in Kenya, in 1898. The construction boss, Lieut. Col. John H. Patterson, also shown, finally hunted them down. The story became a movie, *The Ghost and the Darkness*, which was released in 1996. The mounted lions are now in the Field Museum in Chicago.

(Slaves were known as "black ivory," because the slavers forced their captives to carry elephant tusks to the trading posts, where then all were sold. Mass slavery was not wiped out in Africa until after World War I.)

The notorious lions of Tsavo, however, that killed somewhere between 35 and 135 railroad construction workers in 1898, may have turned to eating humans because of a rinderpest epidemic that wiped out their normal prey, Cape buffalo and cattle, in that part of Kenya.

Hunting with Gun & Movie Camera

True man-eaters have always made the headlines. Until fairly recently, such news stories fed directly into most people's idea of predators as cruel and savage killers—ravenous wild beasts that attacked on sight and made life in the wilderness a daily test of courage.

The *Born Free* books, movies and TV program of the 1960s and '70s pretty much finished

off this notion. Millions of people learned that African lions can behave like oversize golden retrievers, and even lions that aren't used to humans often have very different personalities and roles in their family groups. Today, with nature documentaries available on a dozen cable channels and the Internet, we take this sort of filming (and knowledge) for granted, but it began almost a century ago with

Osa Johnson on the East African savannah with one of her lever-action .405-caliber Winchester Model 95s. The *New York Times* described her as a "crack performer with a rifle."

a couple from Kansas named Martin Johnson and Osa Leighty.

Just five feet tall and no tomboy, when Osa was still in her teens, she became an expert with a rifle and, almost by accident, one of the world's top big-game shots. She also became an explorer, a filmmaker and lecturer, a naturalist, an aviator and finally a best-selling author and entrepreneur and even a *fashionista*. Today she would be a role model; nearly a century ago, when women were the "weaker sex," Osa was simply extraordinary.

In 1910, when she was 16 and without telling her parents, she married a man named Martin Johnson. Johnson had come home to Kansas with photos that he'd taken in the South Pacific, while sailing as the cook on the famous author Jack London's yacht. Martin thought he'd make a few dollars by selling tickets to illustrated lectures about his adventures. He must have been good at it, for he

found not only a career but also a wife and business partner. He had hired Osa to sing at his slide shows and, well, one thing led to another.

Together Martin and Osa made two expeditions of their own to remote South Pacific islands, this time with movie cameras, to film headhunters and cannibals. The results were spectacular. Audiences from New York to Los Angeles were especially fascinated by Osa herself—the "plucky little wife" (barely in her 20s) who shared her husband's hair-raising adventures.

Then the Johnsons shifted their focus to wild animals instead of people. After an expedition to Borneo, they decided to try East Africa. They arrived in Kenya in 1921, just as the age of the motorized safari was beginning. Martin and Osa learned to drive, and then set off into the bush—luckily with the help of Kenya's first game warden, the legendary Blayney Percival.

In Borneo, Martin had learned how to approach and photograph wild animals; Osa had learned how to shoot and when. Osa was also learning to cope with years away from her family and civilization. One of her priorities in the bush became always to create a home. Whether it was a tent or a cabin, Osa decorated and furnished it comfortably and planted gardens and laid out walkways. She brought what we'd call comfort food and packed dressy clothes, not just hunting gear. And she always had pets in camp—birds, orphan monkeys or antelopes and once a baby elephant.

Martin and Osa never had children. Their partnership managed to be loving, equal and professional all at the same time. The credits in their many films always read "Mr. and Mrs. Martin Johnson," but Osa became famous as herself. This was partly because she was often on camera. Sometimes she was clowning around—stopping to "powder her nose" in the wilderness or dancing with African pygmies to a jazz record—but often it was clear that she was at some risk from animals or tribesmen. It was also because audiences knew that it was Osa who handled the guns. Martin worked behind the camera; Osa, when she wasn't on-screen, protected him from whatever he was filming. She also shot most of the meat for them and their camp staff, which she considered her "wifely duty."

While filming elephants once, Martin decided that one bull was such a magnificent specimen that he just had to have the tusks. He turned the camera over to Osa and picked up a rifle. At the shot, the bull turned and charged—followed by six other elephants. Martin fired again and once more, and then he turned and ran. The elephants still came. Osa kept cranking the camera till the very last second—this was great footage!—and then snatched up her rifle and fired one shot. The huge bull collapsed almost on top of the camera, and the other elephants scattered.

In 1923 the Johnsons came home with the first of many African movies. To sell tickets, theaters tried to sensationalize the films, but they showed animals as they really were, not the maddened, bloodthirsty beasts of popular imagination—nor the caged animals that

Borneo, 1920. Osa, apparently dressed for the camera, checks out a crocodile she has shot; it is being pulled ashore by a cable around its neck.

Osa tinkers with a new rifle, a Springfield modified by Griffin & Howe of New York, while Martin looks on. The scope, she wrote, was "wonderful till it got a slight jar. We have come to the conclusion that the open sight is the best in the long run, at least for Africa."

some other filmmakers relied on. Martin and Osa's movies were not only entertaining, they also were praised as an authentic record of wilderness that even then was disappearing fast.

The Johnsons earned the support of the American Museum of Natural History and the Explorers Club. They also became close friends with Carl Akeley, the great naturalist and taxidermist, and George Eastman, head of the Kodak film company, and many other important people. The next time the Johnsons set off for Africa, they had 21 cameras and mountains of supplies carried by six safari cars, four trucks, five mule wagons, four oxcarts and 200 porters. They also packed 18 guns and more than a ton of ammunition.

Osa wrote: "Anyone seeing the arsenal . . . would have been justified in assuming that we were out to kill animals quite as much as to photograph them in their wild state. It was merely a precautionary measure, however, and took into account the series of emergencies that might arise over a period of four to five years."

Their "arsenal" included three .470 Nitro Express double rifles, five bolt-actions

Not until after Martin died, in 1937, was Osa billed under her own name. This is a poster for a movie based on her book called *I Married Adventure*. With a zebra-striped cover, it became the No. 1 nonfiction best-seller of 1940.

(a .275 and a .303, two .404s and a .505) and four lever-actions (three .405s and one .32, all Winchesters). The lighter rifles were for shooting meat, the heavier ones for protection against elephants, buffaloes, lions and rhinos. They also had four shotguns—two pumpguns (a 12-gauge Winchester and a short-barreled 20-gauge Ithaca) and two doubles (a 12-gauge Parker and a 20-gauge Ithaca)—plus two Colt revolvers (a .45 and a .38).

As their success grew, the Johnsons wrote books and magazine articles and appeared in many news stories. Their expeditions became more and more elaborate. By 1930 they were shooting "talkies," or movies with sound. In 1932 they learned to fly and bought airplanes: two Sikorsky flying boats, which could land on water or ground. (One was named *Osa's Ark* and was painted in zebra

stripes; the other, *Spirit of Africa*, got giraffe spots.) Martin and Osa flew more than 60,000 miles over Africa, filming from the air and getting to even more distant areas.

Martin died in 1937 in a plane crash—not in the African bush but in California, while he and Osa were traveling by commercial airliner. Osa was heartbroken, but she recovered from her injuries and went on to become even more famous.

By now she was a member of the American Museum of Natural History, the Society of Women Geographers, the National Wildlife Federation, the Girl Scouts of America, and the Adventurers' Club. The animals in her children's stories were made into stuffed toys called Osa Johnson's Pets. Osa was appointed an honorary chairman of National Wildlife Federation Week. She was even named one of America's 12 best-dressed women.

This led to a line of "luxury sportswear" called Osafari in colors like Maasai Bronze, Kenya Blue and Uganda Flame. *Cosmopolitan* Magazine published Osa's wild-game recipes. Osa became a character in a newspaper comic strip called *Danger Trails*. She authored two best-selling books about her life that led to a TV program called *Osa Johnson's Big Game Hunt*. And more and more. Osa died of a heart attack in her New York City apartment in 1953. A few years later, as a final tribute to an unusual couple and an exceptional woman, her friends and family created the Martin and Osa Johnson Safari Museum in her hometown of Chanute, Kansas.

While they were in Kenya, Martin once wrote: "I got a great film and turned to Osa. She had her half-completed dress thrown over her shoulder, a thimble on one finger, the needle with the thread dangling hanging from her mouth, and her .405 Winchester all ready for action. It struck me as the most ridiculous thing I had ever seen, to see a dressmaker ready to shoot elephants."

Ridiculous, that is, unless one of the elephants turned on him again.

A Bad Day with Buffalo

Ever had a bad day—maybe a broken fingernail, a yucky pimple in the middle of your forehead or, worse yet, an unpleasant exchange of texts with your boyfriend? For Niki Ensign Atcheson, a bad day is when almost a ton of Cape buffalo falls on top of you.

In 1959 Dr. Len Ensign and his lab-technician wife, Marti, decided to leave California and join a bush hospital in East Africa. They packed up their infant daughter, Niki—Nicole—and set off for Belgium to learn French and study tropical medicine. The family eventually settled at Kibuye Hospital Station in what is now Burundi. Life there was not unlike living on a ranch in a remote part of the Dakotas. There were few comforts and endless chores for everyone, including Niki: "By the time I was five, I had helped deliver lots of babies and helped set broken limbs, amputate limbs, sterilize operating-room trays, and just about anything else you can think of."

Between his medical duties, her dad hunted for meat. Niki helped skin the animals and learned to make jerky. But she was too little to carry a gun.

Eventually Niki went to college in the US and got a degree in marine biology. She married into a shellfish-farming family named Taylor, did research in Hawaii and the Virgin Islands, and had two daughters. As she approached 30, however, memories of Africa returned: "I remember puff adders, village drums, the smell of steamy red earth in rainy season and bouts of malaria. I remember sparks from the hunting campfire throwing themselves toward the starry Africa sky like little fireflies in a crazed dance. You get hooked on Africa, and you just can't let it go."

Niki wanted to return to Africa, this time to hunt—for the kind of beast that's able to gore, stomp and mutilate you if you make a mistake.

African hunting can be very pricey, but the family business was prospering and Niki began plan-

Niki Ensign with friends at Kibuye Hospital in East Africa, early in the 1960s. Living in the bush was a never-ending adventure that finally drew her back to Africa when she was an adult, this time to hunt big game.

ning. She took an NRA hunter-safety course, and then it was time to select a rifle. At the time, the family "arsenal" consisted of an air gun with which one of her daughters had done some mischief. Instead of starting with a .22 rimfire, for her first gun Niki chose a .375 H&H Magnum. She is five feet two inches tall; the stock was way too long, and the recoil walloped her.

Niki knew that, with no hunting or shooting experience, she wasn't the ideal client, especially

Niki Atcheson in Zimbabwe with legendary PH John Sharp and one of her favorite trophies: a solitary old Cape buffalo bull. This safari was in 2010, long after she had recovered from her terrible injuries and gone back to hunting. Niki is holding "Baby," her .458 Lott. The Jack Russell terrier is on guard.

to hunt dangerous game. So she contacted safari companies as "Nik Taylor" to hide the fact that she was a girl. Her search led to Jack Atcheson & Sons, Inc., well known as "worldwide hunting consultants since 1955." Keith Atcheson, one of the sons, recommended Russ Broom Safaris. By now her cover was blown, but despite Niki's "girlness," the firm agreed to take a chance on her. A large cash deposit likely helped.

To get ready, Niki said, "I slept with my gun. I vacuumed with my gun. I did dishes with my gun. I gardened with my gun. I shot and shot my gun." Finally, in 1995, a very excited Niki was off to Zimbabwe. She bagged a dugga boy (an old Cape buffalo bull that's gotten so cranky even the other buffalo don't want him around any longer), a huge leopard and some plains game. She also signed up for another safari the following year. That yielded a second dugga boy, a huge old elephant and another leopard. She bought a more powerful rifle and learned to reload her own ammunition.

Along the way, she and Keith Atcheson had both been divorced, and they decided to join forces. With five children and hunting on both sides, their

newly blended family was like the Brady Bunch, if the Brady Bunch had been heavily armed. Keith had another company called Hunters Montana, where Niki began guiding for deer, elk, antelope and bighorn sheep. Today she says that guiding is more rewarding than hunting.

By 2004 Keith and Niki had been on safari many times. She had taken 12 buffalo (Cape, water and bison), two elephants, lions, leopards and all manner of other game. She also had a new rifle: a bolt-action CZ, caliber .458 Lott, that she christened "Baby." In the not-so-gentle world of big-game hunting, the Lott (named for its inventor, Jack Lott) is a "snot-flyer." It kicks.

That year Keith and Niki were back in Zimbabwe with three dugga boys on their wish list. Five days into the hunt she got her shot and slammed a 500-grain bullet into a bull. The buffalo disappeared into the bush, but there was plenty of blood trail to follow. They tracked it for the rest of the day and were up before dawn the next. Mindful that dangerous animals are even more dangerous when wounded, Niki rechecked her rifle and ammunition, and the search resumed. The forest was silent. Then, in a moment of inattention, the wounded bull came for her. The PH got off a shot; no effect. Niki swung up her rifle to shoot, but the muzzle hit the buffalo's nose. She was spun around and flattened facedown on the ground.

The buffalo drove one horn into the back of her right thigh and, with a snap of its neck, flipped her six feet in the air. To get the bull's attention, Keith kicked the buff in its rear end. It spun to face him, and he put the muzzle of his .416 on its forehead and fired. The bull fell, thrashing and kicking, on top of Niki and died. Niki was alive, but she'd been at the convergence of two mortal threats: a maddened animal and the possibility of a bad shot from those trying to save her.

This was her 13th buffalo, and the date was June 13th—but who's superstitious?

Keith, the PH and the trackers rolled the animal off of her. In addition to a colossal puncture wound in the back of her leg, Niki had a broken arm, broken ribs and a broken collarbone and was bleeding in her brain. She could feel body fluids sloshing around inside and believed she was dying.

Then began a 19-hour trip to a hospital in Johannesburg where Niki had five surgeries and skin grafts. Today Niki is fully functional, although the scar on her leg has left her, as she says, "bikini-challenged."

Niki is now a grandmother, but her golden curls and general demeanor are more like a high-school cheerleader's. She still hunts big game too. When describing her ordeal and buffalo hunting in general, Niki is quite matter-of-fact. Ask her, though, about lion hunting, and the smile vanishes and her voice takes on a tone of doom. That's another story.

Hunting for Meat & Sport

Commercial hunting for ivory—or skins, meat, feathers or some other part of a wild animal to sell—is generally illegal everywhere. Hunting animals that hunt us or our livestock is rare, but it still occurs. And many people around the world still hunt to put meat on their own table. Few of us would starve without it, though, so it's probably better to say that many hunters make a point of eating what they kill, and they use this as one of their reasons for hunting.

All around us, even in city parks, the struggle for life and death goes on forever: Spiders trap and eat flies, songbirds pluck spiders from their webs, hawks swoop down on songbirds, and so on. Within a few miles of downtown New York, Chicago and Los Angeles, coyotes kill and eat deer. Visit Yellowstone National Park on your family vacation, and you may see a bear or a pack of wolves eating a bison. The predator-prey relationship means survival.

One of the benefits of civilization is that we no longer need to kill and butcher our own meat; a vast industry has been created to do it for us. Because of this, some people now think that hunting is cruel and should be banned. Most people who oppose hunting buy meat from a market and wear leather shoes and belts and carry leather handbags, all products of this industry. Few of them, however, give a thought to how cattle, pigs and sheep are

Steve Helsley

This Colorado elk was hunted for meat. Now the work begins; it has to be field-dressed, gotten out of the woods, skinned and then butchered. Do this just once and you'll gain new respect for a hamburger—and for hunters.

"processed" for market. They don't understand ethical hunting either, or the relationship between hunting and conservation, or the fact that most hunters don't really like the act of killing—but if they don't do it, they're not hunters.

Which is more natural: stalking and killing a deer in its natural environment with a well-placed bullet and then butchering it yourself, or buying a steak from a cow that was raised in a pen on chemically enhanced feed and then trucked to a factory that slaughtered and cut it up on an assembly line?

There are now too many people in the world for everyone to hunt their own meat; and slaughterhouses supposedly treat animals more humanely than they once did. But many hunters regard what they do as the most honest form of "shopping" for meat, just as many people grow their own vegetables in a garden. And, just as gardeners take care of their fields and plants, hunters watch over their natural resources. The sale of hunting licenses and the taxes on guns and ammunition raise many millions of dollars each year in the US alone, and much of this money goes to wildlife management and conservation.

Hunting also helps keep game populations in balance, since four-legged predators such as wolves and mountain lions were wiped out long ago in much of the US. (Which was done mostly for the benefit of people who raise cattle, pigs and sheep for market.)

Hunting for Trophies

Trophy hunting has an especially bad reputation among people who believe that mankind should no longer kill wild animals, especially for sport. Trophy hunting means finding and killing the best-possible example of some kind of game animal as an example of the hunter's skill. (Hunting demands physical fitness and woodcraft, a certain steadiness under pressure, and skill with a gun or a bow.) Although trophy hunting isn't hunting for food, the meat isn't wasted. In wilderness areas it may go to a nearby village or be eaten by the hunter and camp staff. It's not always possible to do this, but the hunter might bring the meat home, or it might be taken to a butcher shop to be sold.

Often now the meat is distributed to families in need. Back in 1989 a friend of ours named Ron Hickman, with his wife, Marcia Hair, set up a network called Deer Atlanta, in Georgia. They put hunters and butcher shops together with the Atlanta Community Food Bank, and the result was that thousands of pounds of healthy, low-cholesterol, low-fat venison (deer meat) were given to underprivileged people in the city. This program was so successful that it was copied by hunting groups across the country. Now Safari Club International, through its Sportsmen Against Hunger campaign, donates more than

Days of stalking in the Kalahari region of southern Africa resulted in this grand kudu bull with spectacular spiral horns. The hunter is Kim Gattone: "There's something so pure about hunting and stalking. The more arduous the hunt, the more I enjoy it, and it's all the more rewarding to work so hard for the harvest. At home in Montana I hunt to fill the freezer with my favorite meat: elk and antelope."

a half-million pounds of wild game meat and fish to charitable organizations every year.

The trophy itself—the horns or antlers, skull and/or skin is part of the hunter's reward. Keeping a trophy is as natural as hunting itself, and it should be a sign of our respect for the animal. A trophy is also a remembrance of days in the field and the rare experience, the awe and excitement, of being a natural predator once again.

However, man is not only a predator, he is also a competitor. (The two are almost but not quite the same thing.) The larger a rack of antlers, or the heavier a pair of tusks or the bigger a bearskin, the more we value them. "Mine is bigger than yours," so I am a better hunter and provider than you. But this isn't necessarily so; outstanding trophies have been taken easily, by sheer luck, sometimes within steps of camp. And sometimes trophies can be bought with money. A worthwhile trophy, though, usually calls for many days in the field, with hard work and sweat, frustration and disappointment before final success.

In Africa the trophies most in demand are called the "Big Five": leopard, lion, Cape buffalo, rhinoceros and elephant. They're impressive, sometimes-dangerous animals that are challenging to hunt. (The leopard isn't big—rarely more than 200 pounds—but it is very wary, utterly courageous and unearthly quick. A wounded leopard defending itself with fangs and claws has been compared to a chainsaw with its throttle stuck wide open.) Hunting the Big Five is expensive too, and often the bigger or rarer the trophy, the bigger its price tag.

Unfortunately, when money is on the line, people sometimes take shortcuts. They buy or breed animals with bigger antlers or longer manes or whatever, and then they pen them up so that their clients can find and shoot them more easily. The hunting company makes money, and the hunter comes away with a trophy that he or she hasn't really earned.

This gives trophy hunting a bad name even among hunters. It is the very opposite of pursuing a truly wild animal on foot and then killing it cleanly, with a gun or bow: fair-chase hunting for free-range game.

One of the most famous of the old-time white hunters of East Africa, Philip Percival, used to say, "If you want to have a nice hunt, leave the tape measure at home." In other words, forget sheer size and your name in the record books and concentrate on the quality of the experience instead—the wonders of the scenery and wildlife; being in the bush, with its evenings around the campfire with new and old friends; and finding, outwitting and at last taking a fine trophy. That is, an impressive old animal that has made its contribution to the gene pool (left behind many offspring) and is nearing the end of its natural life.

It may not make sense at first, but this kind of trophy hunting is also the surest way to protect wild game. In Africa, for example, tribal people who live in the bush generally regard wild animals as a nuisance. Lions and leopards prey on their goats and cattle (and threaten them and their families), while other game, from elephants to warthogs, raid their crops. Given the chance, they kill these animals any way they can, often with traps or poison, even if it's illegal. But if the tribe gets a share of the money that visitors pay for the privilege of hunting there, wild animals become a resource to be protected. The local people get not only some of the cash but also the game meat. So "if it pays, it stays."

Trophy hunting helps prevent poaching too. Game rangers and their scouts, no matter how well trained or equipped, can't patrol everywhere at once. Sport hunters and their guides and trackers are out on the land, paying attention to what's going on, and often are the first to discover any signs of illegal killing of game.

Hunting is no longer for everyone, but for people who accept that humans are natural predators and who have the desire and the skills, it can be both thrilling and deeply satisfying.

Hunting Gamebirds

Big-game hunting usually requires a rifle or possibly a high-powered revolver (or a bow and arrows, but this book is about guns). We say "usually," because some places limit deer hunters to shotguns loaded with slugs or buckshot. Many people hunt small game—squirrels, rabbits, even foxes—with shotguns, because they're hard to hit with a single bullet. And at least as many people hunt gamebirds, like pheasants, grouse, quail, ducks and geese, and this absolutely requires a shotgun.

So other than for small game and deer in those restricted areas, hunting with a shotgun is called wingshooting. That is, shooting things while they're on the wing, flying.

Oops, one more exception: Turkeys, although they are technically gamebirds and hunted with shotguns, are shot while they're on the ground, so turkey hunting is not wingshooting.

(We've always wondered about this. A wild turkey on the wing is an impressive and challenging target, so why not hunt them with dogs and flush them into the air before we shoot, the way we do other upland birds?)

It isn't that we can't shoot pheasants or grouse or ducks on the ground—or in a tree or while they're swimming on a pond—it's that we shouldn't. It isn't sporting, which is what modern hunting is all about. When hunters have to put food on the table or else starve, any method of harvesting game is acceptable. Today, however, putting food on the table typically means going to the market, and hunting has become a sport (although a sport that connects us with our roots as predators). Therefore, we try, sort of, to make every kind of hunting more challenging. Hunting isn't meant to be slaughter any more; it means fitting ourselves back into the basic predator–prey relationship, which improves our most ancient human skills and gets us attuned to the natural environment.

Hitting a strong, fast-flying wild bird while it's in the air is usually harder than shooting a standing animal with a rifle. But when we

Terry Allen

Happy hunter with a Texas pheasant. Bird hunting means walking the uplands with a keen-nosed dog, and then being able to hit a fast-flying target when it flushes into the air. This is Georgia Pellegrini, author of *Girl Hunter*.

were kids and found out that shotguns fire pellets that spread out in flight, we were horrified. That sounded too easy, like cheating! Then we tried it—and have spent most of the years since then trying to become decent wingshots.

Waterfowl—ducks, geese, snipe and so on—live on the water. Upland gamebirds live on dry ground. "Uplands" are hillsides, meadows, woodlands and so on—any natural area that's drier than a marsh. In North America upland gamebirds include pheasants, ruffed and prairie grouse, chukar and Hungarian partridge, doves, woodcock, several kinds of quail and a few other similar species. Most upland gamebirds live in flocks or coveys. Upland hunters walk the woods and fields with dogs trained to find birds by scent, and then they flush them into the air for a shot. A wild bird rocketing out of its hiding place can be noisy and startling. Some gamebirds can hit 50 or 60 miles per hour. All have different flight patterns. A great big pheasant flushing out of a cornfield and flying away in the open can be a fairly easy target; a ruffed grouse exploding from a hawthorn thicket and dodging away through thick pines is a very difficult target.

Upland birds have learned to be wary for a simple reason: They taste good. Every predator, from foxes to hawks to humans, likes to eat them.

Bird hunting is legally regulated; there are specific seasons and limits, which vary from state to state or country to country, and some species—certain doves, for example—that are gamebirds in one place may be protected "songbirds" in another. And, just as with big game, it's possible to hunt gamebirds that have been specially raised and put

out for the gun. This is usually more sporting than it is for four-legged animals; birds can't be fenced in, at least not if they're going to fly. They're bred in pens, but then they are released. You'll find a lot of difference between pen-raised birds, though. If they're released to fend for themselves when they're young, they learn to behave and fly much more like wild birds than if they're let out the day before (or even the same day) the hunters arrive.

In "Shooting in Fashion" we mention British-style driven-bird shooting. This is more or less the opposite of American bird hunting (which the British call "walk-up" or "rough" shooting): The hunters wait for the birds to come to them. The Guns stand in a long line, usually at the foot of a hill or behind a stand of trees, and shoot at birds that fly over them. The birds—pheasants, partridges or red grouse—are driven toward the Guns by beaters, a line of people walking slowly through the brush, sometimes for a couple of miles. This kind of shooting is done on private estates that have professional gamekeepers to look after the birds, deer and other animals. The "keepers" know where the birds roost and feed and where to station the Guns and how to push the birds toward them.

To people who've never done it, driven shooting sounds too easy to be sporting. You just stand there? And the birds come to you? True but, done properly, with the birds flying over the guns at high altitude and often with the wind behind them, it's anything but easy. As you can probably guess, it's also very expensive—unless your family owns the estate.

Waterfowl

Hunting for waterfowl, sometimes called wildfowling, usually involves ducks and geese, and sometimes snipe and rails. In a few places hunters may take swans or cranes. There are many huntable ducks—mallards, wigeon, two species

of teal, canvasbacks, black ducks and more—and just a few geese. Naturally, the birds spend much of their time on rivers, lakes, ponds or salt water.

Waterfowlers usually hide in blinds to wait for birds to land nearby, either on water or in fields.

Steve Helsley

A day's bag of Canada geese shot over the grainfields where the birds go to feed. Waterfowlers often use decoys and calls to lure the birds out of the sky and into shooting range.

They put out decoys to try to lure the birds out of the sky, and they use duck and goose calls to get the birds' attention as they fly by.

Gamebird and waterfowl species (and hunting seasons) are different in different parts of the US. A deer is a deer, and the males have antlers, but it isn't always so easy in bird hunting and waterfowling, where you have to be able to identify the species and often tell male from female before you pull the trigger. Depending on where you live, you may be limited to just one deer per year, but you might be allowed up to five mallards, for example, or one black duck each day. Exceed the legal limit on any species, and you're a poacher and now fair game yourself—for game wardens.

The Bird Hunter's Blue Sky Rule

Muzzle control is one of the absolute, never-forget-it rules. An AD, or accidental discharge, is just a scary moment if the gun is pointed in a harmless direction. For bird hunters, muzzle control means following the Blue Sky Rule: Don't shoot at a bird unless you can see sky around it. That means the bird is high enough in the air that your shot won't hit another hunter (or a dog) on the ground. The pheasant hunter who accidentally shot one of us forgot the Blue Sky Rule.

Becoming an Outdoors Woman

BOW, Becoming an Outdoors Woman, is an international organization that helps women of all ages learn shooting, hunting, archery, fishing, skiing, kayaking, four-wheeling, camping and other outdoor activities. BOW programs provide hands-on instruction and experience that build confidence and also connections between women. A normal BOW workshop is a three-day weekend in a supportive and non-threatening environment. BOW was launched at the University of Wisconsin–Stevens Point's College of Natural Resources by Dr. Christine Thomas in 1991. Today there are BOW chapters in 47 states and six Canadian provinces as well as one in New Zealand; many of them are connected to universities or government fish and game departments. They're easy to find on the Internet.

Bird Dogs

One of best things about hunting upland birds or waterfowl is having a dog to hunt with you. Dogs are not only great companions but also have keen senses of smell, hearing and eyesight, which all help the hunter find and retrieve downed game. A dog that's one of the pointing breeds (English setter, German shorthair, Brittany and others) sniffs out a gamebird's hiding place, and then stands and points to it with its nose until the hunter has caught up. Then the hunter moves in to flush the bird into the air for a shot.

Labrador retrievers, golden retrievers, cocker spaniels and other breeds are flushing dogs. They smell a hidden bird, and then they flush it by themselves, so the hunter has to keep up and be ready.

Dogs also find the fallen birds. Because of their coloring, which camouflages them in their habitat, dead birds can be hard to find without a dog's sharp nose. A dog also can track and grab a wounded bird that's trying to get away.

Waterfowl dogs aren't used to point. The dog sits by the hunter till it's time to fetch a duck or goose that has fallen in the water or in a field. Labrador and Chesapeake Bay retrievers and other

Terry Allen

Bird dogs (like this springer spaniel) not only find and sometimes flush the game, but they also retrieve the dead birds and find wounded ones.

dogs that don't mind cold water were bred especially for swimming to the birds and bringing them back in their mouths.

Turkeys

Wild turkeys look nothing like the fat white farm birds we see on TV every Thanksgiving. They're beautifully camouflaged to fit into their habitat and much stronger and warier than domestic turkeys. Benjamin Franklin thought the wild turkey, not the bald eagle, should be the symbol of America. At up to 25 pounds, the turkey is the largest of North America's gamebirds. It's also a native species, not an exotic brought in from Europe or Asia. (Pheasants originally came from China, Hungarian partridge from—well, you can guess.) In the 1970s state fish and game departments across America set out to re-establish the turkey, which had disappeared from much of its original range because of overhunting. These programs succeeded beyond anyone's expectations, and now wild turkeys can be found in about every state except Alaska.

As we pointed out earlier, turkeys are the only birds that hunters kill on the ground. To not destroy the meat, hunters try to shoot them in the head; the head is a very small target, so the firearm of choice is a shotgun that delivers a tight cluster of shot big and heavy enough to be lethal out to 50 yards or so. Turkeys are wary, and it can be difficult to get close to them.

National Wild Turkey Federation

Keen-eyed and wary, wild turkeys are a challenge for hunters, who have to lure them into range with calls and decoys. Benjamin Franklin thought the turkey, not the bald eagle, should be the symbol of America.

Turkeys have very sharp eyesight, so hunters camouflage themselves from head to toe. In the spring, they sit in a likely spot and use a call that sounds like a hen to try to lure the males, or toms, into range. In the fall, hunters use calls to attract toms or hens, both of which are legal (in states that have fall turkey seasons).

Shotguns for Birds

Different gamebirds require different shotguns and ammunition. You can't always count on bringing down a big goose or pheasant—flying maybe 60 yards away and armored with thick feathers—with the same light gun and load that's best for small quail or woodcock that flush at 10 yards.

Shotgun pellets spread out in flight, and the farther they go, the more open the shot pattern becomes. Waterfowl and sometimes pheasants are often shot at near maximum range, which is about 50 to 65 yards for most shotgunners. At that distance, the spread of pellets from a light gun and shotshell might not be enough; usually you need to put at least three or four pellets into a big bird to bring it down. So, to keep their shot patterns dense enough to be effective, many wildfowlers and pheasant hunters use guns with tighter chokes and shells that pack a lot of big pellets.

This might be a 12-gauge Magnum or even a 10-gauge, firing up to 1¾ ounces of large pellets in a cartridge that's 3½ inches long. The recoil from such loads can be pretty nasty, so hunters usually shoot them in semi-automatic guns, whose mechanisms absorb some of the kick. (Really, except at long range, a somewhat lighter gun and cartridge work just as well or even better. Extra shot won't make up for bad shooting.)

Old-time market hunters sometimes used 8-gauge and even 4-gauge guns or small cannons called punt guns to kill as many birds as possible, but today the 10-gauge is the largest shotgun legal for hunting.

At the other end of the bird hunting scale are the people who hike the uplands for small, lightly feathered birds that flush at close range and dodge away through the brush. These hunters want light, easy-handling shotguns with cartridges that carry enough shot to do the job but don't tear the birds to pieces (or knock the hunters silly with recoil). More and more upland hunters now carry 28-gauge guns that weigh a lot less than big goose guns and that fire only three-quarters of an ounce of small pellets.

Most shotgun pellets are lead, because it's very dense and heavy and hits hard. But lead is poisonous, so for some uses lead shot is banned. (For duck hunting, for example. Water birds may eat fallen lead pellets by accident, which can kill

Terry Allen

A bird gun—light, quick-handling, often custom-fitted. This is an English double-barreled 12-gauge with a brace (pair) of British red grouse, maybe the speediest gamebird of all.

them.) Then nontoxic shot, made of steel or alloys of molybdenum, tungsten or other metals, has to be used instead.

Punt Guns & Market Hunting

Back in the days when ships were made of wood and driven by sails, one of the most common naval weapons was the swivel gun: a light cannon, four or five feet long and with a bore diameter of 1½ inches or so. At first it was loaded with a ramrod from the muzzle; later versions were breechloaders. Swivel guns were mounted on a ship's rail or in the fighting tops, the platforms on the masts where marines were stationed to shoot down onto the enemy's deck. Swivel guns were smoothbores and usually loaded with clusters of large shot, to cut down gangs of sailors at close range, when the ships had battered each other with their heavy cannons and were now alongside. Giant shotguns, in other words.

A swivel gun also could be put in the bow of a boat that was manned by a crew of oarsmen under the command of a lieutenant or midshipman. It was just the thing for holding off hostile natives

A modern-day punt-gunner fires a blackpowder cartridge. In Britain it is still legal to hunt waterfowl with these cannons, which have to be maneuvered very carefully into range; decoys, however, are considered unsporting.

when landing on a South Sea island to top up the ship's supply of fresh water.

It didn't take long for hunters to realize that a gun like this could also be deadly on flocks of ducks and geese sitting on the water.

Notions of fair chase or sportsmanship didn't enter into it; this was business, pure and simple. Market hunting in great-great-granddad's day didn't mean going to the mall and hanging out at the food court. Into the early 1900s, market hunting in America meant harvesting game, birds mostly, to sell to butcher shops and restaurants. In 1860 a pair of mallard ducks, plucked and cleaned, might bring as much as $1.25 in a city, not counting the value of the feathers. That's about $35 in today's money. (The feathers went to clothing, bedding and furniture makers. Everything from ladies' hats to overstuffed chairs and bed quilts required feathers.)

Market hunters came up with something similar to a naval swivel gun called a punt gun. A punt is a light, shallow boat with a flat bottom and a squared-off bow. Hunters also called them sneak boats, particularly in America. Instead of oars or paddles, a punt has a push pole.

A punt gun is a huge shotgun, or a small cannon, that's aimed out over the front of the

boat. Punt guns have a bore diameter of 1½ to 2 inches or so and can weigh a hundred pounds or more. Big ones can fire two pounds of lead pellets, or scrap metal, at a time. A lucky shot can kill dozens of waterfowl at once. The recoil is ferocious, so big punt guns are mounted on the boat with springs or rubber straps to absorb the shock.

Punt guns are still legal in Britain, where they're heavily regulated and a handful of diehard traditionalists still use them.

Standard operating procedure is for a punt-gunner to pole or sail his boat out to where flocks of birds have gathered on the water to sleep for the night. As the sun comes up, he maneuvers quietly into position, and then, before the birds fly away to their daytime feeding grounds, he fires his one shot. There's rarely any chance for a follow-up; whatever birds aren't down are gone for good. (In the old days, groups of punt-gunners working together could kill more than 500 ducks in one massed volley.) Then the gunner stands up and

Market hunting wasn't just for birds. Bison (American buffalo) were almost exterminated by commercial hunters. They were shot mostly for their hides, but this is a pile of skulls that were collected to be ground up for fertilizer. Before the Civil War there were millions of buffalo on the plains. By 1890 only about 2,000 were left. Today American bison numbers have grown back to about a half-million, and limited hunting is allowed.

poles over to pick up his bag. Usually there are cripples to be finished off with a shotgun.

Market hunting of any sort, with guns or nets or by using bait, began to be banned across the United States in 1900 as waterfowl populations were being hit hard. The largest bag recorded in the US is said to be 3,008 ducks taken over eight days at Bath, Illinois, by three hunters in 1901. But it wasn't just ducks and geese that were being slaughtered. In 1909 President Theodore Roosevelt created the first of what would become the US Forest Service's National Wildlife Refuges. This was Pelican Island, in Florida, where millions of herons and egrets were being killed to provide feathers for ladies' hats.

In 1897 an English sportsman by the name of Sir Ralph Payne-Gallwey tested punt guns. He found that a 175-pound muzzleloading punt gun with a two-inch bore firing six to seven ounces of black powder and two pounds of lead BB shot (about 2,560 pellets) would put two-thirds of its pellets into a 12-foot-square target at 70 yards.

By comparison, a 12-gauge Magnum, the shotgun of choice for many duck hunters today, fires just 75 lead BB shot. From a tightly choked gun barrel, at 70 yards the pellets will spread out to a ragged circle perhaps four feet across.

Using Enough Gun

A punt gun is too much gun. Back in 1966 a book called *Use Enough Gun: On Hunting Big Game* was published in America. The author, Robert Ruark, had died the year before, when he was only 49. Although he wasn't around for very long, Ruark became wealthy and famous thanks to a string of very popular books and magazine stories, many of which had something to do with hunting.

Use Enough Gun was based on Ruark's experiences as a hunter, which began when he was 8 years old, in North Carolina. By 1951 he'd made enough money as a writer to be able to hunt in Africa and India. By the time he finished *Use Enough Gun*, he had been on safari many times.

When it came to hunting and guns, Ruark knew what he was talking about, and he had a lot of valuable things to say about proper hunting manners. At least two of his hunting sayings are still widely remembered today. One of them is that a Cape buffalo "looks like you owe him money." This is the exact quote; it means that he's looking at you.

(We hope that someday you, too, will be able to go to Africa and see Cape buffalo in the wild.

This hunter in Tanzania—*Sports Afield* editor-in-chief Diana Rupp—used enough gun, a bolt-action .375 H&H Magnum, to kill her monster Cape buffalo with one shot. (The PH had her fire one more shot as "stay-dead" insurance, but it wasn't necessary.) Will your bullet hit hard enough or reach far enough to kill? Can you hit what you're aiming at?

Even if he's feeding peacefully, when a Cape buffalo bull spots you, he picks up his head—with those curving, wicked horns—and stares balefully into your eyes, seemingly wondering whether he should come over and flatten you now or finish eating first.)

J. Scott Rupp

Ruark's other famous phrase is "Use enough gun." He meant enough to do the job, to kill quickly and cleanly. Not only the rifle and caliber, but also the bullet has to be selected for the game.

Ruark once shot a hyena with a .220 Swift. Hyenas are not large animals, but the Swift fired a tiny (48-grain) bullet at more than 4,000 feet per second. It was the hottest, fastest commercial load of the day, meant for nothing bigger than groundhogs at long range. The bullet, too small to have much mass or to hold together at that speed, just blew apart into fragments on the hyena's hide instead of penetrating and killing. After shooting the hyena nine times with the .220, Ruark went to the other extreme and reached for his .470 Nitro Express to finish the job. He never fired the Swift again.

Use enough gun.

Too much gun, on the other hand, is punishing to carry, because it's heavy, and to shoot, because of its recoil and even the cost of ammunition. There's no need to shoot deer with a heavy Magnum or Nitro Express cartridge; deer just aren't that big, tough, difficult to kill or potentially dangerous.

Hunting magazines and books have been around for centuries, and for centuries they have published articles about the advantages or disadvantages of one gun or cartridge versus another. This may make good reading, but the basics never change: smaller calibers for small game, bigger ones for medium game, Magnums or Nitros for the big stuff; solid or metal-jacketed bullets for thick-skinned, tough animals, expanding bullets for everything else.

Tactical marksmen and snipers follow this rule too. Using a .50-caliber long-range rifle to wipe out a hostage-taker at 75 yards may cause serious damage farther downrange as the bullet keeps going. (Remember Number 8 in The 15 Commandments.) On the other hand, shooting at an insurgent 1,500 yards away with a 5.56x45mm is a waste of ammo—the round isn't effective at that range. Pick the proper tools for the job.

Don't think that hunting big game with small calibers is somehow more "sporting," either. This was a fad in the 1960s among certain hunters who believed that a high-velocity small bullet was as effective as a bigger, slower one. The bullet's energy may calculate out to be the same, but a bullet needs a certain amount of mass to be effective (as Ruark found out on the hyena). A lightly wounded animal may go for miles, in pain and fear, or get away to die days later of slow blood loss or in the jaws of predators. A hunter owes her game a quick, clean death, and a larger, slower bullet virtually always outperforms a lighter, faster one. Karamojo Bell and Jim Corbett had their own reasons for using light rifles on big game, and they were able to get away with it by being ultra-accurate and careful (a little luck helped too); but don't try this at home.

Keeping Guns Clean & Safe

How NOT to Destroy a Gun—and Where to Put Them

The easiest way to blow up a gun is to fire it while the barrel is plugged. Even if the obstruction seems minor, under the huge blast of pressure created by burning gunpowder in such a confined space, a bullet hitting even just a bit of dirt can become the irresistible force meeting the immovable object. If something's got to give, it's the gun barrel. Can you imagine the energy needed to burst a thick steel tube?

It's a good habit to check your gun's bore before you load and fire. It's all too easy to get "foreign objects" into a gun barrel. One of the authors once filled a double-barreled shotgun's muzzles with snow just by walking through a prairie in the winter. The gun was hanging over his arm, barrels down. The muzzles brushed the tall grass as he moved along, picking up snow. Luckily he has the habit of looking through his gun barrels before dropping a pair of cartridges into them, so he discovered that the muzzles were blocked before it was too late. The snow was powdery light and probably would not have resisted the shot charge—but then again maybe it would have.

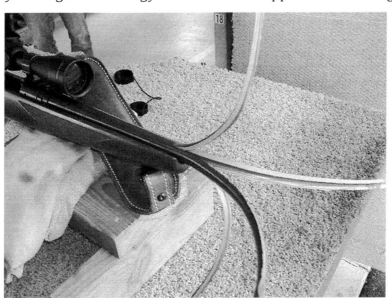

A rifle barrel split like a banana peel. The shooter forgot to remove the bore sighter (a device that goes into the muzzle) before firing a round, and then an irresistible force met an unmovable object and something had to give. Luckily, no one was hurt.

Bad ammunition can leave barrels plugged too, if there isn't enough oomph to push the bullet out. With shotguns, even if the pellets come out, the big plastic shot-cup wad that contains them may stay behind, stuck somewhere near the muzzle.

Either way, if the shooter doesn't realize what's happened and fires again, the barrel is likely to burst or at least bulge. If the rupture happens out near the muzzle, maybe the shooter won't get hurt; if it's farther back, her forward hand is in danger. Either way, shrapnel or hot gasses could blow back into her face. (Wear those shooting glasses!)

Later we'll talk about using the correct ammunition, but here's something that is just about guaranteed to ruin your day. It happens surprisingly often to shotgunners who have both 12- and 20-gauge guns: They fire the 12, then reach into a pocket for a fresh round and, without looking, mistakenly pop a 20-gauge cartridge into the gun. A 28-gauge or .410-bore shotshell is skinny enough to drop right through a 12-gauge

A deluxe, all-in-one maintenance kit made by Outers, with solvents, lubricants, brushes and tools for about every caliber and gauge, plus a convenient stand for the gun while you're working on it. You don't need this much gear to clean your guns, though—just a rag, some gun oil, bore-cleaning fluid, cloth patches and a rod and brush that will fit the barrel.

barrel; a 20 will slide in a few inches and stick. The next time the shooter pulls the trigger, nothing will happen. She might think, Oh, I forgot to reload! If she then puts a 12-gauge shell into the gun and fires it—with the 20 stuck in the barrel ahead of it—all hell will break loose.

A 28-gauge cartridge will do the same thing in a 16-bore barrel. (And we know a woman who got nothing but a dry click! when she tried to shoot a pheasant and found she'd put a tube of lipstick into her 20-gauge shotgun.)

The point is: Never mix ammunition. If you switch guns, empty your pockets or shell vest completely and start over. Some shotgunners have 12-gauge vests and 20-gauge vests and always change them when they change guns.

Pay attention, be observant and think about what's happening. This is especially important if you're hunting in bad weather or moving through thick brush. It isn't just the barrel either. Dirt, snow, twigs, leaves, even grains of unburned powder can get into the action and jam it up. And for

heaven's sake, if you slip and fall with a gun in your hands, make sure it's OK before continuing on. Inspect the gun closely, especially if it hit the ground. Open the action, look through the bore and check the sights and the magazine. Brush off any dirt.

(If you were holding the gun pointed in a safe direction and if the safety was on and your finger was outside the trigger guard when you fell . . . you and anyone around you should be OK too.)

This sort of on-the-spot care is just common sense. Cleaning a gun at home after using it and before putting it away is important too. This can be as much work as you want it to be; some people just love to disassemble their guns and inspect every part, cleaning and wiping and oiling and reassembling. If this pushes your buttons and you know how to do it, go right ahead. But unless you dropped the gun into the lake or were out in heavy rain or a sandstorm, or you have a gas-operated semi-auto that collects gunpowder residue in its action, it isn't necessary. Just run a cleaning rod through the bore and wipe down the outside (see below) to remove any fingerprints, sweat or other gunk.

Cleaning Guns: How & How Often

aybe you'll go on to shoot blackpowder guns or become a serious match competitor, or you'll hunt ducks and geese on salt water or fire 500 rounds a week at sporting clays—these and other specialized kinds of shooting require different methods of gun cleaning. If you progress to that sort of shooting, you'll learn (from your mentor and more-experienced shooters) how to take care of your guns.

Meanwhile, if you have a new gun (BB, pellet, .22) read the care-and-use manual that came with it. If your gun didn't come with any instructions, here's what you should know about basic care and maintenance.

First, every shooter should have these items in a gun-cleaning kit:

1. A cleaning rod skinny enough and long enough to go all the way down the barrel. Shotgun or rifle cleaning rods are usually in three sections that screw together; one section has a handle. For short barrels, just use the section with the handle.

2. A brass bristle brush and a tip (maybe with a slot in it), which both screw into the end of the rod and are the right size for the bore of your gun.

3. Cotton cleaning patches. These are also sized for gauge or caliber.

4. A bottle of solvent to remove powder residue and traces of bullet metal or plastic wadding that builds up in the bore while shooting.

5. A small bottle or spray can of gun oil to lubricate moving parts.

6. A silicone-impregnated cloth to wipe fingerprints, skin oil, sweat, water or whatever from the gun. (Because they're salty, sweat and blood make a gun break out in rust like pimples.) You can use a soft cotton rag instead with a few drops of gun oil on it, but run this through the laundry every now and then. Oily rags can cause fires.

7. An old toothbrush and some cotton swabs (Q-tips) to get solvent and oil into hard-to-reach places. A spray can of pressurized air can be very useful too, to blow dirt away.

Here's what you do with these items:

1. Find a table that you can use, and spread newspaper on it. (This'll get dirty.)

2. Make absolutely sure the gun is unloaded: nothing in the chamber, nothing in the magazine or cylinder. If the gun has a detachable magazine, pull it out. (If there are still cartridges in the gun when it's time to clean it, you've screwed up big-time.)

3. Partly disassemble the gun, if possible. If you can, take the barrel off. If it's a bolt-action, pull out the bolt.

4. This is where it gets dirty: Attach the bristle brush to the cleaning rod, dunk it in the solvent and scrub out the barrel. (Push and pull the brush all the way through several times.) Do it from the breech end if possible. If you have to do it from the front, don't let the rod scrape the edge of the muzzle. (This can hurt a gun's accuracy.) You can put the newspaper on the floor and rest the end of the gun barrel on it or on an old towel on the newspaper, and work the brush up and down like that.

5. Now attach the other tip and push/pull cotton patches up and down the barrel, changing them each time. (They're disposable, so throw them away.) Look through the barrel every now and then at a strong light; the bore should become shiny-bright. If it's a rifle or handgun, you'll see the spiral lines of the rifling. If you can't see down the barrel because

the action blocks the light, you can get a little angled flashlight to stick in the ejection port while you look down the muzzle. When a patch finally comes out clean, put a few drops of oil on it and run that down the bore. Now the barrel is clean and has a light film of oil to protect against rust.

6. Certain parts of the action need a drop of oil to prevent friction and rust. A *drop* of oil—too much attracts dirt and can build up and get gummy.

7. Thoroughly wipe the outside of the gun, both the metal parts and the stock, with the silicone cloth or the slightly oily rag.

8. Put the gun back together. Make sure it's uncocked, and put it away properly. Gunmakers often recommend storing long guns muzzle-down, to keep oil from slowly oozing into a wooden stock or pooling in the action.

All guns need occasional cleaning to prevent rust, to keep the bore unobstructed and to make sure the action works smoothly. This helps ensure that a gun is safe to use and accurate to shoot, and it protects the value of a gun too. Besides, dirt and rust are just plain nasty, and their presence says I don't deserve to own a gun!

If you get into the habit of inspecting a gun before you put it away and at least wiping it down, you'll know that the next time you take it out it'll be good to go.

The Right Ammunition

Bad ammunition can instantly mess up a gun. We told you what a bullet or a wad left in the barrel can do. The next best way to damage a gun (other than neglect) is to fire a round through it that's too powerful. This usually doesn't hurt the barrel, because it's extra-thick at the chamber, where the bang takes place, but if the action can't withstand the extra pressure, something's going to fail there. A well-made action usually won't burst, but it may jam, and then you can't open it.

Factory-made ammunition is extremely reliable, at least in America and Europe, so bad cartridges generally are the fault of shooters who load their own. It's easy to put too little or too much or the wrong kind of powder into a shell, and the results are rarely good.

You're not loading your own ammunition, at least so far, so this isn't a concern yet. But you do need to pay attention to what sort of ammo you feed your guns. For example:

More than a dozen different .22 rimfire cartridges have been produced over the years. There are a half-dozen .300 Magnums out there under various makers' names, and at least four different 9mm pistol cartridges. Twelve-gauge shotgun shells may be 2, 2½, 2¾, 3 or 3½ inches long. No matter what you've heard, the .223 Remington is not exactly the same as the 5.56mm NATO round. Nor are the 7.62 NATO and the .308 Winchester completely interchangeable. There are plenty more such opportunities for confusion too.

Modern guns are clearly stamped with their specific cartridge. Make sure that's exactly what you shoot out of them. The weight of the bul-

These are all 12-gauge shotshells, but obviously they don't all go in the same gun. You have to know exactly what ammunition fits your gun.

Steve Helsley

let or shot charge may vary, depending on what it's meant to be used for, but *every* new factory box of ammunition will indicate caliber, make and whatever other information you need to figure out whether you can shoot it in your gun.

Older guns and older ammunition may not be so well identified. If in doubt, don't shoot. If you can't close the action on a cartridge, there's a problem. Stop. Your mentor or an experienced gunsmith needs to check this out.

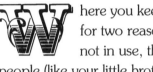

Storing Your Guns

This Sentry steel locker holds five long guns and has a shelf for ammunition. Some gun safes have combination locks; this inexpensive one has a key. Safes come in all sizes, and some are fireproof. Some even have dehumidifiers, to prevent rust. These are expensive, but the guns they're meant for are worth much more. And how do you put a price on safety?

Where you keep your guns is important for two reasons: First, when they're not in use, they should be where other people (like your little brother or sister) can't get at them. The best place is a steel vault or safe specially built for guns and with a secure lock on the door.

Your parents may decide that only they will have the key or combination so you can't take out a gun without their permission. Don't complain. When you get your driver's license, you'll go through the same process with the car—but if you've already showed them that you can handle guns well, your parents likely will be more generous with the car.

Guns should never be stored loaded. If we have to explain why, go back to the beginning and re-read this book.

Accidental shootings are very rare in the United States, but when they do happen, they're extra sad because they almost always happen to friends or family members. This is why some people also put locks on the triggers or block the actions when they put their guns away and keep the ammunition in a completely different place. People who have break-action guns usually store them disassembled in their cases. Manufacturers are now developing "personalized" guns that let only an authorized user fire them.

A GunVault storage box programmed to open only when it recognizes the owner's fingerprints. The box itself should be fastened to something so that it can't be stolen. You are responsible for keeping your guns not only clean and safe, but also out of other people's hands.

Accidental shootings are about impossible if someone has to a) get at the gun, b) unpack it and put it together, and then c) find the ammunition and load it.

By the way, if you store a gun "negligently" (in an unlocked place or without disabling it with a trigger lock or something similar) and an unau-

thorized user causes harm with it, in many places you could be charged with a crime.

The other reason for storing guns securely is to keep them clean and protected from moisture, fire and even damage by insects or small animals. We've seen a wooden gunstock that was chewed by something toothy and have heard of gun barrels plugged up by insect nests. Some gun safes have built-in dehumidifiers to remove any dampness from the air. Ammunition has to be kept dry too.

Depending on your home situation, it might be best to store your guns (and ammunition) at a shooting club, target range or gun dealership that has proper lockers.

There are always exceptions: Plenty of people, even in modern-day America, live in places where dangerous wild animals are common enough that guns are kept out in the open and even loaded. They might be where small children can't reach them, but everyone in the family knows better than to mess with them.

Traveling with Guns

Even if you live in an area where a gun rack in the back window of a pickup truck is still a common sight, always put a gun in a case when it's time to transport it somewhere. If the gun has a trigger lock or some other safety device on it, leave it in place. Naturally, the gun should be unloaded too. A carrying case protects a gun (and its sights) from scrapes and dirt and also hides it. Even if it's perfectly OK to leave a gun in view—in a locked car, say—it still freaks out some people who may call the cops. Needless hassle. Also, leaving a gun in plain sight might encourage a thief to break in and grab it.

There is no federal law against transporting firearms for "lawful purposes." But besides the safety rules there are usually state and sometimes local laws to follow. In general you may transport a gun and ammunition in a car if it's unloaded and locked in the trunk in a case. No trunk? Then it has to be in some other locked container outside the passenger compartment, like a toolbox in a pickup-truck bed or a camper trailer.

Licensed hunters can usually carry their guns in their cars—but often not at night, since hunting after dark is illegal. Carrying guns in boats, ATVs or snow machines may be regulated too.

Traveling with guns on commercial airliners, trains, buses and ships is strictly controlled.

School zones, national parks, military bases and properties that belong to the federal government usually have their own firearms rules.

Wearing a loaded handgun openly in a holster is legal in some places and not in others. Most states require a permit to carry concealed firearms; a few do not. (We've discussed this in "You've Come a Long Way, Baby.")

What we've written here is very general, and laws change all the time. You—and your parents and your shooting mentor—have to know the rules

Steve Helsley

A felt-lined, leather-and-wood case custom-made for a matched set of fine double-barreled shotguns along with special tools and cleaning gear. The case alone is worth more than an ordinary shotgun, and a pair of guns like this may cost more than a high-end car.

for where you live and shoot. This is easy now, since you can find the information on the Internet, on Websites created by your state fish and game department, your town or city, and/or your police department.

By the way, if you're caught violating these laws, no matter what else happens to you (a fine or worse), your gun probably will be confiscated. You might even be banned from possessing a gun for some time.

Flying with guns requires a rugged travel case that is lockable and padded to protect a rifle and scope from airline baggage handlers. This one is aluminum, but some are made of heavy plastic. Traveling overseas with firearms isn't difficult, provided you follow the rules.

Silvio Calabi

Reloading Ammunition

Gunpowder + Primer + Bullet = *BOOM!*

Sooner or later serious shooters usually learn to load their own ammunition. People who shoot a lot of trap, skeet or sporting clays may reload their empty shells as a way to save money, while handgun and rifle shooters often do it because they're looking for some performance edge: a special round that prints extra-tight groups on a target or a super-hot varmint-buster that gives great results out to 1,000 yards. Maybe they're working up a modern load for a century-old double rifle, carefully substituting modern powder for the old Cordite and tuning it to hit hard and accurately at Cape-buffalo distances.

Reloading ammunition doesn't necessarily require a lot of equipment, although it can, but obviously it does require explosive materials. Working with and storing powders and primers is perfectly safe if you know what you're doing and develop good procedures and habits.

If you don't know what you're doing, it's an invitation to possibly serious trouble. At best, ammunition that's loaded incorrectly just won't function; at worst, it can destroy a gun and take you with it.

For now at least, stick with factory-made ammunition. And read on about gunpowder, Atomic Pearls and exploding bullets.

Black Powder

Some scientists believe that life on Earth arose from a sort of primordial soup, a perfect combination of chemicals and energy. Before there were AR-15s and red-dot sights, before there were Mausers and metallic cartridges, even before there were muskets and lead balls, there was the "primordial soup" of firearms—their DNA, if you will: charcoal, sulphur and saltpeter, or potassium nitrate.

Whoever first combined these ingredients into something that went bang has been lost to history. Where it happened has been variously identified as China, India and England. Exactly when isn't known either, but it's certain that by the 13th Century gunpowder was being used in firearms. (The Chinese were putting it into rockets—fireworks, that is—long before then. They may have invented firearms too.) With some refinement, this material would remain the standard propellant for handguns, rifles, shotguns and artillery until the 1880s.

That was when a Frenchman named Paul Vieille came up with something called *poudre B* (*poudre* meaning powder, and *B* for *blanche*, or white), or smokeless gunpowder. After this its predecessor became known, naturally, as black powder. Smokeless powder was so much better in so many ways that it made the black stuff obsolete overnight. More than 125 years later, though, black powder is still with us.

The proportion of the ingredients in black powder has varied through the centuries, but it is

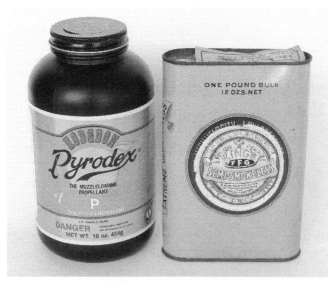

Steve Helsley

Pyrodex is a substitute for black powder that is used in modern muzzleloading and blackpowder-cartridge guns. Like smokeless powder, it is highly flammable but not explosive and therefore safer. The canister of Semi-Smokeless, still sealed, dates from about 1900; semi-smokeless burned cleaner than black powder.

generally about 75 percent saltpeter, 15 percent charcoal and 10 percent sulphur. When black powder burns, it throws off clouds of whitish smoke. It also smells bad (like rotten eggs, from the sulphur) and leaves behind a nasty residue. And finally, although it is what's called a low-order explosive, black powder is dangerously unstable.

Many modern explosives (and smokeless powder) are surprisingly easy to handle, and detonating them takes some doing. Black powder, on the

other hand, can be set off just by a buildup of static electricity. In spite of strict safety precautions, the factories that produce it still blow up periodically.

Black powder is made by thoroughly pulverizing and mixing the ingredients, adding water, pressing the mixture into a cake, and then breaking that into granules. Black powder for shooting comes in a variety of grain sizes ranging from very fine, for priming flintlocks, to coarse, for cannons. State and federal laws regulate how much of it we can have in our possession.

Until dynamite and other high-order explosives like trinitrotoluene (TNT) were discovered, late in the 19th Century, black powder was a critical tool in mining, tunneling, canal building and other big construction projects. Those uses no longer apply, but black powder remains popular for Cowboy Action shooting and several other kinds of target shooting. (Handled properly, black powder can produce very consistent velocities and excellent accuracy.) It's also used by people who hunt with old (or old-style) guns or reenact Civil War or Revolutionary War battles. Blackpowder shooters joke about having to "run around the smoke" to see whether they've hit anything, and they like to refer to smokeless powder as a passing fad.

Black powder likely will be with us for a long time to come for another reason as well: It's one of the key ingredients in fireworks.

Brown and Then Smokeless Powders

For centuries what we now call black powder was simply gunpowder; there wasn't any other color or kind. Whether you were shooting a flintlock pistol across the field of honor or an 18-pounder from the gun deck of a navy frigate, it did the job. But when rapid-firing, breechloading repeating rifles arrived, in the 1860s, the limitations of this powder became obvious. It left a gun barrel

dirty enough to affect its accuracy, and the residue was highly corrosive. Plus there was a limit to how fast it could drive a bullet.

Black powder suited the old muzzleloading, single-shot era. Modern guns, especially machine guns, needed a propellant that burned cleaner and didn't gum up the works; and if it pushed a bullet to greater velocities, so much the better. This would make a bullet more powerful and also reduce how much it dropped on the way to the target.

By the mid-1800s an improved powder had arrived, primarily for artillery. This was brown, or prismatic, powder. It used the same basic ingredients as black powder but in different proportions and with some added moisture in a special form of charcoal. It did perform better, but it was soon overtaken by other developments.

In 1846 two scientists, a German and a Swiss, independently discovered nitrocellulose, also known as nitrocotton or guncotton. The following year an Italian chemist discovered nitroglycerin, the first explosive that was more powerful than gunpowder.

And then, in the early 1880s, while others were still refining prismatic powder, Paul Vieille, the French chemist, altered nitrocellulose to create his *poudre blanche*. (The name was meant to confuse German spies.) This was the first smokeless gunpowder, and it was immediately put to use in a new French military cartridge and rifle. For its weight, *poudre B* produced three times the energy of black powder, so it could launch bullets at much higher velocities. It also burned cleanly, with no more barrel fouling or clouds of dirty white smoke.

European countries went to war with each other every few years, so this was important. (In 1858 a metallurgist named John Scoffren wrote that gunpowder "not only materially affected the art of war, but exercised most important influences on the fate of empires and the progress of civilization.") The Germans bribed a French soldier to bring them a sample of his country's new

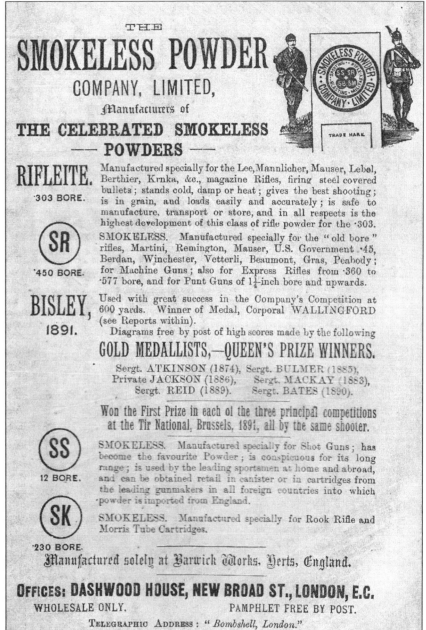

An 1890s English advertisement for different grades of the new smokeless gunpowder. Shooters and gunmakers spent a lot of time working up equivalent loads that would let them keep on using their old guns with the new powder—without blowing them up.

rifle and its ammunition, which they then copied. Meanwhile the British combined nitrocellulose with mineral jelly and nitroglycerin to create their first smokeless powder, called Cordite. By 1900 all the major armies of Europe had new rifles that fired smokeless powder.

Powder cans dating from 1924 to today, with an old muzzle-loading powder horn and a percussion-cap dispenser. The science of propellants has changed tremendously.

You can see why blackpowder shooters joke about having to "run around the smoke" to see if they've hit what they were aiming at. This could be a serious problem if the target was a charging elephant or lion.

Target shooters, police officers and hunters benefited from smokeless powder too. In 1915 in the United States, the .250-3000 Savage was the first cartridge to drive a bullet (just 87 grains) faster than 3,000 feet per second. Twenty years later the .220 Swift hit 4,100 fps with a 48-grain bullet.

Since then smokeless powders have been highly refined for specific applications and to improve accuracy, diminish muzzle flash and reduce barrel wear. Velocities, however, have not increased much. Most modern rifle bullets still leave the barrel at between 2,500 and 3,500 fps.

Both black and smokeless powders can be dangerous, but particular care must be taken with black powder. (It is a genuine explosive.) Smokeless

powder is much more stable, so it isn't considered an explosive, and it has to be burned in a confined space to produce maximum pressure. Putting a match to smokeless powder produces a bright flame but no bang.

Used incorrectly, though, black and smokeless powders both can reduce a gun to jagged pieces of wood and metal.

Bullets That Go BOOM!

If you were 12 years old in the late 1950s, odds are that you were the proud owner of a Daisy BB gun. A fortunate few of us also had a supply of tiny firecrackers called Atomic Pearls. If you stomped on one of these beauties or threw it hard against the sidewalk—*bang!* They were round and about the diameter of a BB, but size varied. A clever operator would sort through his stash of Atomic Pearls to find the ones that fit the Daisy. Exploding bullets!

Atomic Pearls disappeared long ago, so don't get your hopes up. But exploding projectiles are still around. Cast-iron cannon balls were hollowed out and filled with gunpowder perhaps as early as the 13th Century. Getting them to blow up on impact instead of in the cannon required another three centuries of painful trial and error, but eventually exploding artillery shells became standard. Along the way, it occurred to someone to try to put explosives into something much smaller: a bullet.

Originally bullets were round balls. But you already know about Claude-Étienne Minié and his longer, cone-shaped projectile. At about the same time, 1850-ish, the first rimfire .22 cartridges appeared. Then someone figured out how to combine these two advancements: Drill a hole in the nose of the bullet and fill it with powder; then plug the hole with a rimfire blank, reversed so it faced forward. When this loaded-up round hit something hard, *boom!*

Actually, more like bang! You can't pack much explosive into such a small space, which has been the problem with exploding bullets all along.

These were used in muzzleloaders, so it was very important not to pound such a bullet down the barrel of the gun with the usual ramrod, or you'd risk setting off the rimfire cap and exploding the bullet. The tip of the ramrod had to be shaped so that it pressed against the body of the bullet, not its sensitive tip.

Sir Samuel Baker

Sir Samuel Baker was a 19th Century English explorer, big-game hunter and author who spent many years in Africa. Baker's adventures with guns and exploding bullets are worthy of investigation by the *MythBusters* team. In one of his books, he wrote:

"Among other weapons, I had an extraordinary rifle that carried a half-pound percussion shell—this instrument of torture to the hunter was not sufficiently heavy for the weight of the projectile; it only weighed twenty pounds: thus, with a charge of ten drachms of powder, behind a HALF-POUND shell, the recoil was so terrific, that I was spun round like a weathercock in a hurricane. I really dreaded my own rifle, although I had been accustomed to heavy charges of powder and severe recoil for many years.

"None of my men could fire it, and it was looked upon with a species of awe, and was named 'Jenna el Mootfah' (child of a cannon) by the Arabs, which being far too long a name for practice, I christened it the 'Baby;' and the scream of this 'Baby,' loaded with a half-pound shell, was always fatal. It

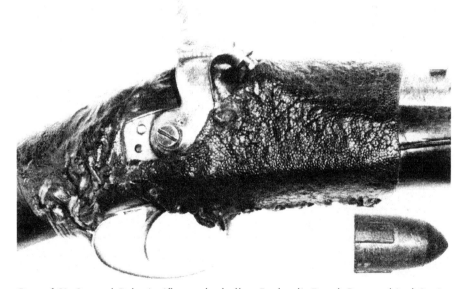

One of Sir Samuel Baker's rifles and a bullet. England's Royal Geographical Society, which owns the rifle, says it's a 4-bore (1-inch caliber); that isn't big enough to fire the sort of bullets Baker wrote about, so this may not be "Baby." It's wrapped with hide, probably from an elephant's ear. Hunters who were in the wilds for months at a time sometimes did this to fix gunstocks that broke or to reinforce them against breaking.

was far too severe, and I very seldom fired it, but it is a curious fact, that I never fired a shot with that rifle without bagging [something]: the entire practice, during several years, was confined to about twenty shots. I was afraid to use it; but now and then it was absolutely necessary that it should be cleaned, after lying for months loaded. On such occasions my men had the gratification of firing it, and the explosion was always accompanied by two men falling on their backs (one having propped up the shooter), and the 'Baby' flying some yards behind them. This rifle was made by Holland, of Bond Street, and I could highly recommend it for Goliath of Gath, but not for men of A.D. 1866."

Baker added that he had designed special ammunition, made for him by a certain Mr. Reilly, for this gun: "an iron lead-coated explosive shell, containing a bursting charge of half an ounce of fine grain powder."

"Baby" must have been a 2-bore, or 1.32-caliber, rifle. But packing a half-ounce of gunpowder into even a bullet that big is not easy. (Half an ounce of powder takes up as much room as 2,000 grains of lead; a half-pound bullet weighs 3,500 grains in total.) The "iron shell" might have held the powder, while the lead coating added mass and a softer surface for the rifling to grip. But this was no easy thing to make; and as a "percussion shell" it still needed a detonator in the nose to set it off when it struck something. These bullets must have been unusually long.

Furthermore 10 drams (0.62 ounce—not much more than Baker claimed was in the bullet itself) of powder is a light charge for a rifle firing a half-pound projectile. The bullet might penetrate very little, if at all, and just blow up on the skin of the elephant or rhino. This wouldn't do much more than cause a superficial burn and maybe scare the beast to death. It might have worked to drive off hostile natives if it was fired against their canoes.

So there are questions about Baker's bullets. But explosive ammunition did exist, at least for a while. Baker wrote about "Baby" in 1866; at that time the Bavarian Army in Germany had a 14.5mm (.570-caliber) explosive bullet for its single-shot Lindner rifle. Three years later, for their 11.5x50R Werder rifle, the Germans loaded up another one. This *Zundegeschoss*, or "primed bullet," had a hollow copper tube filled with priming powder set into its nose. Both of these rifles were breechloaders, which avoided the problem of seating these bullets

from the muzzle without setting them off. We don't know how effective they were.

Twenty years later the introduction of smokeless powder led to smaller bullets, with even less room for explosives. During World War I (1914–1918), the French tried to make an exploding rifle round to shoot at airplanes and observation balloons. They used an obsolete 11mm (.43-caliber) cartridge that fired a bigger slug than their normal 8mm (.32) service round, but it never became practical.

The Germans experimented with new explosive bullets too, also with poor results. Manfred von Richthofen, the legendary Red Baron fighter-plane ace, almost shot himself down with them. His bullets accidentally detonated just after clearing the muzzles of his Spandau machine guns, and the fragments went through the cowling over his airplane engine.

World War II (1939–1945) inspired Germany and maybe other countries to give exploding bullets another try. The German *B-Patrone* bullet produced a puff of smoke when it struck something, but that was all. It wound up being used as a spotter round, to see where bullets were hitting.

Testing in the United States led to the official conclusion that "the explosive effect of a bullet of this size was not sufficiently great to justify the difficulty of its construction."

Military-rifle bullets are generally much smaller now than they were in WWI and WWII (which in turn were much smaller than the bullets of Sir Samuel Baker's day). The 5.56mm bullet for the M16 and M4 rifles and the Russian 5.45mm bullet for the AK-74 are both less than .23-caliber—not even a quarter-inch in diameter. Put explosives in them and they won't go bang!; they'll barely go poof.

Bullets for hunting are often much bigger, but even if they could be made to explode, they probably would be illegal in most places and frowned upon as unsporting everywhere. Whalers sometimes attach explosive heads to their harpoons, but that's another story.

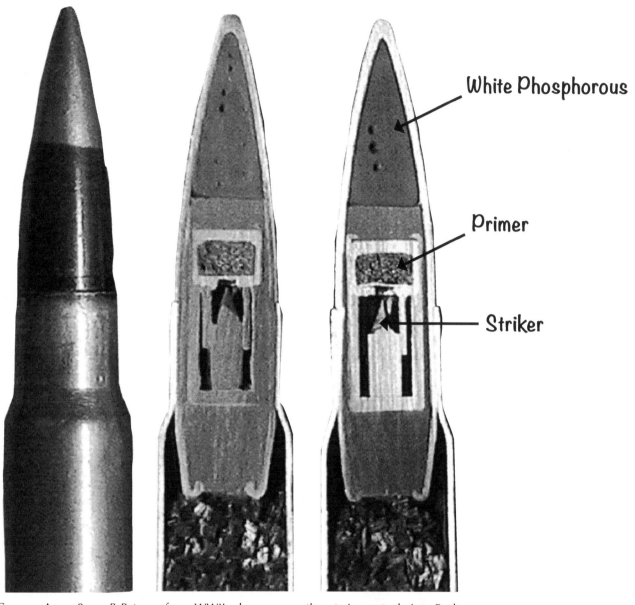

White Phosphorous

Primer

Striker

German Army 8mm *B-Patrone* from WWII, shown more than twice actual size. Each bullet has its own internal primer, which detonated the small charge of white phosphorous in the nose. But with such a small amount of explosive, these were useful only as spotter rounds; the puff of smoke would show the shooter where the bullet was hitting.

Killer Apps

The Stories Behind Famous Guns

Were Arrows Better Than Balls?

Gun writers and historians love to quote a letter written by Benjamin Franklin in February 1776. This was just six months before the American colonies declared their independence from the British Empire and the Revolution broke out for real. Franklin was writing to an officer of the Continental Army named Charles Lee about the prospects for war with England, and he included this:

"But I still wish, with you, that Pikes [*long spears*] could be introduced and I would add Bows and Arrows. These were good Weapons, not wisely laid aside;

"1st, because a Man may shoot as truly with a Bow as with a common Musket.

"2ndly. He can discharge 4 Arrows in the time of charging and discharging one Bullet.

"3dly. His Object [*target*] is not taken from his View by the Smoke of his own Side.

"4thly. A Flight of Arrows, seen coming upon them, terrifies and disturbs the Enemy's Attention to his Business.

"5thly. An Arrow striking in any Part of a Man puts him *hors du Combat* [*out of action*] till 'tis extracted.

"6thly. Bows and Arrows are more easily provided everywhere than Muskets and Ammunition."

The official seal of Britain's National Rifle Association, founded in 1859, has two soldiers, one armed with a longbow, the other with a musket. The argument over which weapon was better for infantry—faster, more accurate or more effective—went on for a couple of centuries.

Although he was a wise man, Benjamin Franklin misunderstood a couple of points about muskets and bows. The English longbow was a superb weapon, but it had been "wisely laid aside" long before 1776 because no one could still "shoot as truly" with it as with a musket, especially in America.

A longbow was very powerful—usually five to six feet long with a draw weight that was far more than a hundred pounds—and it fired a heavy, man- and horse-killing arrow three feet long with an effective range of more than 300 yards. The English and Welsh archers who made life so difficult for French knights in the Hundred Years War (1337–1453) grew up with bows in their hands. Over years of practice they developed the technique and tremendous strength to draw their bows and shoot them accurately. They could, as Franklin wrote, discharge four arrows in the time it took to fire and reload a musket once, and they could do this more or less continuously 30 or 40 times before their strength began to give out. But in Britain these skills had been lost a hundred years before our Revolution, and the English longbow had never come to America at all.

To Ben Franklin's other points: Number 3 was correct. So was Number 4, except that it's possible to see an arrow coming and step out of its way, at least if you know it's coming. (It's hard to dodge 1,000 arrows raining down all at once. But that's what shields were for.) Number 5 is true. Although a longbow is far less expensive to produce than a musket, number 6 was false at least in America, where no one knew how to make proper longbows and the Native American bows were much-less-powerful, short-range weapons.

A thunderous volley of musket fire, belching smoke and (if the sun wasn't bright) flame, was probably just as terrifying as a hail of arrows. A ball, even one fired from a crude musket at a pokey 1,200 feet per second, is invisible and can't be avoided (if it doesn't miss entirely). Finally, it is far, far easier to teach someone to load and fire a musket than to shoot a war bow.

The argument over bows versus guns was likely centuries old by 1776. It probably didn't go away completely until breechloading repeating rifles were perfected almost a century later.

Paul Revere & the 2nd Amendment

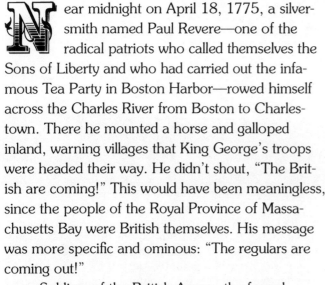

Near midnight on April 18, 1775, a silversmith named Paul Revere—one of the radical patriots who called themselves the Sons of Liberty and who had carried out the infamous Tea Party in Boston Harbor—rowed himself across the Charles River from Boston to Charlestown. There he mounted a horse and galloped inland, warning villages that King George's troops were headed their way. He didn't shout, "The British are coming!" This would have been meaningless, since the people of the Royal Province of Massachusetts Bay were British themselves. His message was more specific and ominous: "The regulars are coming out!"

Soldiers of the British Army—the feared "redcoats," the best infantry on earth—were marching westward in force that night. England had been sending more and more troops to Boston, whose citizens were angry about taxes and regulations that the Crown had put on them. Paul Revere was part of a spy network that had been set up to watch these troops and to quickly spread the word if they left the city in strength. Alerted by Revere and William Dawes, another courier, several dozen more riders fanned out across the countryside that night. Their job was to rouse the Minutemen—colonial militiamen who could report armed and ready for duty "at a minute's notice." This rapid-reaction force had been in existence for more than a hundred years already, since the days of Indian attacks on settlers, and the Minutemen had been active in the French and Indian War of the 1750s too.

At first the fear was that the army had been sent to Lexington, about 15 miles by road from Boston, to seize the patriot leaders Samuel Adams and John Hancock. But when Revere and Dawes reached Adams and Hancock, well ahead of the soldiers, they decided that the British would not have sent 700 men under a lieutenant colonel just to arrest them. The goal had to be the stockpile of colonial military supplies in nearby Concord, where the Massachusetts Provincial Congress met. Revere set off again, but he was captured by a British patrol before he got to Concord. He'd done his job, though, and across the region church bells were ringing the alarm.

Just before dawn on April 19, redcoats and militiamen met on the town common in Lexington. A wild and disorganized skirmish followed. A colonist probably fired first—the famous "shot heard 'round the world"—and then the British returned fire and launched a bayonet charge. Eight militia were killed; the rest scattered. The British then pushed into Concord unopposed. They split up into search parties and found the hidden arsenal, including three cannons that had been buried. Meanwhile, though, Minutemen were pouring in from neighboring villages.

A rear guard of two British infantry companies (about 90 men) took up a defensive position on the far side of the North Bridge, spanning the Concord River between Concord and Lexington, and found themselves facing 400 or more militia. This time the redcoats—exhausted from marching all night, led by an inexperienced young captain and possibly beginning to panic—fired first. Then, badly outnumbered and taking casualties, they did something almost unheard of: They broke and ran, fortunately for them right into the arms of a full British brigade (1,000 troops) that had been sent from Boston as reinforcements.

A long night became a very long day as the British soldiers retreated back to the city. They were attacked along the way at least eight times by the militia.

One of the most famous landmarks in Boston is this statue of Paul Revere. On his midnight ride, Revere didn't shout "The British are coming!" That would have made no sense, as everyone in the Massachusetts colony was British. But the redcoats were coming to seize the colonists' arms.

Both sides were stunned and shaken. Neither believed that the other would really shoot or that the patriot movement, having been simmering for years, would explode into open rebellion against the lawful King. This was the start of the Revolutionary War and the birth of the United States of America—and the spark that lit the flame was the government's attempt to seize colonists' arms and ammunition.

After the Revolution, deciding how the new nation would be governed was a long and difficult process. To gain enough support for the Constitution, the document that established the basic laws and organization of the new United States, the authors added a list of 10 amendments, or explanations, that became known as the Bill of Rights. These include freedom of speech, freedom of the press, freedom of religion and so on.

"Stand your ground!" Colonists and redcoats face off on the town common in Lexington, Massachusetts, on April 19, 1776. The "shot heard 'round the world" has just been fired, and the world will never be the same again.

The Second Amendment reads: "A well-regulated militia being necessary to the security of a free state, the right of the people to keep and bear arms shall not be infringed."

Considering how the United States became an independent country, it's not hard to see why the Bill of Rights gave this particular privilege so much importance. Richard Henry Lee of Virginia, one of the first statesmen to propose that the American colonies break away from England, wrote: "To preserve liberty, it is essential that the whole body of people always possess arms and be taught alike, especially when young, how to use them."

Firearms (and other weapons) had arrived in what became Massachusetts with the first Pilgrims, in 1620. Guns put meat on the table and defended against Indians and helped the colony survive. For the next couple of centuries, as the new nation spread across the North American wilderness, the notion of taking guns away from law-abiding citizens was simply unthinkable.

The Constitution was adopted in 1787. Of the states that joined the union during the next 160-plus years, 45 adopted similar "right to keep and bear arms" provisions in their own constitutions.

It wasn't until the second half of the 20th Century that the meaning of the Second Amend-ment began to be debated in public. The argument focused on whether the right to keep and bear arms was an individual right or a collective right. In other words, does the Second Amendment apply to individual gun owners or only to those in a government militia?

The Constitution also established the three branches of American government: legislative, executive and judicial. The legislative branch (Congress) passes our laws, the executive (the President) enforces them, and the judicial (the courts) interprets them. And so, to a large degree, the courts determine the ultimate meaning of the Constitution, its Bill of Rights and all other laws. In 1868 the Fourteenth Amendment was added to the Bill of Rights. Its "due process" clause has become the legal means for determining if a right included in the national Constitution applies (is "incorporated") to individuals in state cases.

As some states have no "right to keep and bear arms" provision in their constitutions, this too would have to be clarified by the courts.

After a number of legal challenges to the Second Amendment at state and federal levels, the United States Supreme Court took up these matters.

In 2008 the Supreme Court ruled in *District of Columbia v. Heller* that the "right to keep and bear arms" is an individual right. Two years later the Supreme Court ruled in *McDonald v. Chicago* that the federal right was incorporated under the Fourteenth Amendment and so applied to all 50 states.

It is important to understand that no right is absolute. The most common example of this involves the First Amendment: The right to free speech does not allow someone to yell, "Fire!" in a crowded theater if there is no fire. Firearms rights are subject to restrictions too, including many related to age, mental health and criminal convictions. The interpretation of our constitutional rights evolves as the legislative branch of government passes new laws and as the courts provide new rulings on those laws.

Pistols at Dawn: The Duel

For centuries a dispute between gentlemen that went beyond some mild name-calling could turn into a formal fight to the death. Being accused of cheating at cards, for example, or of cowardice was often enough to spark a challenge. So was paying too much attention to another man's wife, or even just a strong difference of political opinions. Personal honor was at stake.

The man who felt himself insulted would "demand satisfaction." The point was not necessarily to kill his adversary but to show a willingness to put his life on the line to stand up for his honor or beliefs. Not to issue a challenge, or to decline one, meant that a man didn't truly believe in the rightness of his position.

(This had its roots in the ancient custom of trial by ordeal. If someone accused of a crime could survive a fight or being dunked into a pond, God was obviously on her side and she was innocent. This was before everyone had a lawyer.)

In Britain and America the era of the pistol duel was about 1770 to 1870. Gentlemen owned pairs of special pistols that were beautifully made and balanced and perfectly matched. When it was time to fight, the duelists' supporters, called seconds, carefully supervised the loading of the pistols "charged smooth and single"—that is, just one ball in a smoothbore, or unrifled, barrel. Each combatant chose one of his own pistols; the other was left with the second.

Holding the guns down by their legs or up in the air, the duelists took their places. The challenger usually chose the distance, which might be very close if the insult was especially serious; the seconds normally decided when or at what signal their gentlemen could fire.

A confident man might wait for his trembling opponent to shoot first and miss, and then take aim and . . . after making his target wait long, ago-

Eugene Onegin and Vladimir Lensky's duel in the snow, painted by Ilya Repin. This is a famous scene from Alexander Pushkin's classic Russian novel *Eugene Onegin*, published in the 1820s. Duelists continued to meet on "the field of honor" for almost another century.

nizing seconds, deliberately kill him. A cruel man might aim for the stomach, to cause a wound that led to a slow and painful death. A more humane one might just wing his enemy in the shoulder or leg, to make a point without resorting to murder. A doctor was often standing by.

If both men missed, accidentally or on purpose (duelists sometimes "deloped," just fired into the ground), the seconds would ask if they wished to take up their other pistols and continue. Often the answer was no; just by showing up, both men had proved their courage, and honor was satisfied. Or they might in fact have another round. If it went as far as three sets of misses, though, the seconds would usually call everything off. This was getting ridiculous!

The seconds—each duelist had one and sometimes two—didn't just stand by. Their job was to see that no one cheated and to get involved if necessary, so they were armed too. If one duelist tried to fire before the signal, his opponent's

Thomas Hager

Many gentlemen owned pairs of perfectly matched and custom-made dueling pistols like these, built by William and John Rigby in Dublin, Ireland, in 1828. The bores were supposed to be smooth, but some gunmakers hid rifling in them in order to make the pistols more accurate—and deadly.

second would shout a warning or even shoot the cheater. There are stories of rigged duels where one side had a man with a rifle hidden in the bushes nearby, to fire at the same instant, and of seconds who opened fire on each other.

Dueling pistols were single-barrel muzzleloaders with flint or percussion locks. Since the owner's life might depend on every shot fired, these guns were made with the greatest care. Calibers were usually 32 or 36 bore (.526" or .506"), and the barrels were typically eight to 10 inches long. The powder and ball were critical too. No detail was too small to overlook.

The code of honor required dueling pistols to be smoothbores, but the benefits of rifling to accuracy were too real to be ignored. Some gunmakers offered "scratch rifling"—bore grooves that were so faint that they could have been caused by over-eager cleaning. This might be missed by the seconds, who inspected and loaded the pistols in the field, often under dawn light. Other makers hid their rifling down in the bores, so the muzzles remained smooth.

Many politicians, military officers, authors, painters, musicians, businessmen and titled aristocrats fought duels, some many times. The more prominent you were, the more likely it was that you'd be "called out." The most famous duel in

American history took place on July 11, 1804, in New Jersey between Gen. Alexander Hamilton and Col. Aaron Burr.

It was a true grudge match, the result of years of bad feelings between the two men. As you may know from school, Burr fatally wounded Hamilton. What you may have forgotten is that Burr was then the Vice-President of the United States and later started the company that became the Chase Manhattan Bank; and Hamilton had been Secretary of the US Treasury.

Dueling took place all over the world and often with weapons other than pistols. It was usually illegal, but the law was rarely enforced until the 20th Century. Still, duels often took place in some out-of-the-way place and at dawn, for secrecy. Islands in rivers between states or countries were popular dueling sites, because they were difficult to get to and there might be confusion over which law applied.

Dueling died out late in the 19th Century, but our fascination with it did not. The "sport" even made one appearance at the Olympics, in 1906, in Athens. The competitors shot at dummies dressed like gentlemen with targets on their chests, not at each other. Before that there was a school in Paris that taught dueling skills by dressing its students in heavy coats and wire-mesh or glass masks and letting them shoot wax bullets at each other. This "bloodless dueling" spread as far as New York City, but it didn't last long. Some might say that Paintball is just a modern form of this.

The temptation to attack an enemy is sometimes overwhelming. Kids in schoolyards do it. Gang members do it. Nations do it. And to this day Her Britannic Majesty Queen Elizabeth II, Monarch of the United Kingdom, has an official champion to stand up for her, should she ever be challenged on the field of honor. He is Lt. Col. John Lindley Marmion Dymoke, Lord of the Manor of Scrivelsby, in Lincolnshire, England. He has never been put to the test. Not yet, anyway . . . .

The Mosin-Nagant 'Three-Line' Rifle

The manufacture of firearms has been going on now for seven centuries. Around the world thousands of makers have produced probably more than a billion rifles, shotguns and handguns in thousands and thousands of different models. As we said at the beginning of this book, it's hard to imagine a more important man-made object than the gun, and a handful of them have become part of popular culture. In the following pages we'll tell you about Winchester lever-actions, Colt .45s, the Gatling gun, the Tommy gun, the AK-47 and others. They were truly "instruments of history"—history that is anything but dry and dull.

A longer list of genuinely significant firearms would include the German Mauser rifle, the British Brown Bess musket and Lee-Enfield rifle, the American Kentucky (or Pennsylvania) rifle, and the Russian Mosin-Nagant "three-line" rifle. The latter was the AK-47 of its day, and it is by far the most important gun that most Americans have never heard of. Millions and millions of Mosin-Nagants have seen more than a century of use around the world. They've taken part in some of the most fascinating episodes of the 20th Century, and they're still lurking around in the 21st Century. We're going to dig deeper into the Mosin-Nagant as a way to show you how something as "simple" as a gun can be used as a sort of magnifying glass through which to look at history.

A Mosin-Nagant Model 91/30, probably refinished for sale in America. This is the sniper version, with the downturned bolt handle and a 3.5X PU scope. The scope's side-mount allowed the shooter to use the iron sights as well. The Russians called the leather straps to which the sling attaches the "dog collar."

Before there were airplanes, Kellogg's Corn Flakes, the modern Olympic Games or Teddy Bears, there were Mosin-Nagants. The rifle was designed for illiterate peasants, so its parts are few, big and somewhat crude. Like a zombie, it's ugly and won't stay dead—and it's been said that a Mosin-Nagant could be used to beat a fire hydrant to death.

In the late 1880s, when Russia was an empire ruled by the tyrannical Romanov family, its government set up a committee to select a modern military rifle, one that used new smokeless-powder ammunition. In 1891 this committee picked a design that combined the turn-bolt action designed by Russian Army Capt. Sergey Mosin *(MO-seen)* and the magazine of Belgian gun designer Léon Nagant *(Nah-GON)*. Most of the rest of the world calls the result the Mosin-Nagant, but in Russia it's still known as the three-line rifle—a "line" equaling one tenth of an inch, thus .30 caliber. It fired the also-new 7.62x54R cartridge. Since it's still used in a few current Russian service weapons, this is now the longest-serving military round in the world.

Manufacturing began in 1892. The rifles were also made in France, because Russian arsenals couldn't produce them fast enough. The Mosin-Nagant's baptism by fire came in 1900, when Russian soldiers helped put down the Boxer Rebellion, in China. Next was the short and lop-sided Russo-Japanese War, which ended abruptly when the Imperial Japanese Navy wiped out the Imperial Russian Navy in late May 1905.

Here's the Russian adversary to the Mauser rifle. This Mosin rifle was at Stalingrad, Leningrad and Berlin. It taught the German army all about sniper rifles.

See Both Rifles in Action in the DVD *"Enemy at the Gates"*, Free with your Mosin Rifle.

Original Soviet Sniper Rifle from WWII

Roza Shanina commanded a squad of female snipers who proved to be the scourge of the German army. These courageous young women used a rifle that was state-of-the-art at the time and is still in service in some strange places!

Get one of Roza's Rifles, Stalwart of the Russian Army. My sniper rifles are in outstanding condition, even though they were manufactured as snipers in WWII. When I found them, they were ready for military service again. But now they're civilians. Call in right away and get one while you can! **You get the rifle, the original accessories, the display stand and DVD, All for only** $799.

A present-day ad offering Mosin-Nagant sniper rifles at a premium price and highlighting their use in World War II. Enemy at the Gates *is as historically accurate (not) as most Hollywood movies; the picture of Roza Shanina in a heroic pose was a publicity photo.*

(President Theodore Roosevelt earned the Nobel Peace Prize by negotiating the truce, signed by the Russians and the Japanese in—of all the unlikely places—Kittery, Maine.)

When World War I began, in 1914, Russia still didn't have enough Mosin-Nagants. Tsar Nicholas II's Ministry of War turned to the United States and ordered a total of 3.3 million of them from Remington and Westinghouse. By early 1917, however, only 356,000 of these rifles had been delivered, and Russia was spinning out of control. Finally rebelling against the backward and brutal government, soldiers were disobeying their officers and peasants were standing up to the Tsar's police. In March 1917 "Bloody Nicholas" gave up his throne to try to head off more trouble. His brother, Prince Mikhail, was smart enough to refuse the crown. A new government was created and collapsed almost immediately. The imperial city of St. Petersburg, which had been re-named Petrograd, was in chaos. Then came the Ten Days That Shook the World, the October (actually November; Russia then used a different calendar) Revolution, when the Bolshevik Party seized power and Russia slid from monarchy into communism.

The new rulers withdrew Russia from the Great War. This freed up a huge part of the German Army to turn and face the remaining Allies—Britain and its Dominions, France, the US, Italy and other countries—and probably made the war drag on longer.

For this reason and because they were afraid of similar workers' revolutions against their own aristocracies at home, Britain, France, Italy and other countries wanted the Bolsheviks to fail. In 1918, before WWI ended, a multi-national force invaded Russia partly to help the White Guard—Russians who were opposed to the Bolshevik Red forces. America was officially neutral on the Bolsheviks but sent 5,000 soldiers to the Arctic port of Archangel, in northwest Russia, in August and another 8,000 to Vladivostok, more than 6,000 miles away in eastern Russia. Their job was to keep war materials, especially Mosin-Nagant rifles that had been made in Massachusetts and Connecticut, from falling into the hands of the Germans—not to mention the Reds or any of the other forces then roaming around in Russia while it was in such confusion.

Some of these American troops had gone to England first, on their way to France to join the fighting in WWI, but Gen. John Pershing moved them onward to Russia. In England they'd swapped their familiar .30-06 Enfields for Mosin-Nagants—rifles that had been ordered by the Tsar's government and shipped from America, then diverted to England after the Bolshevik uprising. Resupply would be impossible during the Arctic winter; this way the Americans would be able to use ammunition already in Russia.

This bit of bright thinking aside, every aspect of the invasion became a complete fiasco. Even the politicians could see this coming: When US Secretary of War Newton Baker bid farewell to Maj. Gen. William Sidney Graves, commander of the Vladivostok force, he shook the general's hand and just said, "Watch your step; you will be walking on eggs loaded with dynamite. God bless you and good-bye."

Until the last of these invaders finally left Russia, a year and a half later, Red, White and foreign soldiers—American, Canadian, British, Australian, French, Italian, Czech, Hungarian and others—all used Mosin-Nagants. When the Americans went home, they abandoned their rifles, thereby handing the Reds even more of the guns they'd been sent there to protect.

The chief advocate of this semi-secret attack on Russia had been Winston Churchill, then Britain's Secretary of State for War, who cried that "Bolshevism must be strangled in its cradle!" Naturally, the Russians never forgot this and, 25 years later, their deep distrust of Churchill caused severe problems when Russia, the United States and Britain were trying to work together to smash Germany in World War II.

Meanwhile, back in the US, Remington and Westinghouse had kept right on making Mosin-Nagants—eventually 1.6 million of them. In order to keep those companies in business, the rifles that hadn't been shipped to Russia were bought by the US War Department. Throughout the Great War, which ended in late 1918, they'd been used for training recruits and given to state militias. (The US Army Manual of 1918 referred to the Mosin-Nagant as the "Russian Three-Line Rifle.") Front-line American battle rifles at the time were the bolt-action Model 1903 Springfield and Model 1917 Enfield.

When WWI ended, Mosin-Nagants began to migrate to the far corners of the world. Vladimir Lenin, the leader of the new Soviet Union (after the Whites lost the civil war, Russia became the USSR, the Union of Soviet Socialist Republics, aka the Soviet Union), supplied them to Afghanistan in its fight against British rule—maybe as payback for Winston Churchill's raid on Russia.

The US Government apparently gave thousands of its Mosin-Nagants to the new nation of Czechoslovakia and sold thousands more to Mexico and other friendly countries. In 1928 American citizens could buy Mosin-Nagants for $3.34 plus a packing charge. (They had cost the American taxpayer about $32 each. A Mosin-Nagant modified for hunting with a shortened barrel, a reshaped stock and bolt handle, sling attachments and better sights cost $7.30, packing charge included.) Hollywood property companies accumulated piles of them, so Mosin-Nagants showed up in movies for decades.

In 1930, after years of tinkering with the original 1891 model, the Soviet Revolutionary Military Council approved a redesign of the Mosin-Nagant that was even easier to manufacture and had sights calibrated in meters instead of the Tsarist *arshin* (equivalent to 28 inches). This was the Model 91/30. Two years later came a sniper version. It had a specially finished barrel bore and a telescopic sight, and the bolt handle was bent downward so it wouldn't hit the scope when the action was opened.

Then, in 1939, began the six-year agony of World War II. You've already read, in "Snipers," what people like Simo Häyhä and Lyudmila Pavlichenko did with their Mosin-Nagants in that chapter of global history.

etween 1892 and 1922 Russian, French and American companies made more than 11 million Mosin-Nagants. By the end of WWII, in 1945, at least 20 million more were manufactured in Russia. By the time production ended everywhere, in the 1960s, millions more Mosin-Nagant rifles had been made—in Bulgaria, China, Czechoslovakia, Hungary, North Korea, Poland and Romania and possibly elsewhere.

A photo, dated 2009, reportedly of a Taliban unit showing off its firepower. Most of the members are brandishing battered AK-47s. The pointy thing angled upward is a *ruchnoy protivotankovy granatomyot*, an RPG. (English-speakers take this to mean Rocket-Propelled Grenade, but it's really Russian for "hand-held anti-tank grenade launcher.") The rifle in the foreground is an ancient Mosin-Nagant Model 91/30 sniper rifle, with its scope just visible and its cleaning rod still under the muzzle.

In addition the guns were used in Cuba, Nicaragua, Egypt, Syria, Turkey, Thailand, Japan, Somalia, the Congo and every country in Scandinavia and Europe. Irish nationalists were armed with Mosin-Nagants (secretly supplied by Germany) during their Easter 1916 uprising against the English Crown. The Mosin-Nagant even became a propaganda tool in the Cold War between the USSR and the US, Communism vs. Democracy. When the Central Intelligence Agency wanted an excuse to get rid of the leader of Guatemala, in 1954, the agency bought Mosin-Nagants—left over from the Spanish Civil War in the late 1930s—from an international arms dealer and shipped them to Guatemala to make it look like Communists were arming the country.

American soldiers faced Mosin-Nagants in Korea in the early 1950s and in Vietnam in the 1960s and '70s, and the rifles still show up in Afghanistan today. They may be obsolete, but that's no comfort to someone hit by a 147-grain bullet fired at 2,800 fps.

After WWII many armies began to dump bolt-action rifles of all kinds and upgrade to automatics—and by "dump" we don't mean "take them out to sea and throw them overboard." Hundreds of thousands of these outdated rifles, including Mosin-Nagants, were scooped up by dealers and wound up for sale in the US. Mosin-Nagants hadn't gotten any prettier, and lacked about all of the desirable features of a sporting rifle, but they were cheap as dirt. Then, when the Soviet Union collapsed, in 1991, the flow of surplus Mosin-Nagants into America jumped again. So did prices: A basic Model 91/30 that sold for $9.95 in 1960 cost $109 in 2012. But now they're "collectibles."

In fact a Mosin-Nagant is a cheap way to start collecting interesting military rifles, and there are reference books and online bulletin boards to help research all the variations. If they're in decent condition, there's no reason not to shoot the rifles either. Some of them, especially those that were rebuilt in Finland, are exceptionally accurate. Every one of them would have a tale to tell. If you know the Mosin-Nagant story, you have a pretty firm grip on world history in the 20th Century.

It's estimated that 100 million each of Mauser bolt-actions and AK assault rifles have been made, versus about 17 million Lee-Enfields and 8 million M16 types (so far). This makes the Mosin-Nagant the third most popular rifle of all time. The AK-47 may have been a worthy successor to the Mosin-Nagant, but when it's time to bury the last rusted-out AK in a hundred years or so, the honor guard will likely be made up of Afghan Mujahedeen warriors carrying Mosin-Nagants—maybe some of those sent over by Comrade Lenin.

Colt: Two Famous .45s

The Single Action Army

To non-shooters it's almost one word: "Coltfortyfive." But shooters know better.

The Colt company has been making handguns for almost 200 years, and the guns certainly have not all been .45-caliber. In fact there are two famous .45-caliber Colts—one a revolver and the other a semi-auto pistol. They're both .45s, but they take different cartridges. They're both more than a hundred years old, and they're both still being made by Colt and many other companies.

In 1872 Colt's Patent Firearms Manufacturing Company won a competition to supply the US Government with a new revolver called the Single Action Army. The SAA was a breechloading six-shooter with a cartridge that was also new: the .45 Colt. At the time, this was the most powerful handgun round yet invented. The Army was so pleased with the SAA that it called it "the best weapon to carry on the person that has ever been produced" and ordered thousands of them.

Samuel Colt had died 10 years earlier, when he was only 47, but he had become rich on an idea that he'd had when he

was a teenager. Colt had always been interested in guns, explosives and machinery. When he was 16, sailing as a cabin boy on a ship to India, he carved a wooden model of a revolver, a pistol that could fire six times before it had to be reloaded. This was in 1831, when most guns were muzzleloaders that fired just one shot at a time.

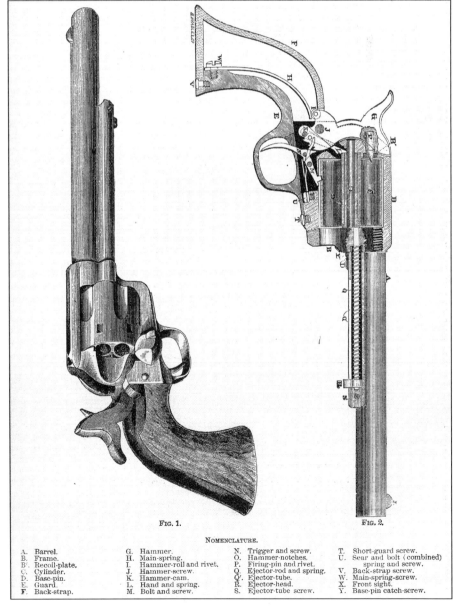

FIG. 1.   FIG. 2.

NOMENCLATURE.

A. Barrel.	G. Hammer.	N. Trigger and screw.	T. Short-guard screw.
B. Frame.	H. Main-spring.	O. Hammer-notches.	U. Sear and bolt (combined)
B'. Recoil-plate.	I. Hammer-roll and rivet.	P. Firing-pin and rivet.	spring and screw.
C. Cylinder.	J. Hammer-screw.	Q. Ejector-rod and spring.	V. Back-strap screw.
D. Base-pin.	K. Hammer-cam.	Q'. Ejector-tube.	W. Main-spring-screw.
E. Guard.	L. Hand and spring.	R. Ejector-head.	X. Front sight.
F. Back-strap.	M. Bolt and screw.	S. Ejector-tube screw.	Y. Base-pin catch-screw.

This is how *Farrow's Military Encyclopedia* of 1895 showed the US Army's new Colt SAA revolver. It recommended using only "the best sperm oil" (whale oil, that is) to lubricate the revolver's moving parts.

Revolving guns weren't new. Most of them had a cluster of barrels that turned to bring each one in line with the hammer so it could be fired. Colt's model had just one barrel; behind it was a cylinder that turned with chambers for six shots.

This was clever, but it wasn't new either. By 1818 a man from Boston named Elisha Collier had produced a flintlock gun with one barrel and seven chambers in a cylinder. After each shot the cylinder had to be rotated by hand. These Collier guns were used by British troops in India, and Colt probably saw one there or aboard the ship. Colt got the rest of his idea from the ship's steering wheel, which always locked into position after it had been turned.

Colt's revolver was like Collier's but with two improvements: First, it wasn't a flintlock; it used the new percussion caps. And second, pulling the hammer back with the thumb to cock it

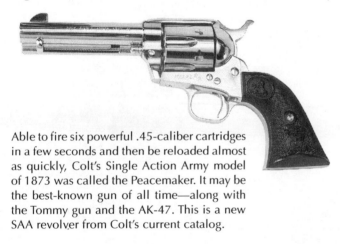

Able to fire six powerful .45-caliber cartridges in a few seconds and then be reloaded almost as quickly, Colt's Single Action Army model of 1873 was called the Peacemaker. It may be the best-known gun of all time—along with the Tommy gun and the AK-47. This is a new SAA revolver from Colt's current catalog.

also mechanically rotated the cylinder to line up the next chamber with the barrel and then lock it there. The shooter could fire the gun six times with just one hand.

Colt made his first real revolver three years later, and after that it took almost 40 years of improvements and different models (and a patent problem) to get to the Single Action Army. What really made the SAA possible, however, was metallic cartridges.

Before these came along, each chamber had to be loaded from the front with a paper cartridge:

Tear the paper, pour the powder into the chamber, then ram the rest of the paper and the ball down after it. Or you had to pour powder from a dispenser into the chamber and follow that with a ball. (The ramrod was built into the gun under the barrel.) Then a percussion cap had to be put on the nipple behind each chamber. The SAA, however, fired factory-made cartridges that just dropped into each chamber from the back.

Colts were already well known before the Single Action Army. They were used in the Civil War and then carried by the soldiers, miners, lawmen, traders, farmers, ranchers and cowboys who settled the West and fought the Indians. Samuel Colt was called the Peacemaker, because people could settle arguments just by pulling out one of his revolvers. His guns were known as equalizers, from the saying "God made men. Sam Colt made men equal."

As good as the SAA was, though, it might have disappeared but for an accident of timing and history. By the late 1800s people all over the world had become fascinated with tales of the Wild West, and the hero of these stories always relied on his trusty Colt. Buffalo Bill's Wild West Show (and others) traveled the Eastern US and Europe staging "Indian battles" and other entertainments, and Colts were used often. Newspaper reporters and dime novelists gave the Peacemaker nickname to the Single Action Army itself and made it famous. Then came the movies. The very first feature film ever made in Hollywood, in 1914, was a Western called *The Squaw Man*. Since then the Colt SAA has had a supporting role in thousands more books, stories, movies and TV shows and the "six-gun" has passed into legend, myth and history.

The SAA could be ordered with different barrel lengths, grips, sights, finishes and engraving and even with detachable shoulder stocks. Every famous sheriff and outlaw seemed to have his own favorite style. Peacemakers weren't all .45s either. Colt eventually made them in calibers from .22 to

.476 Eley (a British military round of the 1880s) and sold them all over the world. The SAA and the .45 Colt cartridge made the transition from black to smokeless gunpowder too. Colt stopped making the SAA for a while, but demand was so great that the company had to bring it back. Today a lot of companies produce their own versions of this classic; Colt still offers it in .45 and .357 Magnum. Certain models have a safety feature that lets them be carried with all six chambers loaded.

The Model 1911

The only problem with the Single Action Army was just that: It was a single-action. It had to be cocked by thumb before it could be fired. Colt followed the SAA with its double-action New Army Model 1892 revolver. No thumb required.

Double-action, however, wasn't ideal either. Cocking the hammer with the trigger takes a long finger pull against a lot of resistance, which makes the gun wobble. It can be done fast, but to be accurate takes lots of practice and skill.

There was another way. The first true machine gun, the 1880s Maxim, operated by recoil energy. The recoil slammed back the bolt, which kicked out the empty shell and re-cocked the hammer, and then a spring closed the bolt again. On its way forward, the bolt picked up a fresh round from the magazine and shoved it into the chamber. All the shooter had to do was squeeze the trigger. Why not use this system on rifles, pistols and shotguns too?

European gun companies came out with the first recoil-operated pistols, but the best one turned out to be another Colt, the Model 1911, and it too was a .45.

A gunmaking genius named John Moses Browning created the M1911 and its new cartridge. Browning was born in 1855 in Utah. He had 21 brothers and sisters, and his father was a gunsmith. By the time he died, in 1926, he held 128 firearms patents and his name was on the Browning Arms Company. But he was more interested in inventing guns than in managing a factory, so mostly he sold his gun designs to other manufacturers.

Designed by John Browning and made by Colt, the Model 1911 became a worldwide success. It was carried by American soldiers and many others through both world wars, Korea and Vietnam. It is probably the most popular combat and self-defense pistol ever made.

These designs included more than a dozen rifles and shotguns, a dozen pistols and five automatic weapons. One of these was the awesome M2 heavy machine gun, which fires the .50 BMG round. BMG stands for Browning Machine Gun. The M2 has now been on duty with American forces continually since 1921. (Generations of soldiers have called the M2 "Ma Deuce.")

Browning began work on the Model 1911 pistol around 1895. It would be called the 1911, because that was the year the US Army selected it as its sidearm.

Always looking for superior firepower, American forces had gone from Colt's SAA to its New Army Model in 1892. Not only was the New Army Model a double-action revolver, but it also fired a different cartridge: the .38 Long Colt. It was easier to shoot than the .45 because it recoiled less, but it was also less powerful. No big deal—until 1899, when American troops were sent to put down the Moro Rebellion in the Philippine Islands. The Moros were Muslim warriors fighting for their independence; as we would say today, they were highly motivated. Soldiers reported that even multiple hits from a .38 sometimes didn't discourage a Moro swinging his bolo knife. The Army shipped some .45 Colt single-actions to the Philippines, and supposedly the bigger, heavier bullets did the trick.

And then along came auto pistols, which were easier to shoot and faster to reload than revolvers (with pre-loaded magazines). The US Ordnance Department invited manufacturers to submit their pistols to be tried out. Meanwhile, Col. John T. Thompson (who later invented the Tommy gun) and a major from the Medical Corps named Louis LaGarde test-fired all sorts of handguns at human cadavers and even live cows, and then announced that the Army's new pistol should not be less than .45 caliber.

The Colt company and John Browning were listening. In 1904 Browning created a new cartridge that fired a .45-caliber bullet weighing 230 grains at 850 fps. It was slightly less powerful than the .45 Colt SAA round, but it was a lot more compact. It was named the .45 ACP, for Automatic Colt Pistol. Then Browning set about perfecting the gun itself.

After years of testing and development, the .45 Automatic Colt Pistol beat out all other competitors. John Browning himself attended the last big trial, where one of his guns fired 6,000 rounds in two days without a problem. Whenever the pistol got too hot, it was dunked in a tank of water. On March 29, 1911, it was declared the winner.

John Browning's 1911 pistol was an instant success all over the world. (Did you notice the one fired at Leonardo DiCaprio in *Titanic*, a movie that was set in 1912?) It was carried by American soldiers and many others through the two world wars, Korea and Vietnam. In WWII Colt couldn't keep up with the orders, so other companies were licensed to produce it too. It is probably the most popular combat and self-defense pistol ever made, exactly the sort of "man-stopper" that Thompson and La-Garde and every trooper wanted.

British and American lieutenants aboard the SS *Mongolia* in April 1917, possibly in a combined training exercise on deck. The American holds an early Model 1911. *Mongolia* carried troops to Europe in the early days of WWI. The US Navy equipped the ship with six-inch guns, with which she fired on, and may have sunk, a German submarine in the English Channel. This was the first American naval action of that war.

In 1985, though, after more tests, it was replaced as the official US sidearm by the Beretta M9. This caused a tremendous uproar. Not only was the beloved .45 ACP giving way to a less-powerful round—the 9x19mm cartridge, originally made for the Luger—the Beretta wasn't even American; it was an Italian pistol!

The selection committee pointed to the advantages of the new pistol. Its magazine held 15 cartridges compared to the 1911's seven. It was double-action, meaning that once the slide had been worked to chamber a round, the hammer could be lowered (for safety) and then fired with the trigger finger. (If it's down, the M1911's hammer has to be thumbed back, single-action, for the first shot.) The 9mm round was used by all other NATO armies, and the US should use the same ammunition as its allies. Even though it was less powerful, a metal-jacketed 9mm bullet could penetrate certain kinds of body armor of the day that would stop the fatter .45 round. And finally, the Army's old M1911s were worn out and had to be replaced anyway.

Furthermore, except for the Ingram MAC-10, no one was making .45-caliber submachine guns any more either. The Thompson, the M3 "Grease Gun" and the Reising of World War II and Korea were long gone, replaced by lighter, handier submachine guns that fired the 9mm round.

The grumbling hasn't completely stopped yet. Some American troops have quietly gone back to the M1911 and the .45 ACP for the same reason that it replaced the .38 Long Colt more than a century ago. They say the 9mm isn't stopping those highly motivated Muslim warriors, this time in Afghanistan.

Well, OK. But here's an interesting thing: The Thompson-LaGarde tests, which in 1904 chose .45-caliber bullets for their "stopping effect at short ranges," also recommended that "soldiers armed with pistols or revolvers should be drilled unremittingly in the accuracy of fire," as there was "no hope of stopping an adversary by shock or other immediate results." In other words, *where* a bullet is put is always more important than how big or powerful it is. (Read "Stopping Power" and "Knockdown Force.")

Back when he was an undercover cop, one of the authors had a bad day at work. He was hit by two .38 bullets and two .45s. He couldn't feel any difference between them.

The Vietnam War. With just a flashlight and a Model 1911 .45 pistol and probably thinking about booby traps and snakes, an American soldier prepares to enter a Viet Cong supply tunnel.

It's hard to find anything that has lasted for a century or more without enormous changes. Your family car doesn't look or drive anything like the first practical automobile, built in 1885. All that a Boeing 787 Dreamliner has in common with the Wright brothers' biplane of 1903 is that they both can fly under their own power. ENIAC, the first fully functional digital computer, was the size of a house, weighed 50 tons and cost a half-million dollars when your grandparents were your age. Compare that to the computer on your desk now.

But imagine a Texas Ranger who traveled through time from John Wesley Hardin's day to appear at your shooting range today. You could hand him a Single Action Army made last week and he'd know exactly what to do with it. (He'd be surprised, though, that firing it didn't make a cloud of white smoke.) He probably would be carrying one himself. Same goes for a Doughboy—as American troops were called in World War I—if you handed him a modern Model 1911.

Winchester: The 'Cowboy' Guns

In 1950 Universal Pictures released a block-buster movie called *Winchester '73*. The cast included some big names but, as you may have guessed, the real star of the movie was a Model 1873 Winchester. The story line was the adventures that the rifle had as it passed through different characters' hands.

The original 1950 movie poster for *Winchester '73*. Actor James Stewart got top billing, but the real star was his rifle. It was called "the gun that won the West," and it was the first of many Winchester lever-action guns. Just like with the Colt SAA, Hollywood helped make it popular.

(It seems like ancient history now, but the fighting between the US Army and the Indians ended only in 1890, in South Dakota. That was just 60 years before *Winchester '73* came out and well within the lifetime of many people who saw it.)

Sam Colt might have objected, but Winchester's Model 1873 rifle was called "the gun that won the West." Back in 1950 some moviegoers perhaps could tell the difference between a Model 73 and, say, a Model 94, but today most people see a lever-action rifle and just think *Winchester!* Other American gun companies, especially Marlin and Savage, made superb lever-actions too, but Winchester gets most of the credit. There have been 16 different lever-action Winchesters: 14 rifles and two shotguns. John Browning, the genius who invented the Colt Model 1911 and so many other great firearms, designed five of them. (He even based his first machine gun on one of them, but that's another story.)

Browning and most other important American gun designers—Eli Whitney, Sam Colt, Eliphalet Remington, John Garand, Gene Stoner, Bill Ruger and so on—were engineers and machinists. Oliver Winchester, however, was a businessman. He knew about advertising, managing money and how to choose employees and products. Winchester was born in Massachusetts in 1810. He became a carpenter's apprentice and a house builder. Then he switched careers and started a clothing company in New York City that made a fortune in men's shirts. In 1855 he bought the Volcanic Arms Company, in Connecticut, which had been started by Horace Smith and Daniel Wesson, who later became famous for Smith & Wesson handguns. Winchester renamed it the New Haven Arms Company.

When the Civil War started, in 1861, New Haven Arms was making a 16-shot lever-operated rifle called the .44 Henry (named for Benjamin Tyler Henry, the man who designed it). At a time when single-shot muzzleloaders were common, this was radical. At first, though, the Union Army didn't want it. Too fragile, they said, and besides, it needed special ammunition, not just powder and ball. But many soldiers bought Henry rifles and ammunition for themselves. The South called it "that Yankee rifle they load on Sunday and shoot all week!" By 1863 the Union and some European governments were buying Henrys.

After the war, in 1866, Oliver Winchester sold his shirt business, and New Haven Arms became the Winchester Repeating Arms Company. The first rifle with the Winchester name on it came out that year. The Model 1866 was an improved

The Henry and the Model 66 both fired the .44 Henry, a stubby little rimfire round. The Model 73 got a slightly bigger centerfire version called the .44-40 Winchester. Colt and Remington and other companies made revolvers for both of these rounds, which made it easier to pack ammunition. But with each new Winchester lever-action after that—models 1876, 1886, 1892, 1894, 1895—came more-powerful cartridges. (This wasn't true for the M92, which was only for handgun ammunition.) Still, the US Cavalry kept its Springfield breechloading carbine through the Indian Wars, which ended in 1890. Even though it was only a single-shot, the Springfield was more powerful and accurate than most Winchesters. It was harder to reload on horseback, but the

A Winchester Model 1886. This one has a full-length magazine tube under the barrel. With almost every new lever-action model, Winchester also brought out more-powerful ammunition.

version of the Henry, and the Henry was based on a gun made by Volcanic Arms.

Like the Henry and the Volcanic, the Model 66 was operated by a finger lever under the stock grip. The lever could be worked very quickly with the rifle at the shoulder and even on a moving horse. Other benefits of the lever-action were that the shooter could uncock the rifle just by lowering the hammer with his thumb, and (as the Confederate Army found out) the magazine tube under the barrel could hold a lot of ammo. They weren't precision target rifles, but Winchesters were accurate enough out to 150 yards or more.

troopers normally used their horses only as transportation; they dismounted to fight. (Never mind what you see in the movies.)

The later Model 1895 lever-action could fire the .405 Winchester, which was introduced in 1904 as a big-game cartridge. Theodore Roosevelt and his son Kermit both brought Model 95 .405s to Africa on their year-long safari in 1910, and they reported that the rifles "did admirably with lions, giraffes, elands and . . . hippos."

It turned out the M95 could even handle the modern, high-pressure .30-06 Springfield round, which came along in 1906. This was partly because of its five-round box magazine, which stacked the ammunition vertically. You can't put cartridges with spitzer (pointed) bullets into a tube magazine because of the risk of setting off a primer with the point of the bullet behind it. However, the box magazine makes the 95 uncomfortable to carry in one hand.

Otherwise, lever-actions generally balance and handle very well, more like a good shotgun than a rifle. They're outstanding for quick shooting at close range, and they're also quite flat, so they fit neatly

The Winchester Model 95 lever-action rifle had a box magazine, which could safely hold cartridges with high-performance spitzer (pointed) bullets. In Africa both Kermit Roosevelt and his father used .405-caliber M95s for big game.

into a saddle scabbard. This is why a lot of ranchers still carry them as working rifles. For some reason, though, while lever-actions were popular in the US, Canada and Mexico and into Central and South America and even Cuba, they never caught on anywhere else. With one exception, sort of: Russia.

As you've read, when World War I began, in 1914, the Russians couldn't make rifles fast enough for their huge army. So along with more Mosin-Nagants from Remington and Westinghouse, Tsar Nicholas II's Ministry of War also ordered 300,000 lever-action rifles: Winchester Model 95 military muskets with bayonet mounts chambered for the 7.62x54R Mosin-Nagant cartridge. The Winchesters were delivered in 1915 and 1916, but most were never used, because Russia withdrew from WWI after the Bolshevik Revolution. Fifty years later, just like many of the surplus Mosin-Nagants, thousands of these Winchesters wound up back in the US, where they were sold on the open market at cheap prices.

In 1955 Winchester came out with its most unusual lever-action, the Model 88, the only lever gun that didn't have an exposed hammer. It had a different bolt, too, that was strong enough for any high-pressure ammunition. The M88 sold well, but it was discontinued in 1973.

Winchester has made all sorts of rifles with all sorts of actions, but the most popular has been the Model 1894, especially in .30-30 Winchester caliber. It was the first lever-action Winchester specifically designed (by John Browning) for smokeless powder. For many years the 94 was America's traditional "deer rifle," and by now close to 8 million

have been made. For a while it was even available as a .410 shotgun.

Back in 1938 Daisy copied the Model 94 with its Red Ryder, and that became the best-selling BB gun. Marlin, too, set some production records with lever guns. One of Annie Oakley's favorite rifles was Marlin's Model 1891, a lever-action .22. This became the Model 1897, and then the Model 39, and finally the Model 39A, and it's been in continuous production longer than any other gun in America.

Winchester produced lever-action .22s also. Now the company is again offering versions of the Models 86, 92, 94 and 95 in calibers that range from .357 Magnum to .405 Winchester. Lever-actions still rule!

When Oliver Winchester died, in 1880, his company passed to his son William, but he died just three months later. William's widow, Sarah, inherited half of the company and an income of $1,000 a day. (That's like $22,000 per day today.) Sarah's and William's only child had died when she was a baby, and Sarah came to believe that the Winchester family was cursed because of all the deaths caused by their rifles. A psychic told her to build a house for all of those spirits and that if construction ever stopped, she herself would die. In 1884 in California she started adding rooms to an old farmhouse. Construction continued around the clock, seven days a week, 365 days a year for the next 38 years. When Sarah died, in 1922, the house had 160 rooms. It's now a National Historic Monument known as the Winchester Mystery House.

Dr. Gatling's Rapid-Fire Gun

The taming of horses, swords made of bronze, the longbow and the crossbow, gunpowder—these advancements all led to tremendous changes in combat. However, it's likely that the machine gun has had a greater effect on warfare than anything else. At least so far.

Once guns arrived on the battlefield, possibly in China in the 12th Century or in Italy in the 13th, inventors immediately began trying to increase their firepower. Early firearms were not only horribly inaccurate but also very slow to load and incapable of sustained fire. Around 1481 Leonardo Da Vinci, in Italy, designed one of the earliest guns that could, at least in theory, produce a high rate of fire. It had three rows of multiple barrels; when one row was being fired, the others could be reloaded.

For the next four centuries all manner of firearms were introduced. One of the most interesting was Englishman James Puckle's repeating gun of 1718. It had a single barrel and a revolving cylinder with six chambers. A hand crank turned the cylinder, and the gun fired whenever a chamber lined up with the barrel. Puckle even came up with interchangeable cylinders that could be pre-loaded for faster firing. Not only that, but he also proposed two kinds of cylinders: one that fired round bullets for use against Christians, the other square bullets for "slaying heathen Turks."

Almost 150 years later, in Indiana, it was an American medical-school graduate and farm-equipment inventor named Richard Gatling who created the first practical rapid-firing gun. He began work on it in 1861 as the Civil War began and earned a patent on it the next year. His design reversed Puckle's gun. Instead of six revolving chambers, Gatling used six revolving barrels, also turned by a crank. Each barrel fired once per revolution. The ammunition was fed by gravity from a magazine that sat on top of the gun. The

A 10-barrel Gatling gun on a tripod with its gravity-fed, rotating magazine. In its first 50 years, the Gatling gun fired paper, rimfire and centerfire cartridges in calibers that ranged from .30 to 1 inch. On a windless day blackpowder Gatlings must have made an impressive smoke cloud during rapid fire.

story goes that Dr. Gatling took the idea from the planting machine he'd invented for farmers that had a cylinder that dropped a seed into a furrow with each turn of a handle. The rate of fire was determined by how fast a team of gunners could turn the crank to revolve the barrels and also refill or replace the magazine.

In spite of Gatling's best efforts to sell it, his gun didn't see much use in the Civil War. (In 1864 he wrote a letter to President Lincoln calling his invention "just the thing needed to aid in crushing the present rebellion.") But early versions of his gun were unreliable, and many Army officers regarded it as wasteful of ammunition and even "ungentlemanly."

The Confederacy surrendered in 1865. By 1876 the US military was reduced from more than 1 million troops to about 26,000, and its funding shrank even more. The Army eventually did buy some improved Gatling guns, but it still had no plan for how to use them. Lt. Col. George Custer could have brought Gatling guns to the Little Big Horn but chose not to. Would a couple of them have changed the outcome?

A modern, hydraulically powered seven-barreled Gatling gun—the 30mm Avenger, mounted under the nose of an A-10 Thunderbolt (also known as a Warthog) ground-attack jet. The recoil is so severe that the gun has to be positioned so it doesn't throw the plane off course.

Meanwhile, both the British (in Africa) and the Russians (in Central Asia) and then other countries found uses for Gatling's invention. Finally in 1898 US forces used Gatlings to great effect in Cuba during the Spanish-American War.

However, the Gatling gun was officially declared obsolete in 1911. Single-barreled, truly automatic machine guns by Maxim, Hotchkiss, Colt and Chauchat—smaller, lighter, faster, more portable and less expensive—ruled the battlefields of World War I. But this wasn't the end of Dr. Gatling's gun.

Already in 1893 Gatling had been granted a patent for an improvement to his gun that used an electric motor to spin the barrels. Correspondence from the US War Department in 1914 indicated

that this motorized Gatling had achieved a rate of fire of 3,000 rounds per minute from 10 barrels. Impressive as this was, it didn't seem terribly useful at the time, and the electric Gatling gun would have to wait a half-century to be rediscovered.

Putting "more lead in the air" became important during World War II (1941–1945) for all sorts of reasons, such as shooting down bigger and faster airplanes. But the rate of fire of single-barreled machine guns is limited by how fast their actions can cycle (eject-reload-cock-fire). In 1946 a 10-barreled .45-70-caliber Gatling that had been made in 1903 was connected to an electric motor and managed an amazing 5,000 shots per minute—about four times as many as any single-barreled machine gun could achieve.

The electric Gatling could handle cartridges of almost any size, including those able to destroy armored vehicles, so designers first built a 20mm (.79-caliber) model. Then they went in the other direction and downsized the Gatling for the Army's 7.62x51mm M14 rifle round. The result was the Minigun, which has been installed in airplanes, helicopters, boats and all sorts of vehicles, even SUVs. Arnold Schwarzenegger used a Minigun in *Terminator*. Its ability to fire up to 6,000 rounds per minute—100 per second—is impressive, but since it weighs more than 65 pounds and 1,000 rounds of ammo weigh another 55 pounds, it's not a gun you walk around with (unless, of course, you're the Terminator).

The saying "Everything old is new again" applies neatly to Dr. Gatling's gun. His design of 150 years ago is now being used to shoot down rockets: The Phalanx Close-In Weapon System is the US Navy's last line of defense against anti-ship missiles, and it is a very bad boy indeed.

To the ancient Greeks, a phalanx was a tight formation of heavily armed infantry. The automated, radar-controlled US Navy Phalanx looks like R2-D2, but its 10 electrically driven barrels can launch 4,500 20mm tungsten or depleted-uranium projectiles per minute. It simply chews incoming missiles to shreds. And then there's the GAU-8/A 30mm Gatling with seven barrels spun by hydraulic pressure. Also known as the Avenger, this is what makes the US Air Force A-10 Thunderbolt ground-attack jet a devastating tank-buster. The recoil of sustained firing at 4,200 RPM is enough to throw the "Warthog" off course, so the cannon is mounted off-axis in the plane's belly to compensate.

When asked why he had invented his gun, Dr. Gatling replied, "It occurred to me that if I could invent a machine—a gun—that would by its rapidity of fire enable one man to do as much battle duty as a hundred, that it would to a great extent supersede the necessity for large armies, and consequently exposure to battle and disease would be greatly diminished." He was, of course, entirely wrong. It only made battle more deadly.

Gen. Thompson's Trench Broom

Indiana's Richard Gatling and Maine's Hiram Maxim brought the world the rapid-firing machine gun. Then an American Army officer from Kentucky made the machine gun portable.

The Thompson Sub-Machine Gun, as it was officially called, was the invention of Brig. Gen. John T. Thompson, West Point class of 1882. Thompson wasn't a combat commander; he was an ordnance officer, a weapons specialist. During the Spanish-American War of 1898, he shipped Gatling guns to American troops in Cuba. Afterward he supervised the development of the famous Model 1903 Springfield Army rifle. He and a medical-corps officer created the tests that decided that the Army's pistol should be no less than .45 caliber, and then Thompson was appointed chairman of the committee that chose the Colt Model 1911 to be the official sidearm of the US military.

Then came the Great War in Europe, which began in 1914. (For reasons that should be obvious,

Gen. John T. Thompson, US Army, retired, shows off a version of his gun without a shoulder stock. At first he called it the "Annihilator."

it wasn't called World War I until after World War II.) Thompson wanted to serve, but America did not enter the war right away, so he left the Army and became chief engineer at Remington Arms. The company built a huge factory to make rifles for Britain and Russia, which were allied with the French and the Italians against the Germans. Thompson reenlisted in 1917, when the US finally got into the war, and was put in charge of all of the Army's arsenals and production of small arms (firearms that can be carried).

The Great War proved that old-fashioned military tactics didn't work against modern weapons such as submarines, airplanes, tanks, breechloading artillery, flamethrowers, poison gas and even radios, barbed wire and buried mines. British officers, for example, thought the newfangled machine gun was only to be used against native tribesmen in places like Africa and India. They were still in love with the horse and sent cavalry charges against the Germans. The Germans, however, had no problem with machine guns, and they used them to slaughter the British and their allies.

Both sides took cover in trenches dug across the battlefields of France and Belgium, and there the troops stayed while the generals tried to figure out what to do next.

Gen. Thompson thought that what American soldiers needed was not their long-range bolt-action Springfield rifles but handy, fast-firing weapons for combat at arm's-length— "trench brooms" for cleaning the Germans out

A Model 1928 Thompson Submachine Gun with a 50-round drum magazine. It was meant for the close-quarters trench warfare of WWI, but the military didn't buy it until WWII. Meanwhile, though, crooks and then cops made it famous.

of their ditches. To keep things simple, it had to use standard military ammunition. The .30-06 Springfield round was too powerful, so Thompson chose the .45 ACP (Automatic Colt Pistol) cartridge from the Model 1911—which he'd helped develop. He called his invention a submachine gun, and the word stuck. A submachine gun is lighter and smaller than a machine gun and fires pistol ammunition.

The war ended before Thompson finished his new gun, but he stayed with it. The US Army and Marines tested it in 1920 and '21. *Scientific American* Magazine called it "the most efficient man killer of any firearm yet produced." The military wasn't interested.

WWI was supposed to be the war that ended all wars, so afterward America again drastically cut the size of its military. Many high-ranking officers thought they'd never need Thompson's gun. Some of the older officers still thought of machine guns as "cheating" too, while the Marines saw themselves as precision riflemen not given to "spray and pray" shooting.

Gen. Thompson's company, the Auto-Ordnance Corporation, turned instead to police departments and the general public. (Until the National Firearms Act of 1934 there were no restrictions on the sale of machine guns in America.) To Thompson's dismay, one market did immediately adopt his product: criminals! The first recorded use of a Thompson in gang warfare was in Chicago on September 25, 1925. Because of its impressive *rat-a-tat-tat* noise, it was nicknamed the "Chicago typewriter." Pretty soon every bootlegger and bank robber had a Thompson. In response the FBI started buying them too.

True success, however, had to wait until the next world war, which started in 1939. American soldiers and their allies loved the Thompson. They called it the Tommy gun, and it was ideal for house-to-house combat in Europe and against Japanese troops dug into the Pacific Islands. The Tommy gun was still on duty with the American military as late as the Vietnam War, which ended in 1975.

Ten years later US forces switched from the Model 1911 .45 pistol to the Beretta M9, which fired the 9mm round. The Thompson could have been adapted to fire the same cartridge, but by then it was obsolete for other reasons. Compared to an Uzi, a Heckler & Koch or other more modern submachine gun, the Thompson is big and heavy.

In 1921 Auto-Ordnance had slowed the gun's rate of fire to about 800 rounds per minute and settled its weight at around 12 pounds, nicely balanced. This helped tame the recoil of the big .45 ACP cartridge; keeping the muzzle on target was much easier than legend has it. Fired from the shoulder, it was reasonably accurate out to 100 yards in full-auto or single-shot mode. Fired from the hip, it really could sweep out a trench, as Gen. Thompson had wanted. The gun was also well made and simple, with few moving parts. Without tools, it could be disassembled for cleaning in less than two minutes.

Different models used straight 20- and 30-round stick magazines or round drum magazines that held 50 or 100 cartridges. The 100-round drum was not only heavy (and took forever to load) but also so wide that the gunner couldn't fire from the shoulder because he couldn't get his arm around the magazine to hold the front grip.

"Tommy gun" is still a household word, and it still may be the most recognizable gun

Some kids have all the luck. Christina Helsley, at age 15, firing a Model 1928 Thompson with a 100-round drum magazine. The weight helps keep the muzzle down. Note the ear and eye protection and gloves. And the smile.

Steve Helsley

ever made. Auto-Ordnance is still in business too, producing semi-automatic Thompsons for people who want a piece of history that still shoots up a storm.

Russia's AK-47 Assault Rifle

Chances are that no matter where you live or what language you speak, you know what an "A-K" is, or at least you think you do. AK-47 stands for Automatic by Kalashnikov of 1947, and it is the most famous and widely used of all assault rifles. The AK seems to be everywhere—on TV, in movies and in newspapers and magazines. It is estimated that *100 million* AK rifles have been made. So far, anyway. That's one for *every 70 people* on earth.

(The runner-up as the world's most popular assault rifle is the American M16, but it's far back in second place. Over 50 years about 8 million M16s have been built.)

The AK's inventor, a Russian soldier named Mikhail Kalashnikov, didn't set out to be a gun designer. When he was drafted into the Soviet

Army in 1938, just before World War II, he was a clerk for the Turkistan-Siberian Railway Department. During his training to be a tank driver, he designed a number of things that improved his tank's operation. His officers noticed, so after he recovered from injuries received in 1941 during the 19-day Battle of Bryansk, he was reassigned to work on creating new weapons.

The USSR, then armed with the Mosin-Nagant, was pushing hard to develop an assault rifle. This became known as "Stalin's contest," and Senior Sergeant Kalashnikov wound up winning it. (Joseph Stalin was the Premier of the Soviet Union during World War II.) No one could imagine just how significant Kalashnikov's accomplishment would turn out to be.

Andrey Ugarov

One of the world's most famous gun designers, Maj. Gen. Mikhail Kalashnikov, being declared a Hero of the Russian Federation at his 90th birthday celebration in Moscow.

Generally armies have two small-arms cartridges: one for handguns and submachine guns, the other for rifles and light machine guns. For the Soviet Red Army these were the 7.62x25mm and the 7.62x54mm. The smaller one often didn't penetrate well, while the other one was needlessly big and powerful for close combat. When Kalashnikov began his design work, the Battle of Stalingrad had just ended. During that bloody six-month horror, which was one of the turning points of WWII, the fighting often had been not just house to house but room to room in bombed-out buildings. The attacking Germans eventually were captured or killed, but the Russians had seen the need for a new fast-firing rifle that was lighter and handier than the Mosin-Nagant.

The ordnance department designed the cartridge first. It should be a medium-power round that didn't create too much recoil in automatic fire and was compact enough that a soldier could carry a lot of them. The Soviet pistol and submachine-gun round launched an 86-grain bullet at 1,390 fps, and the rifle cartridge produced 2,880 fps with a 147-grain bullet. The new 7.62x39mm split the difference: a 122-grain bullet at 2,320 fps. Soviet forces adopted it in 1943.

The first rifle to use it was the SKS-45, which is short for Semiautomatic Carbine by Simonov of 1945. The SKS had a fixed 10-round magazine and was used by China, East Germany and many other Communist countries also. Meanwhile Kalashnikov and his team were finalizing the AK design. It would have a detachable magazine, usually for 30 rounds, and be capable of semi-automatic or automatic fire. It was approved in 1947 and went into full production in 1949.

The AK-47 arrived too late for the big war, so it was fired in anger first in East Berlin in 1953, when Soviet troops were ordered to put down an uprising of their dissatisfied German "comrades." Three years later the Red Army used tanks and AK-47s to smash a revolt in Hungary, another country that had been trapped inside the USSR ("behind the Iron Curtain," as Winston Churchill put it) when World War II ended.

Since then AKs have played major roles in scores of revolutions, wars, terrorist attacks and political assassinations, not to mention thousands of crimes. Because so many of them have been made and they're so easy to buy, the AK-47 is the weapon of choice for villains everywhere, from drug cartels in Central America to warlords and poachers across Africa. It is so well known that in some places boys are named "Kalash." The rifle even appears on the national flag of Mozambique!

For his work, Kalashnikov received the Stalin Prize First Class in 1949. Many more awards followed. In 1994, on his 75th birthday, Kalashnikov was promoted to Major General by Russian President Boris Yeltsin. On his 90th birthday Kalashnikov was declared a Hero of the Russian Federation by President Medvedev for creating "the brand every Russian is proud of."

While Russian politicians want the world to believe that Kalashnikov alone invented the AK, in 2009 Kalashnikov admitted that Hugo Schmeisser, a German engineer who was captured at the end of the WWII, had a lot to do with it. Schmeisser had led the design team that created the German StG 44, the first modern assault rifle. StG stands for *Sturmgewehr*, which is German for "assault rifle."

The basic military-grade AK-47, with wooden stocks and bayonet. Since 1947 about 100 million of these rifles have been manufactured. Because they're so common and easy to use, AK-47s became the weapons of choice for bad guys everywhere.

The basic AK-47 isn't very accurate but, just like its predecessor, the Mosin-Nagant, it is famous for being a tough, reliable, low-maintenance weapon that uneducated fighters can quickly learn to use. It can be buried under an anthill in Uganda for years, and then dug up, wiped off, oiled, loaded and fired. Rain, snow, mud, dust, heat or freezing cold doesn't faze the AK. Kalashnikov once said, "Anything that is complex is not useful, and anything that is useful is simple."

(This is classic Russian thinking. Here's another good example of Russia's basic approach to engineering: In the early days of the Space Race, when the US and the USSR were competing to see who could land a man on the moon first, NASA announced that it had spent a million dollars to create a pen that could write upside-down and in zero gravity. The Russians said, "Hey, that's great. We use a pencil." The story isn't true, but it's accurate, if you see the difference.)

The AK has been manufactured in countries from Finland to Yugoslavia to Ethiopia. Through more than 65 years, many variations of it have appeared, including the AKM, the RPK and the AK-74. The latter was the Soviet answer to the American M16, a lighter assault rifle that fires a smaller cartridge, the also-new 5.45x39mm Soviet. This "Automatic by Kalashnikov of 1974" became the standard-issue Soviet military rifle and, as usual, there are different versions for different uses plus add-ons like grenade launchers and night sights.

The Russians are changing over again, this time to AK-100 series rifles. A lot of these (the AK-101, AK-102, AK-103, AK-104, AK-108) are meant to be sold to other countries, so they're chambered for the NATO 5.56x45mm and 7.62x51mm rounds.

The Russians are keeping the AK-105 and AK-107, which fire the 5.45x39mm round, for themselves, and today there's a newer version called the AK-12.

The point is that Mikhail Kalashnikov's famous rifle of 1947 became a "system" and inspired a lot of other guns. (Just like the American ArmaLite AR-15/M16.) There's even a semi-auto model called the Saiga that's popular with Russian hunters.

The latest descendant of the AK-47 is this AK-12, available in "light" and "heavy" models for different cartridges. It made its public debut in January 2012; rumor has it that development is still underway.

In the late 1980s semi-automatic versions of the AK began to arrive in the US, mostly from China. Efforts to ban them began almost immediately, which likely just got more people interested. Now AKs are made in the US too—and, like Daisy BB guns, they're available with pink stocks.

The machine gun's effect on the early 20th Century was profound. The impact of the AK-47 on the second half of the 20th Century was equally significant. As the gun's production continues, although more slowly than before, generations of people yet unborn will come to know what "A-K" means. In his book *The Gun*, C.J. Chivers reflects on when the "AK era" might end: "This will not be a short time. It will not even be decades. But in another half-century, or century, the rifles will have broken, one by one, and the chance exists that they will no longer be a significant factor in war, terror, atrocity, and crime."

Rocket Guns: Still Sci-Fi

For the past 50 years rockets have been propelling all sorts of things into space, including monkeys, people, moon and Mars rovers, satellites and reusable shuttles. Before that, during World War II, the Germans fired rockets loaded with explosives against England. And more than a century before that the Sultan of Mysore, in India, had a rocket artillery corps that fired self-propelled shells (not very accurately).

You may wonder whether the rocket principle has ever been adapted to guns. Why not a bullet that's a self-propelled mini-missile?

In 1929 readers of comic books first met Buck Rogers, the action hero of the 25th Century.

He had a pistol that fired exploding rockets instead of bullets, so it wasn't long before a rocket pistol hit the market. But the Model XZ-31 was a toy—a popgun made by Daisy, the BB-gun company. It was followed by the XZ-38 Disintegrator Pistol and then the U-235 Atomic Pistol, also from Daisy.

Science fiction can become science fact pretty quickly. By the early 1960s a real version of the XZ-31 had been invented: the Gyrojet, a futuristic-looking semi-automatic pistol with a new kind of ammunition made by a company in California called MBAssociates.

The Gyrojet was tested by the National Rifle Association in October 1965. The Mark I model fired 13mm (.51-caliber, or just more than a half-inch in diameter) solid-fuel rockets that were 1.4 inches long and looked like .45 ACP cartridges. Each rocket weighed 240 grains before firing and 188 grains after, when the fuel had been used up. The gases from the propellant escaped through four holes in the rocket's base that were angled to make the rocket spin for stabilization. (There was no rifling in the barrel.) The rocket's burn time was 0.12 second, by which time it was 45 feet downrange and had reached a maximum velocity of 1,250 fps. Then it began to slow down.

Daisy's Buck Rogers-inspired toy ray guns. The XZ-31 (bottom), an XZ-35 (right) and the wooden prototype. No inventor has yet been able to make rocket guns work well.

Smithsonian Institution

At 10 feet the rocket could penetrate a one-inch pine board; at 45 feet and maximum energy, it could punch through seven boards. At 100 yards the Gyrojet had about the same energy as a 158-grain .357 Magnum bullet at the same distance: 440 foot-pounds.

The Mark I pistol held six rounds. When the trigger was pulled, the hammer struck the front of the rocket, pushing it back onto a firing pin that touched off the primer. As the rocket moved down the barrel, it re-cocked the hammer for the next shot . . . or launch.

The pistol was light—just 1 pound 12 ounces, or about a pound less than a Colt Model 1911 .45— and firing it produced almost no recoil. But there were major problems. Accuracy was awful. The best 10-shot group the NRA was able to obtain was 15 inches across, and this was from a rest at 25 yards. (A 1911 Colt would keep its bullets within about three inches under those conditions.) At close range, before the rocket achieved full velocity, penetration was poor. Firing the rocket produced a huge muzzle flash. Finally, humidity in the air could get in

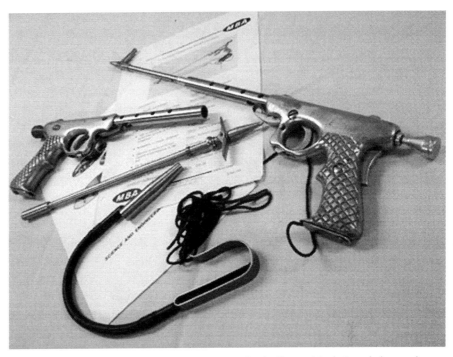

The real thing. MBAssociates Gyrojet guns, including a Mark I and the underwater harpoon model. A Gyrojet appeared in a James Bond movie, and the guns were even field-tested in combat in the Vietnam War, but they were inaccurate and unreliable.

through the vent holes and dampen the fuel, turning a rocket into a dud.

MBA had grand plans for its Gyrojet. The company imagined rocket-firing machine guns, assault rifles, carbines and even an underwater spear. The pistol appeared in the 1967 James Bond film *You Only Live Twice* and even had a limited field test during the Vietnam War, but none of the company's dreams came true. The Gyrojet is now a collector's item and the answer to a trivia question. Best estimates put total production at about 600 pistols. Today a live Gyrojet 13mm rocket can sell for $150.

The Gyrojet wasn't the only attempt to harness rocket power in a firearm, but it is the best known. It's probably pretty much what Philip Nowlan, the creator of Buck Rogers, had in mind.

A .45 ACP cartridge (left) next to fired and unfired Gyrojet rounds. Note the rocket-exhaust vents in the base; the nose of the projectile got flattened by whatever it hit. Gyrojet rounds are collectors' items.

Silencers: Naughty or Nice?

One of the first commercial silencers was produced in the early 1900s by Hiram Percy Maxim, the son of Hiram Stevens Maxim, the man from Maine who was knighted by England's Queen Victoria for inventing the self-powered machine gun.

Percy Maxim came up with his silencer as a way "to meet my personal desire to enjoy target practice without creating a disturbance. I have always loved to shoot, but I never thoroughly enjoyed it when I knew that the noise was annoying other people."

Today if you mount a silencer on the muzzle of your rifle in England, you're a considerate sportsman. Do the same thing in the US, though, and you're a "racketeer, drug trafficker or professional killer" (as someone once testified to a Congressional committee). Somehow Maxim's item of neighborly consideration wound up blacklisted by our feds.

England has very restrictive gun-control laws, while Americans enjoy exceptional firearms freedom. So why this huge difference in attitude about a harmless—beneficial, actually—shooting accessory?

With the National Firearms Act of 1934, the US Government for the first time regulated machine guns, sawed-off shotguns and rifles, hand grenades and . . . silencers. The activities of notorious gangsters were the motivation for trying to control the guns and explosives, but the reason for going after silencers isn't clear any more. The country was in the Great Depression at the time, with millions of people poor and hungry, and some researchers now think that poaching game animals (killing them illegally) with silenced firearms was the problem.

Whatever the reason, the 1934 law required anyone who wanted to own these items to register with the US Treasury Department, to have their background checked for criminal history, and then to pay a $200 tax. The National Firearms Act still stands; since then some states have added more restrictions and made the penalties worse if a silencer is used in committing a crime. So much for Percy Maxim's good intentions.

Percy Maxim, son of the man who invented the machine gun, wanted shooters to use silencers so the noise didn't bother the neighbors. Instead, at least in the US, silencers somehow became associated with professional assassins.

'Turning Off the Noise'

Sound is air in motion. The noise when we trigger off any firearm comes from the high-pressure gas of the burning powder leaving the barrel behind the bullet. It travels outward from the gun's muzzle in a wave, which causes sudden changes in air pressure that our ears translate into sound. This is what makes the *bang!* or *boom!*

Sound levels are expressed in decibels, shortened to "dB." Sounds vary from zero decibels to 194 dB, which is the loudest possible sound. A whisper in a quiet library measures 30 dB, while normal conversation reaches 60 to 70 decibels. City traffic runs at about 85 dB. Each time the dB number goes up by 10 points, the sound is 10 times louder.

A .338 Lapua Magnum sniper rifle built on a Savage action and outfitted with a synthetic stock, a bipod and a screw-on, can-type suppressor. "Turning off the noise" when you shoot is pretty cool. It also has a lot of benefits.

When noise levels reach 90 to 95 decibels, we suffer at least temporary hearing loss. A loud rock concert registers about 115 dB, but the music can hit 150 dB. At 125 dB we feel physical pain in our ears. Just a quick blast at 140 dB causes permanent damage. Hearing tissue dies at 180 dB.

Firing an air rifle makes a sound that measures only 88 to 94 decibels. But from just three feet away, a .22 pistol makes 155 dB and a .223 rifle round reaches 163 dB. In either case, shooters who aren't wearing good ear protection will suffer immediate hearing damage. Maybe only a small amount, but it's permanent and it adds up.

So what does a silencer do? First, it is more accurate to describe it as a "muffler," as the British do. (If your family car didn't have a muffler, the noise would be awful.) Silencers don't create complete silence; they muffle the sound waves to make them less intense. Although federal law in America still refers to these devices as silencers, in the shooting trade they're now better known as suppressors, so that's what we'll call them.

There are two types: integral, which is built into the barrel, and screw-on. The screw-on kind is sometimes called a "can," because that's what it looks like, sitting out on the end of the barrel. Both are fatter than the gun barrel, because they have internal chambers that contain sound-absorbent material and baffles—fins that trap the combustion gas of the exploding cartridge.

A suppressor works by slowing and cooling the gases, which greatly reduces the pressure wave that we receive as noise. (This is exactly what a car muffler does too.) A suppressor can drop the level of a gunshot by 40 dB or more. That's a lot.

An integral suppressor reduces the velocity of the bullet somewhat, because the gases that are pushing it down the barrel bleed out through vents in the bore and then are trapped in the outer baffles.

A can-type suppressor screwed onto the muzzle doesn't slow the bullet. All the gases stay in the barrel and push the bullet to its maximum

Supersonic Bullets

In addition to the *bang!*, if the bullet is traveling at supersonic speed—faster than 1,125 feet per second, the speed of sound at sea level—there also will be a *crack!* as it breaks the sound barrier. Most rifle bullets are supersonic; most handgun bullets are not.

If you fire the rifle, you hear both together. If the rifle is fired at you from a hundred yards away, you may hear the crack of the bullet passing by before you hear the bang (if it hasn't slowed to subsonic speed by then). At least we hope you hear it.

Subsonic Bullets

To eliminate the other noise of firing a gun—the sound-barrier *crack!*—the velocity of the bullet has to be reduced to less than the speed of sound. Subsonic versions of some ammunition are available or can be loaded. However, as we say in "How Far & How Hard," the energy of a bullet comes from both its mass and its velocity. If a bullet is slowed down, its energy and impact are reduced. Fortunately, we can get some or all of this energy back by using a bullet that is a bit heavier.

speed as it gets to the muzzle; whatever the suppressor does to the gases after that no longer affects the bullet.

So the ultimate in a "silenced" rifle is one with an integral suppressor built into its barrel that fires subsonic cartridges loaded with heavier bullets to help compensate for the reduced velocity. No *bang!*, no *crack!*—and a high-powered rifle that makes less noise than some BB guns. If the gun is a semi-automatic, you'll hear the empty shell casing being ejected and the action opening and closing.

Police officers and soldiers sometimes use suppressed weapons when they're invading a building and don't want to alert the people inside (or scare the neighbors). Military marksmen sometimes put cans on their sniper rifles to help conceal their positions. Very few sportsmen use suppressors, at least in America, but we think this will change as hunters begin to understand the benefits: Less noise means less spooked game and fewer annoyed non-hunters.

Very little research has been done on who owns or uses suppressors in the US, but what there is suggests that legal, licensed suppressors

are not a problem and that suppressors, even illegal ones, are seldom used in crimes. In fact, they show up so rarely at crime scenes that the Bureau of Alcohol, Tobacco, Firearms and Explosives keeps no records on them. Still, the federal penalties for possession and use of unlicensed silencers are severe, even if the "silencer" is nothing more than a plastic soda bottle, a tennis ball or a roll of toilet paper jammed onto the muzzle.

We can blame this at least in part on Hollywood. Who hasn't watched a villain on TV or in a movie prepare to whack somebody by screwing a silencer onto the muzzle of a pistol or rifle? (It seems so premeditated and evil.) Unfortunately a lot of people, including some legislators, base their opinions on what they *see* in movies.

In a legal case in California (*The People vs. Phen Pal*), the trial judge said, "A silencer is used only for killing other human beings." This makes him eligible for our Montaigne Award. (Lord Michel Eyquem de Montaigne was the 16th Century author who observed: "Nothing is so firmly believed as what is least known.")

The judge might have been surprised to learn that silencers are legal in 37 states if federal requirements are met. In 1996 a survey found that private individuals in the US owned about 60,000 suppressors, and at one point about 2,000 new permits for them were being issued every year.

More than a century ago Percy Maxim got it right. Silencers can enhance our enjoyment of the shooting sports. The best way to improve people's shooting abilities is to reduce the noise, which magnifies the fear of recoil. The best way to make shooting less objectionable to the general public is by making it less noisy. This is understood in parts of Europe and Britain, New Zealand and other places where there are fewer restrictions on suppressors. Many British .22 rifles are used to shoot garden pests, and they're suppressed out of consideration for the neighbors.

In the chapter "Cool Guns 4 U" we list our top fun guns to own and shoot. Here we want to add a recommendation to one of our recommendations: If you like the Ruger 10/22, you'll love one that's suppressed. Several companies make complete conversions that include special barrels for subsonic .22 Long Rifle cartridges loaded with heavier, 60-grain bullets. These rifles are so quiet that your first reaction is to laugh in disbelief. "Turning off the noise" when you shoot is pretty cool.

Do Guns Make Heroes?

The Congressional Medal of Honor

These days guns often get a bad rap, especially in the news, where they're usually mentioned in connection with some terrible crime like a school shooting. However, guns are only tools, and tools have their proper uses; by themselves, guns are neither "bad" nor "good." If guns are used to commit crimes, guns also can be used to stop crimes. In some cases guns may be the last resort—the only way to defend what's right—and people who use guns to help others sometimes become heroes.

The dictionary defines a hero as "a person of distinguished valor or fortitude." But if you're confused about what it means to be a hero, you're not alone. The word is one of the most misused in the English language. Someone who uses a cell phone to report a fire or who rescues a puppy from a swimming pool is called a "hero." These are worthy acts, but they aren't heroic.

A true hero puts his or her own life on the line for others. Anyone may become a hero, but there are two professions—law enforcement and the military—where this happens most often. When peace officers or soldiers perform exceptional deeds, it is often with the aid of guns. But a gun alone can't make a hero.

The 19,000 American peace officers who have died in the line of duty since 1791 are remembered on the National Law Enforcement Officers Memorial, in Washington, DC. Individual police departments also recognize the bravery of their officers.

For our armed forces there are memorials across the country and even the world. Individual acts of military heroism are recognized with medals, the highest of which is the Congressional Medal of Honor. It is awarded by the President on behalf of the Congress to a member of the military who "distinguishes himself or herself conspicuously by gallantry and intrepidity at the risk of his or of her life above and beyond the call of duty while engaged in an action against an enemy of the United States." It was established in 1862 and first awarded one year later to Private Jacob Parrott, Company K, 33rd Ohio Infantry, US Army, for action behind enemy lines during the Civil War.

The Medal of Honor has been awarded 3,461 times, most recently (as of this writing) to former

Lt. Michael Murphy, US Navy SEAL, won the Medal of Honor in Afghanistan. On June 28, 2005, his four-man recon team was attacked by more than 50 Taliban. To call in an evacuation helicopter, Murphy crawled out into the open, where a radio would work. Already wounded and now exposed, he was shot but completed his distress call and then rejoined his men. By the time help arrived, Murphy and two other SEALs were dead.

US Army Staff Sgt. Clinton Romesha received the Medal of Honor from President Obama on February 11, 2013. In October 2009, 300 Taliban fighters attacked Combat Outpost Keating in the mountains of Afghanistan, which was held by 62 coalition soldiers. The Taliban were so confident of overrunning the camp that they videotaped their attack. But, thanks to Sgt. Romesha and others, they failed. Marine sniper Sgt. Dakota Meyer earned the Medal of Honor just four weeks earlier, also in Afghanistan.

US Army Staff Sergeant Clinton Romesha for his actions during the siege of Combat Outpost Keating in northeastern Afghanistan on October 3, 2009. For 12 hours Romesha rallied his troops, saved wounded comrades and led counterattacks, although he was injured by shrapnel.

Sgt. Romesha survived; not all medal winners do. On October 3, 1993, US forces were engaged in Somalia, in northeastern Africa. An army Black Hawk helicopter had been shot down over the city of Mogadishu. It wasn't known if the crew had survived the crash landing, and there were no "friendlies" nearby. In another Black Hawk, hovering over the crash site, were Sgt. 1st Class Randall Shughart and Master Sgt. Gary Gor-

don of the fabled Delta Force. From the air they could see hundreds of Somali warriors rushing through the city streets toward the downed helicopter. Twice they asked for permission to land and defend the survivors, if there were any, knowing that they would face almost certain death.

At first their requests were denied, but they persisted. When their commander was convinced that they fully understood the risks, he granted permission.

On the ground they fought their way to the helicopter and removed the only survivor, Chief Warrant Officer Michael Durant, from the wreckage. By then the Somalis were on them. In the firefight that followed, both Shughart and Gordon died, as did at least 25 of the enemy. Durant was taken prisoner but ultimately released. For their "extraordinary heroism and devotion to duty" Shughart and Gordon were awarded the Medal of Honor posthumously—that is, after their deaths. The story of their bravery and that of the other soldiers with whom they fought on that harrowing day is told in the book and movie *Black Hawk Down*.

Other movies tell Medal of Honor stories from wars past. These will give you a better understanding of what it means to be a hero:

We Were Soldiers—Vietnam (1964–1975), Walter J. Marm Jr., 2nd Lieutenant, US Army.

Chosin—Korea (1950–1953), Walter E. Barber, Captain, US Marine Corps.

To Hell and Back—WWII (1939–1945), Audie Murphy, 2nd Lieutenant, US Army.

Sergeant York—WWI (1914–1918), Alvin C. York, Corporal, US Army.

The story behind each Medal of Honor is described in an official citation. The citations are in a book called *The Congressional Medal of Honor: The Names, The Deeds—Civil War through Somalia,* by Harley Stuart Shane. They tell stories of courage that can produce a tear in the eye or a lump in the throat. In many cases the recipient was killed in the process of earning the Medal of Honor.

As this is written, there are 79 living Medal of Honor recipients. That number shrinks as elderly veterans die. Someday you may have the honor of meeting one of them. If so, shake his hand and thank him for his extraordinary service.

Delta Force Master Sgt. Gary Gordon (left) and sniper Sgt. 1st Class Randall Shughart. Heroes both, they died defending their brother soldiers during a horrific prolonged gunfight in the streets of Mogadishu, Somalia, on October 3, 1993.

Notice that we wrote "him": So far no woman has been awarded the Medal of Honor, but this will change. Go back to the beginning of this book and re-read "The Silver Star" in "You've Come a Long Way, Baby."

And whenever you use the word hero, remember these stories and be sure you're applying the word correctly.

Poetic Heroism

Nineteenth Century high-school students likely had a better understanding of heroism, because they were required to read classical literature that idealized bravery, combat, sacrifice and love of country. One of the most widely read series of poems of that time was the Lays of Ancient Rome, by Lord Thomas Macaulay. (He wrote them in India while he was serving in the British colonial administration.) One poem is about an attack on ancient Rome by an invading army that has to cross the River Tiber to reach the city. Rome's only hope is to tear down the bridge, but someone must defend it while this is done. Horatius, "captain of the gate," and two companions volunteer to stay behind while the bridge is destroyed, cutting them off from retreat. It means almost certain death.

For generations of schoolchildren, this was the very epitome of heroism:

But the Consul's brow was sad,
And the Consul's speech was low,
And darkly looked he at the wall,
And darkly at the foe.
"Their van will be upon us
Before the bridge goes down;
And if they once may win the bridge,
What hope to save the town?"

Then out spake brave Horatius,
The captain of the Gate:
"To every man upon this earth
Death cometh soon or late
And how can man die better
Than facing fearful odds,
For the ashes of his fathers
And the temples of his Gods."

Cool Guns 4 U

All About the .22—and the Right One for You

Our (the authors') ideas of what guns are cool are different now than when we were 14. We talked about this with the kids who helped with this book. No surprise, they're into AKs, sniper rifles, Glocks, Desert Eagle pistols and all sorts of heavy hardware like that. (Too much TV, too many video games.) Been there, done that. Most of what we used to think were cool guns—guns we just had to have—got shot once or twice and then went into the safe, rarely to see daylight again. Or got traded away.

So there's "cool," and then there's "used and enjoyed a lot." When it comes to your own money, where do you think it's best spent?

Ruger's semi-auto .22 pistol. This is a Mark III Hunter, the direct descendant of the 1949 Mark I, which was the very first Ruger.

Every shooter has to have a .22 rimfire. The lack of recoil and the low noise make it easy to shoot accurately, and the ammunition is really cheap. So why not two .22s—a rifle and a handgun?

Just about every big gunmaker has some sort of .22 in its catalog. To pick just one example, the Ruger 10/22 rifle and Mark I pistol have been around since 1964 and 1949, respectively, and so far Ruger has made enough of them that it could supply every resident of New York City and Chicago combined. Both of these guns are highly reliable and not expensive, whether you buy new or second hand, and plenty accurate. The Mark I pistol has morphed into the Mark III and the 22/45 Lite;

several models are available. There are now six different versions of the 10/22 rifle and even a long-range handgun version. The 10/22 is so popular that we've added a section about it below.

These are both semi-automatics. Until you get some experience under your belt, it's easy to forget to "safe" the gun (decock it, or at least flip on the safety catch) between shots. Remember: A semi-auto reloads itself. And if you also forget about muzzle control—the Third Commandment of gun safety—you could put a bullet somewhere it wasn't meant to go. Like into your leg. Or the dog. Or worse.

It depends on how you learn too. If you shoot at a range under the eye of your mentor or an instructor, a semi-auto can be OK. If you live in the country and learn by going out by yourself, the best gun to start with is a pump-, lever- or bolt-action .22 rifle that you have to crank by hand after every shot. New, a lot of these are more expensive than a Ruger 10/22, but good second-hand guns are easy to find and cost less.

Same goes for handguns. Muzzle control is even easier to forget about with a pistol, because the barrel is so short and you hold it (or wave it around!) with just one hand. It might surprise you that, at least new, .22 handguns generally cost more than rifles.

A couple of other things to keep in mind about choosing guns for yourself: Until you're 14

The single-action Ruger Bearcat .22 is one of the few revolvers still being made in sizes that fit small hands.

or 15 or so, an adult-size rifle may be too long for you. You won't be able to bring it to your shoulder to fire it safely and accurately. (You won't be able to look down the sights properly.) Many gunmakers now offer shorter stocks for kids. And when it comes to handguns, the weight of the gun and the size of the grip may also be a challenge for you at first. There used to be a fair number of revolvers, single and double action, that kids could manage, but not any more. Well, except for Ruger's Bearcat and Single-Six .22s. (You'd think Ruger wanted to be your gun company, wouldn't you?)

The Terrific .22

The .22 rimfire is very accurate in the right guns. It produces no recoil and not much noise, and it just happens to be both useful and great fun to shoot. It has been around for a very long time. In fact it was the first metallic cartridge made in America, more than 150 years ago.

Rimfire means that, instead of a separate primer, the cartridge has priming compound in the rim of its case. When the firing pin or hammer hits the rim, it sets off the primer, which lights the main powder charge. (The hit also deforms the case, so we can't reload and reuse it.) Louis Nicolas Flobert invented rimfire ammunition in France in the mid-1840s by shaping a percussion cap to give it a rim and then sticking a ball into it, to make a self-contained round. This became an indoor shooting-gallery cartridge called in English the .22 BB Cap, for "bulleted breech cap." Flobert cartridges have no gunpowder; the bullet (or ball) is driven just by the primer.

Smith & Wesson took this idea a step further and, in 1857, used it in a new cartridge for the company's first revolver, the Model 1. The S&W .22 had a little 29-grain bullet in a rimfire case, but it also was loaded with four grains of powder, so it had more punch than a Flobert.

The S&W Model 1 was a self-defense "belly gun" meant to be used across a card table, but even for that the original .22 cartridge was pretty puny. A hotter version in a longer case with *five* grains of powder came along in 1871. This was dubbed the .22 Long, so naturally the first one became the .22 Short.

Pretty soon someone added one more grain of powder, lengthened the case again and upped the bullet from 29 to 40 grains. Presto, the .22 Extra Long! And then in 1887 came yet another version, with the 40-grain bullet of the Extra Long in the slightly shorter case of the Long. This was

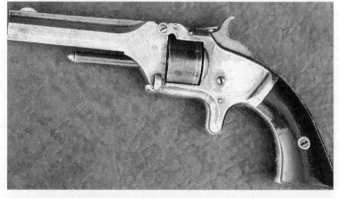

The rimfire .22 Short cartridge was created in 1857 by Smith & Wesson for the company's new Model 1 pocket revolver, a hideaway gun meant for self-defense at close range. The gun disappeared, but the .22 cartridge lives on.

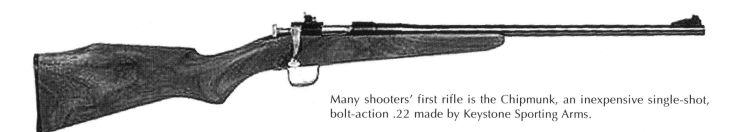

Many shooters' first rifle is the Chipmunk, an inexpensive single-shot, bolt-action .22 made by Keystone Sporting Arms.

christened the .22 Long Rifle. It was converted to the new smokeless powder, and then it went on to become the most popular cartridge in the history of Planet Earth. And never mind its name; the Long Rifle round works in any .22 that's chambered for it, whether they're long guns or handguns.

Many more .22 variants have appeared, but by now most of them have disappeared. One that hasn't is the .22 WMR, or Winchester Magnum Rimfire. It fires a 30-, 40- or 50-grain bullet at up to 2,200 feet per second, making it about twice as hard-hitting as the .22 LR. In 2002 the Hornady ammunition company squeezed down the neck of a .22 Magnum case for a .17-caliber bullet. The .17 HMR (Hornady Magnum Rimfire) steps out at 2,350 to 2,550 fps. The bullets are so tiny, though (just 17 or 20 grains), that the muzzle energy is a lot less than the .22 Magnum's.

But forget the .17 and the Mag. We're here to talk about the .22 LR. The .22 Short and Long are still around, but ammunition-industry experts say that more than 1 billion Long Rifle rounds are sold every year—just in the US. That's a lot of tin cans, dump rats, woodchucks, squirrels, rabbits, paper bull's-eyes and other targets.

You'll find all sorts of LR ammunition—labeled Standard Velocity, High Velocity and Hyper Velocity—with bullets from 30 to 40 grains, copper-plated or plain lead, hollowpoint or solid. You can even get .22 tracer rounds and cartridges loaded with tiny shot pellets, for small pests (although they aren't very effective). And finally there is subsonic .22 ammunition, which is quieter.

Some guns shoot one brand more accurately than others, so try a few and see if there's any difference. If absolute accuracy down to the last

eighth of an inch doesn't matter, buy the cheapest ones you can find. Hollowpoints are best for hunting small game, because the bullets expand, to kill more quickly.

Steve Helsley

Cartridges (from left): A .22 LR round costs as little as 4¢; factory-loaded .223s are about 60¢ each; and a single .600 Nitro Express cartridge can cost more than $25.

Twenty-twos (British and Canadian shooters call them two-twos) are really cheap: as little as 4¢ or 5¢ a round—sometimes even less, if there's a big sale. In comparison, a single .223 cartridge costs about 60¢, and one .600 Nitro Express round can easily cost $25! (Then again, what do you think it costs to hunt an elephant?)

The .22 is the biggest little round of them all.

Things to Do with the .22

Around 1900 a British gunmaker fastened seven single-shot .22 rifle barrels together in a cluster and added a hammer that fired all of them at once. These "volley guns" were meant for combat, but hunters discovered that they could drop a duck or goose at twice the range of even an 8-gauge shotgun. There were safety problems, though, because a .22 bullet can travel a mile or so, much farther than the heaviest birdshot pellets.

So that idea didn't last long. But it is just one of many things the .22 can do. It's not only the ideal plinking and small-game hunting round (and poachers everywhere like it because it's quiet and cheap), but it's also used in world-class target competition. There are 15 different shooting contests in the summer Olympic Games for pistol, rifle and shotgun, and six of them are fired with .22s. There's even a winter event called biathlon, where competitors race around a course on cross-country skis with rifles on their backs, stopping to fire at targets along the way. Norwegian soldiers started doing this in the 1860s as a training exercise called military patrol. It was demonstrated at the Olympics in the 1920s, '30s and '40s, and it got so popular that in 1960 it became a regular medal event. At first

Modern biathlon competition grew out of an old skiing-and-shooting exercise called military patrol. At the 1928 Winter Olympics, held in Switzerland, the German army team (shown here) finished fifth out of nine. Norway won.

it was shot with army rifles, but then the .22 LR became the standard cartridge.

If you want to become a professional shooter (read "Professions with Passion"), you're going to burn up a few hundred thousand rounds in practice, and that means .22s. Most of the famous trick shooters in America used .22 rifles and pistols. They preferred to be called exhibition shooters, but to their amazed audiences what they could do with guns were tricks, if not outright magic. With her Marlin lever-action .22, Little Sure Shot (Annie Oakley) could hit a dime tossed in the air 90 feet away. Ad and Plinky Topperwein, a husband-and-wife team who worked for Winchester from 1901 till about 1950, also did miraculous things with .22s. Plinky would shoot the buttons off of Ad's vest and cigarettes out of his lips. (Ad's name was Adolph. "Plinky" was a nickname that came from plinking, or fun shooting. Mrs. Topperwein's real name was Elizabeth.)

Ad once shot at 72,500 small wooden blocks thrown in the air and missed only nine of them. His longest run without a miss was 14,540. Plinky once broke 967 out of 1,000 clay pigeons. They set these records not with shotguns but with .22 rifles.

The Anschutz Model 1827 biathlon rifle. It's carried on the skier's back in a special sling. She cycles the action by flicking the straight-pull bolt back and forth with one finger. Extra magazines, one for each target stage, are mounted on the stock forend. Some biathlon "rifles" now fire lasers.

In 1959 a Remington pro named Tom Frye broke Ad's record with the company's Nylon 66 .22 semi-auto rifle: 100,004 out of 100,010 wooden blocks. It took 13 nine-hour days of shooting. Then in 1987 John Huffer, known as "Chief AJ," used a Ruger 10/22 to set a different wooden-blocks-in-the-air record: 40,060 hits in a row without a miss. (These dudes must have hated wooden blocks.) Actually, he used 18 Ruger 10/22s, which assistants reloaded and handed to him.

Military forces use Ruger .22s as special sniper rifles. Plenty of cops carry .22 pistols as backup guns or when they're off duty. Blank .22 cartridges provide the power for tools like industrial nail guns and the captive-bolt guns used to kill animals in slaughterhouses.

Once one of your authors was at a remote spot on the Zambezi River in Zimbabwe. At night elephants started coming into camp to feed. This meant destroying the trees: pulling branches down and eating them—leaves, twigs, wood and all. Elephants will push over trees and uproot them to get to the branches. Dennis, the PH (Professional Hunter), yelled at them to leave. The first night they did. Then they ignored him. Next he chased them out of camp with the Land Rover. This worked only once or twice. Finally he said, "If you hear some shooting tonight, it's just me after the ellies again. With a .22."

Sure enough, late that night came *bang!bang!bang!bang!bang!* And then trumpeting and squealing and running.

The next day the miscreants, three young bulls, were seen huddled together in a dry riverbed, sulking like kids who'd been punished for shoplifting. They stayed out of camp after that.

But never think the .22 is harmless. As you know, where you put a bullet is much more important than how powerful it is. Although the power of a .22 LR is less than 5 percent of a .30-06's, it can do real damage. The bullet leaves the muzzle around 1,250 fps and generates 140 foot-pounds of energy. This can be deadly on soft tissue out past 250 yards. There are many stories of covert agents from World War II up to today using .22 pistols to assassinate enemies. Peter Hathaway Capstick, the safari hunter and author, wrote about two adult elephants that were killed with single shots from a .22 rifle. In each case the bullet penetrated the thin skin behind the animal's foreleg and got to the heart, where it caused enough bleeding to lead, eventually, to death.

And finally there's this interesting story of survival with a .22 pistol from a friend of ours:

"My personal favorite defense gun has always been a Beretta Jetfire loaded with .22 Shorts. I never go hiking without it in my pocket. My other rule is to use the Buddy System— never hike alone, so one of us can go for help if something happens. One time I was hiking with my brother-in-law in northern Montana. Out of nowhere came this huge brown bear, and man was she mad. We must have been near one of her cubs. Anyway, if I hadn't had my little Jetfire, I wouldn't be here today. Just one shot to my brother-in-law's kneecap and I was able to escape just by walking at a brisk pace!"

Think it's true?

The Awesome Ruger 10/22

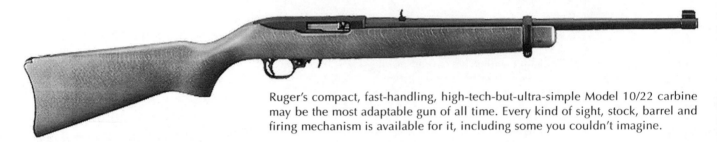

Ruger's compact, fast-handling, high-tech-but-ultra-simple Model 10/22 carbine may be the most adaptable gun of all time. Every kind of sight, stock, barrel and firing mechanism is available for it, including some you couldn't imagine.

In 1960, Ruger (Sturm, Ruger & Company) came out with its first rifle: a handy semi-auto carbine called the Deerstalker that fired the .44 Magnum revolver cartridge. It was meant for hunting medium-size game at close range in thick woods or the jungle. It sold well, but its real claim to fame is that Bill Ruger made a .22-caliber version of it called the 10/22. When this arrived, in 1964, it was about the most high-tech, fastest-handling .22 anyone had *ever* seen. It cost $54.50, which wasn't cheap; that's like $450 today.

Shooters began buying it immediately, and they haven't stopped. The 10/22 must be the most popular .22 rifle in history. The original version was short, with an 18½-inch barrel, and weighed just a bit more than five pounds. The

This is a Ruger 10/22 also—dressed up with an accessory kit to look like a German MG-42 machine gun from World War II.

model name came from the fact that it held 10 rounds, and its magazine was unique for a .22. Instead of stacking the cartridges on top of each other in a box, it held them separately in a spool that rotated to feed each one into the action. Very smooth and reliable.

The gun was also ahead of its time because it was completely modular. The main pieces—the trigger mechanism and trigger guard, the barrel and the stock—can be swapped out easily by loosening just one screw. This is part of why the 10/22 has become a bestseller. Ruger now sells a half-dozen

different 10/22 models, but dozens of other companies make hundreds of accessories for the little Ruger. Every imaginable kind of sight, stock and barrel are available for the 10/22 along with suppressors, 50-round drum magazines and other things you *couldn't* imagine. You can dress up a 10/22 to look like an AR or AK assault rifle or a World War II German MG-42 machine gun. There's even a gadget that turns two 10/22s into a sort of mini-Gatling gun. Crawl around on the Web for a few minutes and you'll see what we mean.

Most of these things require no alterations to the rifle. Buy the kit or the parts, and you can install them without special tools or skills.

Cool as this stuff can be, the basic goodness of the 10/22 is what makes it so great for kids (kids of all ages, that is), once they've become safe with a semi-auto. It's light, accurate and reliable. The stock is the right size. It will fire and feed any Long Rifle ammunition, and it requires only the most basic cleaning and maintenance. We recommend learning to shoot well with the factory-installed sights before you add a scope. Your best bet for the first accessory is an extended magazine (unless it's illegal where you live) and a hand-crank tool that will help you stuff ammo into it.

With all these wild Airsoft-looking accessories, you might start to think that the 10/22 is some sort of toy. Wrong. It's not a fake MP5; it's a real .22 rifle. Real police officers and soldiers, including US Navy SEALs and Israel's Defense Forces, use 10/22s.

Israeli Special Forces reportedly use scoped and suppressed Ruger .22s to kill neighborhood dogs quickly and quietly, to prevent them from barking during undercover operations. (The rifles were nicknamed Hush Puppies.) Israeli marksmen also have used 10/22s for "crowd control" in the West Bank and the Gaza Strip, the territories Israel seized in 1967. The goal was to take out key protestors by shooting them in the legs with something "less deadly" than the 5.56mm assault-rifle round but more effective than a bullet made of rubber, plastic or wood.

This is one of those ideas that sounded reasonable but didn't work as planned. Possibly because

they're shorter than adults, several children were killed by .22 bullets that were aimed low at grown-up legs. Israel's Judge Advocate General decided that the 10/22 was a true live-fire weapon and should not be used for crowd control. An investigation showed that the .22s were more deadly than the army expected, especially in upper-body injuries. It also turned out that soldiers thought the Rugers were less harmful because of the suppressors. *Hey, how dangerous can it be if it's so quiet?*

Once again: It isn't the size or the energy of the bullet (or the noise) that matters so much as where the bullet hits. Even highly trained snipers can't always guarantee what a bullet will hit, particularly in a crowd. And soldiers don't always understand ballistics either. But now you do.

A news photo of an Israeli soldier aiming a scoped and suppressed Ruger 10/22 with a folding bipod on the forend. As a crowd-control weapon, the .22 rifle turned out to be more deadly than expected. US Navy SEALs reportedly use 10/22s also.

Starting Shotgun Shooting

The hardest-kicking gun that most people ever encounter is an ordinary 12-gauge shotgun. That's because it generally fires a fairly heavy load—1 to 1¾ ounces of shot pellets—at around 1,200 to 1,500 fps. By comparison most rifles or handguns fire bullets that weigh less than half an ounce (that's 220 grains); even at twice the speed of birdshot, this doesn't create as much recoil as the 12-gauge.

So if you want to shoot clay pigeons—which is a lot more fun than punching holes in paper targets—don't start with a 12-gauge gun.

However, your first shotgun should not necessarily be the smallest one: the .410. Recoil is created by both the mass of the projectile and its velocity, and it's possible to pack nearly a 12-gauge load of birdshot into even a .410-bore shotgun. Furthermore, since .410 guns usually weigh a lot less than 12-gauges, there's less mass in the gun to absorb recoil. So a .410 loaded with the wrong ammunition can kick uncomfortably hard. Your shooting mentor will, or should, know all about this.

On the other hand a .410 with light cartridges throws only a small quantity of shot pellets that spread out quickly, so a .410 is effective only at short range. (This is why many people put overloaded cartridges in the .410.) A shooting coach who understands this will lob clay pigeons at slow speeds and easy angles, and with some practice and instruction, a beginner should soon be breaking the targets with a .410. There will be more noise and recoil than with a .22, but nothing you can't handle with proper preparation.

The next step up in shotgun bore size is a 28 gauge. A 28 that fits you, firing light loads, should do very well. All else being equal, it will kick only a bit harder than a .410—and possibly less, depending on the gun.

However, there's a downside to both the .410 and 28: Cartridges are expensive. For this reason alone, mentors often start new shooters with bigger 20-gauge guns or quickly move them up to 20s, with ammunition that costs only about half as much. Here, too, if the shot load is light, the gun is comfortable to hold and the stock is nicely padded at the butt, recoil should be no problem.

Now we have to change our earlier advice to stay away from semi-autos. Because the self-loading mechanism in the gun absorbs some of the recoil energy, a semi-automatic 20-gauge can be more comfortable to shoot than some .410s and 28s. The key is to find one that fits you—many makers offer "youth" shotguns with shorter stocks and barrels—and, at least at first, to load only one cartridge at a time.

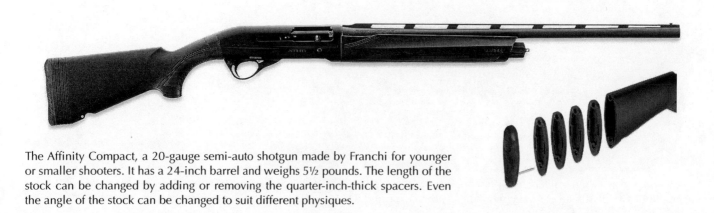

The Affinity Compact, a 20-gauge semi-auto shotgun made by Franchi for younger or smaller shooters. It has a 24-inch barrel and weighs 5½ pounds. The length of the stock can be changed by adding or removing the quarter-inch-thick spacers. Even the angle of the stock can be changed to suit different physiques.

Guns That Fit Girls

Most people are surprised to learn that guns have to fit. Think of other sporting gear, though, such as skis, golf clubs and so on, and it makes sense. How could the same shotgun or rifle fit both a 5'2" woman and a 6'2" man, with their differences in arm length?

But a gun's length of pull (the distance from the trigger to the end of the butt) isn't the only measurement that matters. Equally important is the drop of the stock: how far its comb lies below the line of the barrel. (If you don't know what the comb is, refer back to "Parts of a Bolt-Action Rifle" in "Talking the Talk.") If the drop is too little or too much, your eye won't line up with the sights when you snug your cheek down onto the stock.

There's more. Shooters may have a dozen or more dimensions of a gun's stock made to measure, including the thickness of the grip (and its shape and angle), the length and shape of the forend, and the thickness and profile of the butt. A right-handed shooter with wide cheekbones may have the stock bent slightly to the right, so her shooting eye lines up on the barrel. A large-busted woman might have the toe of the buttstock angled outward, so that it doesn't dig into her breast.

Fit is especially important in wingshooting, where you bring the gun to your shoulder and cheek instinctively instead of deliberately. A stock shaped to your upper body helps make sure the gun shoots where you're looking. Custom stocks, by the way, are almost always wood, not plastic, because wood can be cut and shaped much more easily.

These finer points of gunfit are for later in your shooting life, when you know what you want—and when you've stopped growing. Meanwhile, some guns come with spacers that let you adjust stock length and sometimes drop too. Also keep in mind that many shooters, including very good ones, never alter their guns' stocks. This is because gunmakers have figured out good average dimensions for adult and youth guns that fit most shooters pretty well.

Up until about age 15, many girls are taller than the boys in their class, but they may be lighter and not as strong. All of these factors affect how well you can hold a gun—and this helps determine how accurately you can shoot it and even how safely you can shoot it.

The best advice we can give about gunfit is: Try before you buy, and have your mentor along for help and guidance. A "girl's gun" may have a pink stock, but the shape of that stock is a lot more important than its color.

The Thompson/Center Dimension is a light, accurate and highly cool bolt-action rifle. Adding or removing spacers in front of the recoil pad changes the length of pull. Switching bolts, magazines and barrels—a process that takes just one tool and a couple of minutes and can be done by anyone—changes the caliber from the no-recoil .204 Ruger all the way up to .300 Winchester Magnum, with eight other options (.223 Remington, .22-250 Remington, .243 Winchester, 7mm-08 Remington, .270 Winchester, .308 Winchester, .30-06 and 7mm Remington Magnum) between. This means the rifle can "grow" right alongside its owner, through the teenage years and from shooting targets at the range to hunting game from prairie dogs to moose. The Dimension is easy to carry and to shoot, and it is very reasonably priced—especially compared to the cost of owning several rifles of different calibers. It even comes in a left-handed version.

Professions with Passion

Shooters Can Find Interesting Careers

Firearms may be the single most important man-made item in history. Guns launched and settled wars, elevated one country over another, "pacified" wildernesses for colonization and civilization, fed and protected families, and both aided and stopped crime. Many modern manufacturing processes were developed to build guns, and the oldest documented manufacturer of anything still in business today is a gunmaker. Beretta, in northern Italy, has a receipt dated October 3, 1526, for 185 musket barrels sold to the city of Venice. Beretta is now one of the world's largest and most successful suppliers of sporting, police and military firearms.

In addition to Pietro Beretta, men named Whitney, Lefaucheux, Forsyth, Colt, Winchester, Remington, Gatling, Maxim, Mauser, Lee, Lebel, Whitworth, Mannlicher, Rigby, Browning, Thompson, Kalashnikov, Garand and many more—designers or manufacturers of guns—played crucial roles in history. Cities in England, France, Germany, Austria, Belgium, Italy, Russia, Spain and the United States became centers of gun manufacturing. School systems and professional associations were created to support gunmaking.

In the Digital Age making guns is still important, and manufacturing processes and even materials are changing quickly. There are many professions (besides being police officers or soldiers) that involve working with guns too, not just making them. Some use the latest in computer technology; at least one has hardly changed in 500 years. In the

The oldest career of them all, especially for women, has always been taking care of the family. There are many parts of the world where this full-time job still requires, at least occasionally, a gun.

following pages you'll meet women who are hunting guides, lodge managers, scientists, magazine editors, business executives, authors, chefs and artists.

Do any of these careers spark your interest?

Gunmaker: Craftsman

A gunmaker builds firearms, either mass-production guns or guns that are made one at a time to a buyer's specifications, or something in between. Whether they are individuals or large companies, gunmakers often focus on certain markets: They build only rifles or only shotguns or a particular type of handgun. They may concentrate on military or police needs, big-game hunting or competitive trap shooting. A few gunmakers specialize in building replicas of historic guns.

Gunmaking is like any other kind of manufacturing. There are tools and methods to learn, and some people get into it because they invented a new widget or came up with a better way to do something. In one important aspect, though, building guns is different from producing refrigerators or door hinges. Gunmakers are usually personally interested in what they do, proud of what they make and always looking for ways to improve their products even more.

There's no better way to pick a career. Why would you want to spend 30 or 40 years doing something you didn't like?

In any company that builds guns there are specialists: craftsmen who carve and checker wooden stocks, machinists who bore the barrels and cut the rifling, actioners who make and assemble the lockwork, and finishers who put all of the pieces together and test them. Whatever they do, and whether their work is done by hand or by machine, these are skilled workers

The Fausti sisters—from left: Elena, Barbara and Giovanna—have become some of Italy's best-known gunmakers. When their father retired, they took over the gun company he had founded in 1948. The sisters have grown the business significantly by adding new models, including shotguns designed for women, and by setting up a sales office in the US. When Barbara married Fabio Rizzini, the son of another Italian gunmaker, the sisters bought his family's gun company and added it to Fausti. Elena deals with the company's suppliers while Barbara and Giovanna manage marketing and sales—Giovanna for the US and Barbara for the European and Eastern markets.

who usually learned their trade in a technical school or as apprentices.

When it comes to super-expensive, custom-made guns, which require a lot of hand-craftsmanship, the best of these workers often become self-employed; they set up workshops at home, and gun companies send them jobs. In Europe they're known as "outworkers to the trade." Many of them are in great demand and earn good livings.

Gunmaker: Mechanical Engineer

A gun is a machine. If you're interested in how guns function and in creating new guns or improving old ones, you can enroll in a four-year college program to become a mechanical engineer. Designing a firearm that is safe, reliable, accurate and commercially practical—meaning that it can be built at a reasonable cost and sold at a fair profit—is a challenge. It requires knowledge of mechanical forces and the physical properties of all of the materials used in a gun, as well as how to produce the various parts and pieces. Whether they create automobiles, household appliances or firearms, mechanical engineers rely on CAD-CAM processes—computer-aided design and computer-aided manufacturing.

All but the smallest companies also need employees besides those who actually design and produce guns, including accountants, managers and salespeople. These people don't specialize in guns, but they have to know a lot about them in order to do their work well.

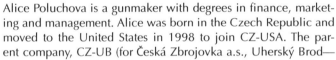

Alice Poluchova is a gunmaker with degrees in finance, marketing and management. Alice was born in the Czech Republic and moved to the United States in 1998 to join CZ-USA. The parent company, CZ-UB (for Česká Zbrojovka a.s., Uherský Brod—"Czech weapons factory at Uherský Brod"), is descended from one of the world's largest and oldest manufacturers of small arms, which began as a royal armory, survived two world wars and three changes of government, and became a private company. Alice is not only the head of CZ's American division, she is also a competitive pistol and shotgun shooter and big-game hunter. CZ-USA sells several rifles, shotguns and pistols sized for smaller shooters.

Gunsmith

A gunsmith works with used guns instead of building new ones. She repairs faulty guns or modifies them to suit the owners' wishes, or she may restore valuable old guns for collectors. Some gunsmiths are generalists who have learned how to work with a huge variety of guns. They may mount a scope or a recoil pad on a customer's rifle one day, and the next day fix a broken extractor or clean and refinish a shotgun that got rusty. Other gunsmiths become specialists who focus on one type of gun or shooting. For example, they fine-tune competition pistols (known as "race guns") or big-game rifles to make them faster and more reliable. Some gunsmiths now even have TV shows, and many work with computers.

Many gunsmiths work for themselves, and many buy and sell guns. Some gunsmiths are self-taught tinkerers, but they're a dying breed. Today anyone who wants to work on firearms is well advised to go to a vocational school to learn the trade properly.

Gunsmith Dale Tate of California, who was trained in London, opens up the chokes in a pair of shotgun barrels with a honing tool. A gunmaker builds guns; a gunsmith repairs or modifies them.

Armorer

Large police departments and every branch of the military service have gunsmiths, called armorers, who maintain weapons. This can be especially interesting work, as armorers often also customize guns (ammunition and accessories too) for special uses such as sniping or close-quarters shooting, arctic or desert warfare, or match competition. Armorers often advise manufacturers on field-tested improvements to guns, ammunition, sights, holsters, carrying slings and unusual features like sound suppressors.

The people who design, build and maintain the guns used in movies and TV shows are called armorers also. Many of those guns are real but have been modified in some way, for safety or special effects. Hollywood machine guns, for example, are often converted to operate on natural gas, so they don't have to fire live ammunition to make them cycle realistically. As you can see, this kind of work takes not only good gunsmithing skills but also engineering know-how and imagination.

Engraver

These days, more and more of the engraving that decorates guns is being applied with a laser or by acid etching, because it's a lot cheaper. The best and most expensive guns, however, always will be engraved by hand. There are different kinds of engraving, but they all amount to "drawing on steel," and they all require a steady hand, an artist's eye and a

Engraver Lisa Tomlin at work in her studio in Virginia. Her daughter Kelly (who took this photo) plans to become an engraver as well.

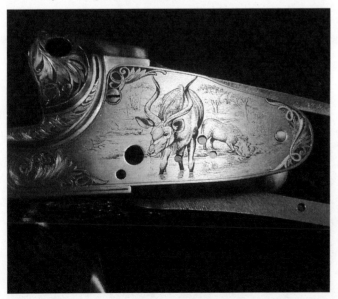

A kudu and warthog by engraver Lisa Tomlin take shape on the lockplate of what will be a very expensive double rifle. Lisa also creates the decorative scrollwork. The best engravers often have several years' worth of work lined up.

knowledge of metals. The tools are simple: a small assortment of chisels and gravers (the scribers used to cut grooves or make dots in the steel); a special padded vise that swivels, to hold the gun, and a good chair; strong, even light from a big window or a lamp; and some sort of magnifying lens. Some engravers also use an electric cutter like a dentist's drill.

It's possible to go to school to become an engraver, but many engravers learn by themselves or as apprentices to established masters. (Naturally they practice on a piece of scrap metal, not a fine gun.)

Some engravers, especially when they're starting out, work for studios that decorate not only guns but also knives, money clips and other things. If they love the work and show a talent for it, they may go out on their own as independent craftsmen. The best engravers often have several years' worth of commissions lined up. Their work doesn't make guns shoot any better, but it adds many thousands of dollars of value and satisfaction for their owners.

All engravers, whether self-taught or schooled, have the natural ability to draw. If you have it—and by now you'd know it if you do—this can be an interesting, creative and well-paid way to make a living.

Forensic Scientist

Crime labs have been supporting the criminal justice system in the United States since the 1920s, but it wasn't until *CSI* started on TV that the public got interested in them. Officially known as criminalistics or forensic laboratories, they are staffed with specialists such as document and fingerprint examiners, toxicologists, crime-scene and laboratory technicians, photographers, firearms examiners and others.

Technicians are generally the ones who gather evidence (strands of hair or fibers, shards of glass, bullets, blood, fingerprints, ashes, tissue and bone, weapons and so on) at crime scenes. Back at the lab, scientists analyze these materials to try to unravel exactly how a crime was committed.

Forensic firearms examiners collect evidence and examine it with optical and electronic instruments, and then interpret their findings. Sometimes they testify in court. Often they test-fire guns, and then compare bullets and cartridge cases with suspect firearms to see if they can be tied to a crime. Firearms examiners handle all types of guns and ammunition and are very involved in shooting. They work with police officers, prosecutors and other forensic experts who may be examining the same guns for DNA evidence or fingerprints. This can get tricky; lifting a fingerprint from a bloody gun with Superglue fumes might affect the bloodstains, which also need to be examined.

There are about 400 crime labs serving federal, state and local law-enforcement agencies in

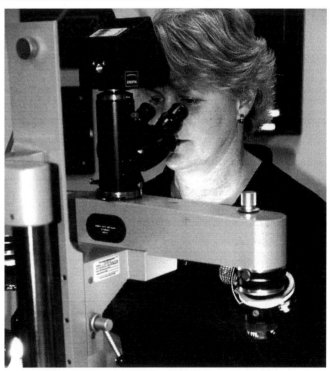

Laura Jane Hodge, a special agent/forensic scientist with the Tennessee Bureau of Investigation, using a comparison microscope. Firearms examiners often test-fire guns and then compare bullets and cartridge cases with suspect firearms to see if they can be tied to a crime.

the US. A Bachelor of Science degree in biology or chemistry is usually the minimum requirement for getting a job in one of them. If you like firearms and science and the notion of putting criminals in prison, you'd be hard-pressed to find a more interesting and rewarding career.

Shooting Instructor

hatever kind of shooting you decide to concentrate on, you'll be able to find a professional (that is, paid) instructor to help you get better at it. Get really good at it, and you may want to become an instructor yourself.

By now most of the many different kinds of shooting competition are supervised by organizations—the International Practical Shooting Confederation, for example, or the National Sporting Clays Association—and many of them have set standards for instructors. Knowledge of guns and the ability to shoot safely and accurately are just two of the necessary skills; an instructor also has to be able to teach. Teaching is a two-step process: An instructor has to analyze a student's shooting—break it down into separate steps to see where mistakes are being made—and then fix the mistakes. (Some shooting organizations have developed specific teaching methods.) Teachers also need the ability to communicate clearly—and patience and consideration are helpful too.

Chapter two ("You've Come a Long Way, Baby") introduced you to one of the top shooting instructors in America: Il Ling New. She is a great example of how far someone can go in this field, but many instructors teach shooting part-time and have a day job that pays the mortgage.

Il Ling New, who teaches at Gunsite Academy in Arizona, is one of the best-known rifle and handgun shooting instructors in America. For more about her, read "You've Come a Long Way, Baby."

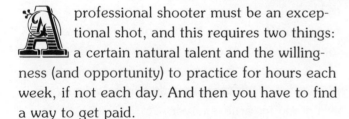

Professional Shooter

A professional shooter must be an exceptional shot, and this requires two things: a certain natural talent and the willingness (and opportunity) to practice for hours each week, if not each day. And then you have to find a way to get paid.

Companies sometimes hire expert shots to help sell their guns by demonstrating them at carnivals and other public events (search for "trick shooting" on YouTube) or at private demos for military or police buyers. Certain world-class competition shooters may get a paycheck for a few years from a gunmaker. Members of national shooting teams may have their living expenses paid so that they can practice and compete without the distraction of a job.

Many such expert shooters get some sort of support from companies in exchange for using (demonstrating) their products. The teaching pro or the club champion at a popular sporting-clays course might get a new gun each season and have his or her ammunition provided. A well-known hunting guide might get guns and ammunition and maybe even a truck, especially if he or she is featured in a TV series. But this isn't earning a living; the pro and the guide still have to attract paying clients.

Very few people are full-time professional shooters. The chances of becoming one compare to becoming a professional skateboarder or playing in the NFL or NBA.

Elizabeth Lanier of Virginia is one of only four women who are Level III sporting-clays instructors in the US. Elizabeth founded a group called GRITS, Girls Really Into Shooting, to introduce women to the fun of shooting, and she also organizes bird hunting trips for women.

Professional Hunter

 well-known African hunter named Peter Hathaway Capstick wrote this in a 1984 book called *Safari, the Last Adventure:*

Professional Hunter Wanted:
Young active man interested in low and infrequent pay to play bwana in remote bushveld. Must be proven raconteur and socialite without liver trouble, expert card player, bartender, caterer, barbecuer, philosopher, African historian. Experience in sanitary engineering, local architecture, labor relations, navigation, medicine and pharmacology, botany, zoology, ichthyology, mineralogy, entomology, butchery, taxidermy, dietetics, optics, photography and radio operation essential. Applicant should speak at least two black African languages fluently as well as English and one other modern European tongue. A solid knowledge of mechanics, driving, gunsmithing, toxicology, ballistics, tracking, marksmanship, hand loading and experience as a professional bodyguard are required.

Benefits are: Twenty-four-hour day, unlimited fresh air, including rain, sun and dust, no medical, dental or life insurance and no retirement benefits. Applicant should supply his own rifles. Vehicles on a per diem basis.

Capstick meant this to be a contrast to the popular impression that people had of a White Hunter in Africa as some sort of minor god who looked like a movie star and could sweep both beautiful women and charging elephants off their feet with equal ease. The reality, as Capstick knew very well, was much less glamorous.

Up until Capstick's day they all were men, but no more. They're no longer called "white" hunters either. Anything that seems to be a racial term makes people nervous (never mind actual skin color), and many safari professionals these days are, in fact, black. So today they're all known as PHs, Professional Hunters, and they have to take certification courses and pass examinations to earn the title.

More women are being certified as African PHs, or Professional Hunters. One of the best-known is Elaine Ness, here with a happy client in Namibia. The hours are long, the conditions can be awful and the pay isn't great, but for a certain kind of person, there's no other life.

Most southern African countries have two kinds of PH licenses: plains game and dangerous game. Taking clients after lion, elephant, rhino, Cape buffalo and leopard is a lot more risky than stalking antelope. The PH has to be ready to deal

with an animal that can kill her client, herself or other people in the vicinity, and this calls for a higher standard of skill. Almost every year a few PHs die on the job—killed by wounded animals or in accidents with vehicles, sometimes shot by poachers or even accidentally by their own clients.

Almost anyone can become an African PH, given enough determination and effort. The work, however, only gets harder after passing the test and joining a safari company. The hours are long, the conditions can be awful, the clients can be inept (or worse) and the pay isn't great. But for a certain kind of person there's no other life.

For some reason the term PH is used only in Africa. In the rest of the world they're called hunting guides, and the regulations governing them are different from state to state and country to country. If you think you'd like to guide hunters where you live, log onto your government Website and start clicking around for "becoming a hunting guide." It's not an easy or well-paid life, but it'll keep you outdoors for at least part of each year.

Hunting Lodge Staff

Not that long ago, even Americans who lived in cities could go hunting just by driving a few miles out into the country. As cities got bigger and bigger, however, and outlying farms were swallowed up and became suburbs, game country got farther and farther away. A few enterprising landowners saw opportunity: Instead of—or along with—growing crops, raising cattle or logging timber, why not open up their property to hunters? And charge a fee?

As this idea grew and became successful, landowners added services and comforts. They

Victoria Rich/Dentinger Design

Ann Kercheville is the president and co-owner (with her husband, Joe) of Joshua Creek Ranch, in the Texas Hill Country, one of the best-known bird hunting lodges in the US. Her professional background is in financial analysis and business management, but she is equally familiar with shotguns, hunting dogs and pickup trucks.

managed their property especially for game, whether birds or deer or other species, and often added more animals. They hired employees. They built lodges for their visiting hunters, added kennels full of trained dogs and stables of saddle horses, and bought hunting trucks and boats. A few of these ranches or preserves have their own mini-airports for private planes.

If you're lucky enough to belong to a family that owns thousands of acres of undeveloped land somewhere, this might be an option. If not, don't lose interest—instead think about working for one of the hundreds of these operations scattered around the US. Many young people spend a few seasons as hunting guides, horse wranglers or camp cooks before moving on to careers—sometimes with companies run by clients they met while hunting. Lodges also need chefs and chambermaids, mechanics and maintenance people, accountants and managers and more.

Booking Agent

The hunting industry—here meaning lodges, preserves, hunting outfitters and safari operators—has grown so large that it has itself created a new kind of business: the booking agency. An owner or manager who is busy running a lodge may turn to an independent booking agent to help find customers. The agent tells potential clients about the lodge, and then books (arranges) their visits; in return the agent receives a commission, a percentage of whatever the client spends at the lodge.

A booking *agency* is usually a full-service company that markets a number of different destinations and kinds of hunting and may even sell airline tickets. A booking *agent* may be just one person who knows a particular hunting operation well enough to act as its representative. Either way, knowledge and experience are key. Booking agents answer questions from prospective clients about the game, the guns, ammunition, gear and clothing needs, the staff, meals and accommodations, travel arrangements and hunting and gun laws. The best agents spend a lot of time in the field learning about and staying in touch with the places and people who they work with.

Niki Atcheson and her husband, Keith, are booking agents for hunters. This is the skull of the Cape buffalo that nearly killed her in 2005. Niki's story is in "Game: Animals & Birds."

Game Warden

Every state and most countries have game wardens: police officers who are charged with keeping an eye on hunters and anglers (and sometimes boaters, snowmobilers, hikers, backcountry skiers and others who participate in outdoor recreation). Wardens spend much of their time in the field checking fishing and hunting licenses and enforcing the laws about bag limits and what sorts of game and guns and hunting or fishing methods are legal in their district.

Wardens are federal and state government employees, armed and generally well trained and equipped, who work in uniform and have government vehicles (pickup trucks, boats, snow machines, even airplanes and helicopters) for their work. They may use the Internet and forensic investigation techniques to break up a gang of wildlife smugglers; or they may go out on snowshoes with dogs to find a lost hunter or hiker. If dangerous animals have to be dealt with—such as a bear that's killing sheep or a mountain lion that attacked a hiker—game wardens are called in. Some states and countries employ professional hunters to track down such "problem" animals.

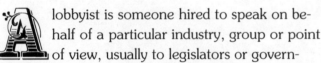

Gun Lobbyist

A lobbyist is someone hired to speak on behalf of a particular industry, group or point of view, usually to legislators or government agencies that make rules about that particular business or activity. When the auto companies, for example, are concerned about proposed new regulations for cars—having to do with gas mileage, say, or the number of airbags required—they hire lobbyists to tell senators and representatives why they're for or against those regulations. Then companies or organizations with a different opinion send *their* lobbyists to speak to the regulators.

The point is to ensure that the people who set the rules hear every side of a particular topic before they make their decisions. As you can imagine, there is often a great deal at stake (money, jobs, environmental issues, even political or religious beliefs), and lobbying can be a very rough-and-tumble process. Lobbyists on one side work to get a bill signed into law, while the opposition does everything it can to frustrate those efforts. Legislative lobbying is a very challenging career and not for the faint of heart. Like pro football or hockey, it's a "full contact" job.

A lobbyist should be an expert in her field and has to have a solid understanding of government and the legislative process. (Many lobbyists are also lawyers.) Lobbyists also need strong interpersonal skills; they must be articulate and persuasive and able to plan strategies that will accomplish their goals.

Practically every industry, organization or activity has its lobbyists, including the gun business, the shooting sports and hunting. If this interests you, you should know that some of the top firearms lobbyists are women.

Gunshop Staff

any a gunshop owner or gun-department employee at a sporting-goods store was once a kid fascinated with guns. However, the day-to-day work of retail sales and owning a small business can easily overwhelm the enjoyable aspects of being in the gun trade. Many gunshop owners say, only half-joking, that they used to do a lot of shooting until they got into the shooting business.

Managing cash flow, tax records and employees can be a job unto itself. So is figuring out how to bring in more customers, and then having the right mix of guns, ammunition and other products on hand for them. In addition, anyone involved in selling (or manufacturing or repairing) firearms has to be specially licensed. This involves a great deal of paperwork too, as gun and sometimes ammunition sales have to be carefully recorded and reported.

If you think your knowledge of guns and human nature makes you the prefect candidate for a gunshop, get a job at one as soon as you're old enough and see for yourself. If it works out, your boss, the store owner, will be thrilled to find a good employee to whom he can sell the business when he wants to retire. Women who work in gunshops are still a rarity, so you may have an advantage as more and more women buy guns and become shooters.

Shooting Writer, Editor, Media Professional

orldwide, thousands of magazines, newspapers, Websites, blogs, books, TV shows and other media deliver information to shooters—about guns, ammunition and gear, shooting techniques, places to shoot or hunt, interesting people, collectible or historic firearms, how to cook wild game, and much more. Providing this sort of content (it used to be called "writing") can be a very interesting career.

Successful gun writers and TV personalities may travel all over the world, get guns and gear, be invited to tour gun factories or go on safari, and meet famous people. Some of them become famous themselves, in a small way.

Just as in almost *every* other firearms-related career, simply knowing a lot about guns or being a world-class shot isn't enough. To write successfully about guns (or hunting, skeet shooting, firearms history or whatever) means becoming a good writer too. TV shows are visual, but before filming begins someone has to write a script.

Ryan Damstrom

Diana Rupp—here with a mountain goat taken in British Columbia in 2005—became an editorial assistant at *Sports Afield* Magazine in 1991 when she was fresh out of college. She went on to other outdoor media, including *Wing & Shot, Wildfowl* and the Northwoods Group, before returning to *Sports Afield* as its editor-in-chief in 2002. In addition to directing the magazine, Diana writes articles and books, appears on *World of Sports Afield* TV and gives presentations to hunting and conservation groups. She lives in California with her husband and favorite hunting partner, Scott, also an outdoor-magazine editor.

Elena Micheli-Lamboy grew up in the Val Trompia, northern Italy's famous gunmaking region, and went to school in England and Germany. She earned a Ph.D. in languages and linguistics, and then combined her background and talents into a unique career. Today American and European gun companies that do business with each other hire Elena as a consultant, interpreter and translator. She married one of her former clients, and she and her family now live part of each year in Italy and the rest of the time in upstate New York.

A writer thinks clearly, and then expresses those thoughts in sentences that are equally clear. Don't worry about imagination just yet; focus on vocabulary and grammar. Pay attention in English class. If you're interested in the topic, the creativity will come.

As the saying goes, if you want to write a magazine article or a book, you have to read one first. Writers read—a lot. Then you'll begin to see how stories and books are put together. Some you'll like, and some you won't. Why? What's the difference? The same goes for TV shows: What is it about certain shows that you like? Can you come up with similar ideas—or better ones? How would you film a story in video?

Join your school newspaper or Website. When you think you may be ready for a larger audience, get in touch with the editors of your local newspaper or a magazine and tell them your idea. Just about all publishing and TV companies are on the Web

as well as in print; they all need writers, and they're always looking for fresh talent.

The media world includes much more than only writing or content creation. Magazines and books need editors, the people who assign stories to writers, and then prepare the texts for publication. An editor has to be an expert in grammar, punctuation and spelling, and then knowledgeable enough about guns or shooting to judge the article or book: *Is it any good?* TV shows have directors and producers who do the same things.

Media companies need other employees too, including accountants and salespeople. Whether they sell the companies' products or advertising in shows, magazines and Websites, the salespeople especially have to know about guns, shooting or hunting.

Kim Gattone also has been able to combine her passions and her profession. Once a world-class mountaineer and endurance athlete who worked for *Outside* Magazine, Kim became a bird and big-game hunter. Now, as the North American and European advertising-sales manager for *African Hunting Gazette*, Kim helps clients develop their marketing programs. One of them, PH Jamie Traut, guided Kim to this trophy oryx in Namibia.

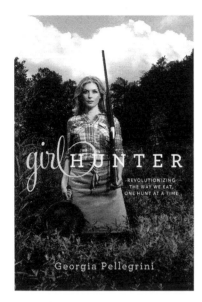

Georgia Pellegrini left a job at a Wall Street investment bank to become a well-known "foodie" specializing in hunting and cooking wild game. She attended the French Culinary Institute, then worked at several famous restaurants while learning to shoot and hunt. On her Website and in her blog and books (*Girl Hunter* is her second book), she emphasizes that women don't need to "tag along" with men but should seek challenges in the culinary, shooting and hunting world themselves. She also creates Girl Hunter Weekends, featuring "good times, great guns, and cream and butter."

As a hunter, Melissa Bachman does it all—rifle, shotgun, handgun and bow; as a TV personality, she is equally well-rounded. To gain experience and to prove herself, at first Melissa worked without pay for North American Hunter Television. Now Melissa not only appears on camera, she also writes, films, directs and produces TV hunting episodes—and now gets a paycheck. Her passion for hunting appears in everything she does. This is a free-range whitetail deer that she took late on a winter day in Texas in 2012.

Acknowledgements

Lisa Damian, Chris Dorsey, Laura Evans, Naomi Farmer, Ron Hickman, Karen Holub, Beverly Huffman, Torrey Johnson, Christina King, William King, Robert Mannen, Bronwyn McGary, Jay Menefee, Chuck Michel, Jason Morton, Scott Olmsted, David Penn, Elaine Sandberg, Mike Stumbo and Chris Zealand helped us with this book. Lt. Col. Andrey Ugarov (Russian Army, ret.) came up with the "true gen" about Lyudmila Pavlichenko. Jacquelyn Borgeson and Conrad Froelich at the Martin and Osa Johnson Safari Museum were especially helpful too. Terry Allen kindly supplied some of the best photos in the book.

We also are grateful to the late collector extraordinaire George Swenson, many of whose photographs and guns appear in this book. And once again our wives—Sue, Marilyn and Kathy—cheered us on and listened to us, for the umpteenth time, tell the stories that we put in this book. (Our own kids are long grown up and have moved away, so they didn't have to listen. But they all got a good education in shooting when they were young.)

Great thanks also to Karim and Hayden Baker; to Lisa, Chris and Hannah Mayers; and to Carrie, Annie & Lisa Herbertson: mothers, sons and daughters who "proof-tested" the manuscript of these books and whose enthusiasm and comments were so helpful.

Silvio Calabi
Steve Helsley
Roger Sanger

Bibliography

Adams, C. and Braden, R. (1996). *Lock, Stock, & Barrel.* Long Beach, CA: Safari Press.

Agnew, M.S.C. *Journal of the Royal Highland Fusiliers,* Vol. 24, No. 2.

"Air Guns": Retrieved February 8, 2012, from www.straightshooters.com.

Atkinson, J.A. (1978). *The British Dueling Pistol.* London: Arms & Armour Press.

Ayed, N. (2008). "Mideast Dispatches: Deadly Merriment, the fallout from celebratory gunfire": CBC News.

Baker, D.J. (2000). *The Heyday of the Shotgun.* Shrewsbury, UK: Swan-Hill Press.

Baker, S.S.W. (1867). *The Albert N'yanza, Great Basin of the Nile, and Explorations of the Nile Sources.* New York: Macmillan and Co.

Baldick, R. (1965). *The Duel: A History of Dueling.* London: Chapman & Hall.

Balleisen, C.E. (1945). *Principles of Firearms.* New York: John Wiley & Sons, Inc.

Ballistic Resistance of Body Armor, NIJ Standard-0101.06. (2008). National Institute of Justice. Retrieved from www.ojp.usdoj.gove/nij.

Barnes, F.C. (2009). *Cartridges of the World* (12th ed.). Iola, WI: Gun Digest Books.

Barsness, L. (1974). *Heads, Hides and Horns: The Compleat Buffalo Book.* Fort Worth, TX: Texas Christian University Press.

Beginner's Digest. (1960). Washington, DC: National Rifle Association of America.

Bell, W.D.M. (1949). *Karamojo Safari.* New York: Harcourt, Brace and Co.

Bell, W.D.M. (1960). *Bell of Africa.* London: Neville Spearman & The Holland Press.

Bell, W.D.M. (1960). *The Wanderings of an Elephant Hunter.* London: Neville Spearman, Ltd.

Berg, A. and Sherman, L. (2004). "Pistols at Weehawken."

Bethell, N. (1977). *Russia Besieged.* New York: Time-Life Books.

Blackmore, H.L. (1961). *British Military Firearms 1650-1850.* London: Herbert Jenkins.

Body Armor: Retrieved February 18, 2012, from http://nij.gov/nij/topics/technology/body-armor/safety-initiative.htm.

Bolotin, D.N. (1995). *Soviet Small-Arms and Ammunition.* Hyvinkää, Finland: Finnish Arms Museum Foundation.

Boomgaard, P. (2001). *Frontiers of Fear: Tigers and People in the Malay World, 1600 - 1950.* New Haven, CT: Yale University Press.

Booth, M. (1986). *Carpet Sahib — A Life of Jim Corbett.* London: Constable and Co., Ltd.

Boothroyd, G. (1970). *The Handgun.* New York: Crown Publishers, Inc.

Bradbury, J. (1985). *The Medieval Archer.* Woodbridge, UK: The Boydell Press.

Bradford, C.H. (1996). *The Battle Road: Expedition to Lexington and Concord.* Ft. Washington, PA: Eastern National.

Braun, J., et al. (2007). *The Complete Guide to Paintballing* (4th ed.). Hobart, NY: Hatherleigh Press.

Bredero, A.H. (1994). *Christendom and Christianity in the Middle Ages* (1st English edition ed.). Grand Rapids, MI: Wm. B. Erdmans Publishing Co.

Brokaw, T. (1998). *The Greatest Generation.* New York: Random House.

Brophy, W.S. (1992). *The Springfield 1903 Rifles*. Harrisburg, PA: Stackpole Books.

Brown, E.J. (1951). *Rimfire Rifleman*. Harrisburg, PA: Stackpole.

Buck, B. "The Eyes Have It." Retrieved February 23, 2012, from www.shootingsportsman.com/technoid-talk/2011/february/the-eyes-have.

Campbell, D. (2011). "Winchester Model 1895: A Look Back." Retrieved March 21, 2012, from www.americanrifleman.org/articles/winchester-model-95/.

Campbell, W. (1864). *My Indian Journal*. Edinburgh: Edmonston and Douglas.

Canfield, B.N. (2000). *U.S. Infantry Weapons of the First World War*. Lincoln, RI: Andrew Mowbray Publishers.

Capstick, P.H. (1984). *Safari, the Last Adventure*. New York: St. Martin's Press.

Carol, G. Retrieved February 8, 2012, from www.gcaudio.com.

Carter, G.L. (2002). *Guns in American Society: An Encyclopedia*. Santa Barbara, CA: Oxford.

Charles, H., Howard, H.P. and Aflalo, F.G. (1911). *The Encyclopaedia of Sport and Games* (IV). Philadelphia: J.P. Lippincott.

Chinn, G.M. (1951). *The Machine Gun* (I & III). Washington, DC: Bureau of Ordnance—Dept. of the Navy.

Chivers, C.J. (2010). *The Gun*. New York: Simon & Schuster.

Clark, P.A. (2007). "Criminal Use of Firearm Silencers." *Western Criminology Review,* Vol. 8, No. 2, 44-57.

Conan Doyle, A. (1902). *The Great Boer War*. Hinhead, UK: Undershaw.

The Congressional Medal of Honor. (1984). Forrest Ranch, CA: Sharp & Dunnigan Publications.

Cooch Behar, The Maharajah of. (1908). *Thirty-Seven Years of Big Game Shooting in Cooch Behar, the Duars, and Assam*. Bombay: The Times Press.

Corbett, J. (1946). *Man-eaters of Kumaon*. New York: Oxford University Press.

Corbett, J. (1947). *The Man-Eating Leopard of Rudraprayag*. New Delhi: Oxford University Press India.

Corbett, J. (1952). *My India*. New York & Bombay: Oxford University Press.

Corbett, J. (1953). *Jungle Lore*. London: Oxford University Press.

Corbett, J. (1954). *The Temple Tiger and More Man-Eaters of Kumaon*. New Delhi: Oxford University Press India.

Corbett, J. (1955). *Tree Tops*. New Delhi: Oxford University Press India.

Cottam, K.J. (1998). *Women in War and Resistance*. Newburyport, MA: Focus Publishing/R. Pullins Co.

Cottam, K.J. (1998). *Women in War and Resistance: Selected Biographies*. Newburyport, MA: Focus Publishing/R. Pullins Co.

Crudgington, I.M. and Baker, D.J. (1989). *The British Shotgun, Volume II: 1871-1890*. Hampshire, UK: Ashford.

Czech, K.P. (2002). *With Rifle and Petticoat: Women as Big-Game Hunters, 1880-1940*. Lanham and New York: The Derrydale Press.

Dater, P.H., MD. (1993). *The Art of Silence*. Boise, ID: ATI Star Press.

Dater, P.H., MD. (2000). *Sound Measurements*. Boise, ID: ATI Star Press.

Davidson, S. (2009). *A Parent's Guide to Paintball*. Vancouver, Canada: Liaison Press.

Davis, T.L. (1943). *The Chemistry of Powder & Explosives*. Hollywood, CA: Angriff Press.

De Calzo, N. and Collier, P. (2003). *Medal of Honor*. New York: Artisan.

Dixon, O.K. (2005). *The Life of Billy Dixon*. Abilene, TX: State House Press.

Ellis, J. (1975). *The Social History of the Machine Gun*. Baltimore, MD: The Johns Hopkins University Press.

Enright, K. (2011). *Osa and Martin - For the Love of Adventure*. Guilford, CT: Lyons Press.

Esper, T. (1965). "The Replacement of the Longbow by Firearms in the English Army." *Technology and Culture, Vol. 6, No. 3, 382-393*.

Ezell, E.C. (2001). *Kalashnikov—The Arms and the Man*. Ontario: Crown Grade Publications.

Farquharson, W.J. (1977). ".45-70 at Two Miles." *Rifle, Vol. 9, No. 6, 36-40*.

Farrow, E.S. (1895). *Farrow's Military Encyclopedia* (2nd ed.). New York: Military-Naval Publishing Co.

Farrow, E.S. (1904). *American Small Arms* (First ed.). New York: The Bradford Co.

Federal Firearms Regulations Reference Guide (ATF Publication No. 5300.4). (2005). Springfield, VA: US Dept. of Justice, Bureau of Alcohol, Tobacco, Firearms and Explosives.

Fischer, D.H. (1994). *Paul Revere's Ride*. New York: Oxford University Press.

Flayderman, N. (2007). *Flayderman's Guide to Antique American Arms* (9th ed.). Iola, WI: Gun Digest Books.

Fleming, B. (1993). *British Sporting Rifle Cartridges*. Oceanside, CA: Armory Publications.

Fox, R.A. Jr. (1993). *Archaeology, History, and Custer's Last Battle*. Norman, OK: University of Oklahoma Press at Norman.

Freemantle, T.F. (1901). *The Book of the Rifle*. London: Longmans, Green, and Co.

Gangarosa, G.J. (1999). *FN Browning - Armorer to the World*. Wayne, NJ: Stoeger Publishing Co.

Geibig, A. (1995). *Die Kunst der Konstrukteure*. Coburg, Germany: Kunstsammlungen der Veste Coburg.

Geibig, A. (2002). *Die Kunst der Konstrukteure*. Coburg, Germany: Coburger Landesstiftung.

Geibig, A. (2005). *Der Herzöge Lust*. Coburg, Germany: Kunstsammlungen der Veste Coburg.

Gilbert, M., Leo Reminger & Sharon Cunningham. (2003). *Encyclopedia of Buffalo Hunters and Skinners*. Union City, TN: Pioneer Press.

Gordon, J.D. (1997). *Winchester's New Model of 1873: A Tribute*. Self-published.

Greener, W.W. (1910). *The Gun and its Development* (9th ed.). New York: Bonanza Books.

"Gyrojet Handgun." *American Rifleman, Vol. 113, Issue 12, 80-81*.

Hackley, F.W., Woodin, W.H. and Scranton, E.L. (1967). *History of Modern U.S. Military Ammunition, Volume 1 1880-1939*. New York: The Macmillan Co.

Hackley, F.W., Woodin, W.H. and Scranton, E.L. (1967). *History of Modern U.S. Military Small Arms Ammunition (I — 1880-1939)*. New York: The Macmillan Co.

Hamilton, D.T. (1916). *Cartridge Manufacture*. New York: The Industrial Press.

Hanger, G.G. (1816). *Hanger to all Sportsmen*. London: J.J. Stockdale.

Hardy, R. (1992). *Longbow: A Social and Military History*. Goldthwaite, TX: Bois d'Arc Press.

Hatcher, J.S. (1962). *Hatcher's Notebook*. Mechanicsburg, PA: Stackpole Books.

Hawkins, G.W. (1897). *Treatise on Ammunition*. London: Harrison and Sons.

Held, R. (1957). *The Age of Firearms*. New York: Harper & Brothers.

Herne, B. (1999). *White Hunters: The Golden Age of African Safaris*. New York: Henry Holt and Co.

Howe, W.J. (1960). "The Quick-Draw Craze." *American Rifleman, Vol. 107, No. 2, 14*.

Howe, W.J. (1961). "Nonmercuric, Noncorrosive Primers." *Beginner's Digest, Vol. 109, No. 1, 34*.

Howell, C.G. (1959). "Fast Draw—No Bloodshed." *Guns, Volume 5, No. 9-57, 14-41*.

Hoyem, G.A. (1981). *The History and Development of Small Arms Ammunition* (I-III). Tacoma, WA: Armory Publications.

Humphry, A.P. and Fremantle, Lt. Col. T.F. (1914). *The History of the National Rifle Association During its First Fifty Years, 1859 to 1909* (First ed.). Cambridge, UK: Bowes and Bowes.

Huntington, R.T. (1972). *Hall's Breechloaders.* York, PA: George Shumway.

Israeli Ruger 10/22 Suppressed Sniper Rifle. Retrieved March 26, 2012, from www.ruger1022.com/docs/israeli_sniper.htm.

Jaleel, J.A. (2001). *Under the Shadow of Man-Eaters / The Life and Legend of Jim Corbett.* Hyderabad, India: Orient Longman, Ltd.

James, E.C. (1951). *A Boy and His Gun.* New York: A.S. Barnes and Co.

Johnson, M. (1929). *Lion - African Adventure with the King of Beasts.* New York & London: G.P. Putnam's Sons.

Johnson, M. (1935). *Over African Jungles.* New York: Harcourt, Brace and Co.

Johnson, O. (1940). *I Married Adventure.* Philadelphia & New York: J.B. Lippincott Co.

Johnson, O. (1941). *Four Years in Paradise.* Philadelphia & New York: J.B. Lippincott Co.

Jonas, G. (2005). *Vengeance: The True Story of an Israeli Counter-Terrorist Team.* New York: Simon & Schuster.

Keith, E. "Elmer Keith on Combat Quick Draw." *Guns, Vol. VI, No. 2-62,* 22-44.

Kent, D.W. (1990). *German 7.92mm Military Ammunition 1888-1945.* Ann Arbor, MI: self-published.

Kirkland, K.D. (1990). *America's Premier Gunmakers.* New York: Mallard Press.

Klein, J. Another Made in USA "less-lethal" weapon kills in Palestine. Retrieved March 26, 2012, from http://mondoweiss.net/2011/01/another-made-in-usa-%E2%80%9Cless-lethal%E2%80%9D-weapon-kills-in-palestine.html.

Kontis, G.E. (2011). "Enemies of the Gun Barrel." *Small Arms Review, Vol. 15, No. 3,* 37.

Korwin, A. (2003). *Gun Laws of America.* Scottsdale, AZ: Bloomfield Press.

Lapin, T.W. (1998). *The Mosin-Nagant Rifle.* Tustin, CA: North Cape Publications.

Lenk, T. (1965). *The Flintlock: Its Origin and Development* (G.A. Urquart, Trans.). New York: Bramhall House.

Little, J. and Wong, C. (2001). *Ultimate Guide to Paintball.* New York: McGraw-Hill.

Logan, H.C. (1959). *Cartridges.* Harrisburg, PA: The Stackpole Co.

The Manual of Field Sports. (1862). London: Tallis & Co.

Marcot, R.M. (1989). *Hiram Berdan.* Irvine, CA: Northwood Heritage Press.

"Market Hunting." Retrieved January 2012 from www.museum.state.il.us/RiverWeb/harvesting/harvest/waterfowl/industry/market_hunting.html.

Marwick, R.D. and Cardona, E.C. (2012). *Soviet Women on the Frontline in the Second World War.*

Mattenheimer, A. (1868). *Cartridges for Breech-Loading Rifles.* Darmstadt & Leipzig: Eduard Zernin.

McIntosh, M. (1990). *The Big-Bore Rifle.* Traverse City, MI: Countrysport Press.

McKee, T.H. (1918). *The Gun Book for Boys and Men.* New York: Henry Holt and Co.

McPherson, M.L. (1997). "Replicating Billy Dixon's Legendary Long-Shot." *Precision Shooting, Vol. 42, No. 9,* 74-85.

Melton, C.W. (2001). *Between War and Peace.* Macon, GA: Mercer University Press.

Mention, P. and Ramio, C. (1988). *Cartridges of the Gras System* (H.B. Malric, Trans.). Oceanside, CA: Armory Publications.

Michel, C.D. (2011). Michel & Associates, PC, Attorneys at Law. Personal communication.

Money, A. (1896). *Pigeon Shooting.* New York: Shooting and Fishing Publications.

Moore, C.J.R., Meade, Lt. H.H. and Jahns, Lt. L.E. (1920). *History of the American Expedition Fighting the Bolsheviks.* St. Petersburg, FL: Red and Black Publishers.

Mottelay, P.F. (1920). *The Life and Work of Sir Hiram Maxim.* London: John Lane.

Mueller, C. and Oldson, J. (1968). *Small Arms Lexicon and Concise Encyclopedia.* Hackensack, NJ: Shooter's Bible, Inc.

Murcot, R.M. (1989). *Civil War Chief of Sharpshooters Hiram Berdan.* Irvine, CA: Northwood Heritage Press.

Neal, W.K. and Back, D.H.L. (1969). *Forsyth & Co.: Patent Gunmakers.* London: G. Bell & Sons, Ltd.

Nedelin, A. (1999). *Kalashnikov Arms.* Moscow: Military Parade, Ltd.

Norton, C.B. (1880). *Breech-Loading Small Arms.* Springfield, MA: Chapin & Gould.

Ordog, G.J., MD, Dornhoffer, P., MD; Ackroyd, G.; Wasserberger, J., MD; Bishop, M., MD; Shoemaker, W., MD; Balasubramanium, S., MD. "Spent Bullets and Their Injuries: the Result of Firing Weapons Into the Sky." *The Journal of Trauma - Injury, Infection, and Critical Care, Vol. 37, Issue 6.*

Partington, J.R. (1960). *A History of Greek Fire and Gunpowder.* Cambridge, UK: W. Heffer & Sons, Ltd.

Payne-Gallway, S.R. (1882). *The Fowler in Ireland.* London: John Van Voorst.

Payne-Gallway, S.R. (1892). *Letters to Young Shooters (First Series) on the Choice and Use of a Gun.* London: Longmans, Green and Co.

Peterson, H.L. (Ed.) (1967). *Encyclopedia of Firearms.* London: The Connoisseur.

Phillipps-Wolley, C. (1894). *The Badminton Library* (II). London: Longman, Greens and Co.

Plaster, J.L. (1993). *The Ultimate Sniper.* Boulder, CO: Paladin Press.

Poole, E.R. (Ed.) (2010). *Complete Book of the AK-47.* New York: Intermedia Outdoors, Inc.

Press, T.A. (2012). "Ohio man cleaning gun killed Amish girl." Puntgunning: www.wildfowling.com/Puntgunning/puntgunning.htm.

Reid, Maj. R.J. (ret.) (2005). "The Development of Artillery Ammunition." Proceedings from Winter Meeting, Larkhill, UK.

Riordan, J. (2008). *The Sniper.* London: Frances Lincoln Children's Books.

Rod and Gun in Canada, Vol. XVI, No. 9. (1914).

Rorabacher, J.A.L. (1970). *The American Buffalo in Transition.* Saint Cloud, MN: North Star Press.

Ruark, R. (1966). *Use Enough Gun: On Hunting Big Game.* New York: The New American Library.

Ruark, R. (1987). *Horn of the Hunter.* Long Beach, CA: Safari Press.

Rush, R., USA (ret.). (2006). *NCO Guide* (8th ed.). Mechanicsburg, PA: Stackpole Books.

Sandoz, M. (1960). *The Buffalo Hunters.* London: Eyre & Spottiswoode.

Sapp, R. (2005). *The Gun Digest Book of Sporting Clays.* Iola, WI: Gun Digest Books.

Sapp, R. (2009). *The Gun Digest Book of Trap and Skeet Shooting* (5th ed.). Iola, WI: Krause Publications.

Schmidt, P.A. (1996). *Hall's Military Breechloaders.* Lincoln, RI: Andrew Mowbray.

Schreier, J. and Konrad F. (1967). "The Origin of the .22 Rim Fire." *The Gun Report, Vol. XIII, No. 1,* 30-32.

Schuster, M.A.; Franke, T.M.; Bastian, A.M.; Sor, S. and Halfon, N. "Firearm Storage Patterns in U.S. Homes with Children." *American Journal of Public Health, Vol. 90, No. 4,* 588-594.

Scoffern, J. (1858). *Projectile Weapons of War & Explosive Compounds* (3rd ed.). London: Longman, Brown, Green, and Longmans.

Selby, H. (2011). "Harry Selby's Rigby .416." *Sports Afield, Vol. 234, No. 3,* pp. 44-49.

Senich, P.R. (1982). *The German Sniper.* Boulder, CO: Paladin Press.

Senich, P.R. (1988). *The Complete Book of U.S. Sniping.* Boulder, CO: Paladin Press.

Senich, P.R. (1982). *The German Sniper 1914-1945.* Boulder, CO: Paladin Press.

Skennerton, I. (1984). *The British Sniper.* Australia: Self-published.

Smith, A. (2003). *The Machine Gun.* New York: St. Martin's Press.

Smith, W.H.B. (1964). *Small Arms of the World* (7th ed.). Harrisburg, PA: Stackpole.

Smith, W.H.B. (1957). *Gas, Air, & Spring Guns of the World.* Harrisburg, PA: The Telegraph Press.

Staff. (1961). "How Far Will a Gun Shoot?" *American Rifleman Beginner's Digest, Vol. 109, No. 9,* 22-24.

Staff, N.R.A.T. (1961). "Did Body Armor Protect?" *American Rifleman, Vol. 109, No. 10,* 28.

Stange, M.Z. (1997). *Woman the Hunter.* Boston: Beacon Press.

Stevens, R.B. (1998). *The FAL Rifle* (Classic ed.). Ontario: Collector Grade Publications, Inc.

Stonehenge (Walsh, J.H.) (1870). *British Rural Sports* (9th ed.). London: Routledge.

Strickland, M. and Hardy, R. (2005). *The Great Warbow: From Hastings to the Mary Rose.* Stroud, UK: Sutton Publishing, Ltd.

Sweeney, P. (2008). *AK & SKS.* Iola, WI: Gun Digest Books.

Swenson, G.W.P. (1972). *The Pictorial History of the Rifle.* New York: Bonanza Books.

Taylor, J. (1994). *African Rifles and Cartridges.* Huntington Beach, CA: Safari Press.

Temple, B.A. (1977). *The Boxer Cartridge in the British Service.* Brisbane, Australia: Watson Ferguson and Co.

"Toepperwein, Adolph." Retrieved March 29, 2012, from www.tshaonline.org/handbook/online/articles/fto09.

Trench, C.C. (1972). *A History of Marksmanship.* London: Longman.

Upton, Maj. Gen. E., USA. (1878). *The Armies of Europe and Asia.* London: Griffin & Co.

VanGelder, A.P. and Schlatter, H. (1927). *History of the Explosives Industry in America.* New York: Columbia University Press.

Venola, R. (2005). "Iraq: Lessons from the Sandbox." *Combat Arms.*

Venturino, M. (1993). "How Far Will a Sharps Shoot?" *Black Powder Cartridge News, Vol. 1, No. 3,* 9-11.

Walker, J.F. (2009). *Ivory's Ghosts: The White Gold of History and the Fate of Elephants.* New York: Atlantic Monthly Press.

Webster, D.B. (1963). "American Wall Guns." *American Rifleman*, August.

Wilson, R.L. (1986). *Colt: An American Legend.* New York: Abbeville Press.

Index